Paul Sheehan's work has appeared in the *New Yorker*, the *New York Times*, and the *Atlantic Monthly*, but most of his writing has been for the *Sydney Morning Herald*, where he is a senior writer. He has served as the *Herald*'s chief of staff, day editor, and New York correspondent. He was a Nieman Fellow at Harvard University, and was educated at the Australian National University and Columbia University in New York. A piece he wrote for the *New Yorker* was selected for the *Best American Essays 1997*.

AMONG THE
BARBARIANS

THE DIVIDING
OF
AUSTRALIA

PAUL SHEEHAN

RANDOM HOUSE
AUSTRALIA

Published by
Random House Australia Pty Ltd
20 Alfred Street, Milsons Point, NSW 2061
http://www.randomhouse.com.au

Sydney New York Toronto
London Auckland Johannesburg
and agencies throughout the world

First published in 1998
Copyright © Paul Sheehan

National Library of Australia
Cataloguing-in-Publication Data

Sheehan, Paul, 1951– .
   Among the barbarians: The Dividing of Australia.

   ISBN 009 183636 0.

   1. Multiculturalism—Australia. 2. Twenty-first century—
   Forecasts. 3. Natural resources—Australia. 4. Australia
   —Politics and government—1990. 5. Australia—
   Forecasting. I. Title.

994.07

Design by Gayna Murphy
Typeset by Bookhouse Digital, Sydney
Printed by Griffin Press Pty Ltd
A Division of PMP Communications

10 9 8 7 6 5

For the colourblind.

Take the women out of publishing
and you don't have a publishing industry.
The women who made this book possible
were Deborah Callaghan, Jennifer Byrne,
Jane Palfreyman and Jody Lee.

CONTENTS

THE TROGLODYTE

THE ABUSE STARTED FLOWING immediately. It came by letter, by fax, by phone, by e-mail, by radio interview.

Geraldine Willesee, SBS radio:
Paul Sheehan hit a grubby rock-bottom ... his story got truly scary ... From which dung-heap did he dredge this offensive, patently stupid and dangerous garbage ... badly researched bile ... the worst of gutter journalism.

Sonja Marsic:
Mr Sheehan's article was a betrayal of all that is truly Australian.

Camilla Nelson:
It's a pity that Paul Sheehan's psychosexual problems have turned out to be so unutterably boring ...

This outrage was prompted by a story published in the *Sydney Morning Herald* on 25 May 1996. It was the first step in describing one of the greatest political myths in Australian history.

Published under the front-page headline THE MULTI-CULTURAL MYTH, the story described an industry of tax-fed lawyers, political operatives and racial axe-grinders that has grown like an enormous parasite out of Australia's heroic commitment to cultural diversity. The openness and tolerance of Australians is one of the themes that defines this book. The two extremes—moral fraud and moral potential—are intimately and painfully connected.

The other seed from which this book grew was a story published in the *Sydney Morning Herald* on 12 August 1995, entitled, 'Australia Superpower' about Australia's potential to become the world's first eco-superpower. This concept was followed up by Thomas Friedman, the Pulitzer Prize-winning foreign affairs columnist for the *New York Times*, who wrote:

> *The clash between France and Australia, observed the Australian writer Paul Sheehan, will be the first real confrontation between a traditional superpower and an ecological superpower.*

The story generated light, but not heat. The heat came the following year with the publication of 'The multicultural myth', which prompted a torrent of emotional responses. Despite the flow of outrage and bile, most of these responses were positive.

> *Eureka!* wrote Nick Jones. *Finally an attack on reverse racism.*

> D. Eastman:
> *Thank you for debunking the newest form of cultural cringe and self-loathing.*

AK Singh:
I sit nightly gnashing my teeth at the passing parade of 'ethnic leaders' on television speaking on behalf of me and the 'ethnic community' ... Where do they get their mandate from?

The very first letter to arrive had come from Nina Webb of Canberra:

Before the self-proclaimed custodians of ethnicity rush in for the kill, let me put on record the support of one Australian of non-Anglo background and birth for 'The multicultural myth.'
    The shamans of the post-war ethnic groups did not encourage the qualities which Sheehan rightly identifies as being the essence of what makes Australia not just a lucky country but a great one to live in: equality, mateship, tolerance. It was not, after all, in their interest to do so. Their power came from division, not cohesion. For today's mandarins of multiculturalism, it still does ...

The bulk of the letters were from people who felt themselves to be members of a silenced majority. They believed their tolerance had been abused and their voices patronised and dismissed. But the most powerful responses and the most interesting, if not enlightening, letters were hostile. Some of the insults were marvellous, and all of them were useful.

Noel McGuire:
The problem with the troglodytes opposed to multiculturalism ... is they find it distasteful working

*alongside Buddhists and Moslems, as if they're less than
human.*

Paul seems to be well on the way to gaga land ...

Al Grassby, former Minister for Immigration in the
Whitlam government:

[It] seemed to have been written in the twilight of 1939.

Angela Chan, chairwoman of the Ethnic Communities
Council of New South Wales, and long-time close associate
of Al Grassby:

*Instead of Mr Sheehan denigrating the increase in
[discrimination] case-load as some ethnic plot to take
advantage of the compensation system, he should have
perhaps questioned the increase as indicative of the
actual number of people being discriminated against in
a supposedly tolerant society in Australia.*

Penny O'Donnell, communications department, University
of Technology, Sydney:

*Australia cannot afford another generation of journalists
like Paul Sheehan ... What kind of example of tolerance
does this offer to media students in National
Reconciliation Week?*

Jane Gibian, writing in a student publication at Sydney
University:

*Cultural imperialism and insensitivity ... demonstrates a
thinly disguised anxiety regarding his own identity ...*

John Minns, office of the Department of History and Politics at Wollongong University:

Racist—in the worst traditions of yellow journalism.

Stepan Kerkyasharian, Chairman the Ethnic Affairs Commission of New South Wales:

*I now await the sequel—*The Myth of Quality Journalism.

E. Vasilopoulos:
Biased, irresponsible and disturbing.

Graham Barry:
Good rabble-rousing jingoistic stuff—nonsense.

Caroline Alcorso, Director of the Working Women's Centre in Sydney:

An incoherent concoction of misleading assertions and half-truths.

Gary Crokett:
... sloganistic nonsense ... a flawed, directionless and myopic grab-bag of assertions ... vulgar and insulting ...

Malcolm Long, then Managing Director of SBS, speaking on ABC radio:

It's a bitter little document.

Yet nowhere in 'The multicultural myth' was there any criticism of Australia's ethnic diversity. Just the opposite. What was rejected was the notion that Australia does not have a distinct dominant national culture that binds and forms society. The story also emphatically rejected the large tax-fuelled industry whose members used, with great effectiveness, the accusation of racism to snuff out criticism or even debate.

The person who went to the most trouble in attacking the article and its author was Geraldine Willesee of SBS, who wrote a heated, hyperbolic, six-page response intended for publication. Ms Willesee, the daughter of a former Labor senator, was the reader who asked, 'From which dung-heap did he dredge this offensive, patently stupid and dangerous garbage?' Strangely, the memo which opened 'The multicultural myth'—a complaint about racism against 'Anglos' at SBS radio—came from Ms Willesee herself. She wrote it, a fact she admitted in her response. That was the dung heap from which the story first sprang.

Her reaction to the story, and all the other hostile responses, shared several characteristics.

They were personal. They concentrated on the writer rather than the arguments.

Nearly all who identified their place of work were on the public payroll. Most were part of the multicultural industry. There was no middle ground, no possibility of concession. Opponents were extremists and racists and xenophobes. Pauline Hanson had not yet given her maiden speech in Parliament, so the Frankenstein's Hanson had not yet been created in the news media's laboratory, otherwise they would have all used the convenient new label of Hansonism. (The relationship between Pauline Hanson and the news media is examined in the chapter 'Love at First Sight'.)

While the two stories from which this book grew, 'The multicultural myth' and 'Australia—eco-superpower', were being prepared and published, in the United States a book entitled *The Good Life and Its Discontents,* by the economist Robert Samuelson, captured the neurosis mirrored in Australia today.

Our attitudes are shaped more by unattained ambitions than actual achievement. We seem to have lapsed into a selective view of the national condition and into tortuous self-criticism.

Three years earlier, that great Australian export Robert Hughes summed up the same neurosis in just three words, the title of his bestselling book, *Culture of Complaint.*

'The multicultural myth', in attacking this culture of complaint triggered the standard response against all those who have ever threatened the industry's power and, more importantly, its funding.

To summarise the hate mail:

The author of The multicultural myth *is a desperate, ranting, racist, xenophobic, jingoistic, unintelligent yellow journalist from gaga land who writes biased, flawed, directionless, myopic, vulgar, insulting, strange, wildly inaccurate, truly scary, malicious, misleading,*

glib, bitter, offensive, patently stupid, dangerous, irre-
sponsible, disturbing beat-ups, incoherent concoctions,
inflammatory rubbish, badly researched bile, sloganistic
nonsense and garbage, a betrayer of all that is truly
Australian, an insensitive cultural imperialist that
Australia cannot afford, a hegemonist whose thinly dis-
guised cultural anxiety has led to a grubby rock-bottom
dung-heap, the worst of gutter journalism. In short, a
troglodyte with boring psychosexual problems.

And this is the voice of tolerance.

PART ONE

Eucalypts are thirsty beasts, and they love firestorms, which farmers don't ... They are the tree of Siva. They are the tree of the future. They are the enemy of the farmer, the friend of the hunter–gatherer. 'Your days are numbered,' they say to us.

David Foster, *The Glade Within the Grove*

1
THIS DOG BITES

THE EUCALYPTUS IS THE pyromaniac's tree. It loves fire. It is aggressive, adaptable, pragmatic. With fire as its great ally, it has colonised the Australian continent to the snowline, to the edge of saltwater mangroves, to the limits of sandy deserts and the last remaining rainforests. A dominant army, its discreet colours flying—the red gum, the blue, the grey, the black, the stringy-bark, the ghost, the scribbly, the ribbon, the coolibah, ironbark, bloodwood, jarrah, mugga, yellow box, red box, white mallee, yellow mallee, red mallee, rose, salmon, tallowwood, sugar, blackbutt, river red and river peppermint. An American scholar, Stephen Pyne, left this homage in his brilliant but largely forgotten book, *Burning Bush: A Fire History of Australia*, published in 1991.

> *Eucalyptus has given the bush its indelible character. It is not only the Universal Australian, it is the ideal Australian—versatile, tough, sardonic, contrary, self-mocking, with a deceptive complexity amid the appearance of massive homogeneity; an occupier of disturbed environments; a fire creature.*

The eucalypt asks for trouble. As drought withers the bush, turning it into fire fuel, the eucalypt, especially the stringy

1

bark, drapes incendiary streamers of tinder. The oil in its leaves is flammable. When fire inevitably comes, the eucalypt sheds its tough bark like protective plates. Eucalypts infiltrate places disturbed by fire. Fire opens areas to sunlight, allowing eucalypt seedlings a chance to outgrow more shade-tolerant rivals. During fires, seeds rain down from the charred canopy. The fluffy ash buries them in an environment of mineralised biochemicals. Fire purges the ground of antagonistic micro-organisms. Fire sweeps competition away.

Fire and drought. The crown of the eucalyptus is continually reshaped for maximum efficiency. (The name eucalyptus comes from the Greek *eu*, meaning 'well', and *kalyptos*, meaning 'covered'.) The canopy drapes downward to reduce leaf temperatures. The leaves are hard, to reduce moisture loss. They are shed infrequently, to preserve energy. As dry periods extend, the root system can grow vast as it compensates for the poverty of the soil. It obsessively retains and recycles nutrients. Seedlings can remain dormant for decades.

It is only in recent years, with the rapid advance of science and the development of environmental history, that the full power of Australian history is being described and understood. Stephen Pyne, a professor at the University of Arizona, provides a compelling history of the natural drama that has shaped Australia; in *Burning Bush,* he retells the history of Australia as a history of fire. He describes the eucalypt as a tree that burns 'readily, greedily, gratefully'.

The calendar of modern Australian history is marked with great conflagrations. Red Tuesday, 1 February, 1898; Black Friday, 13 January 1939; another, even worse, Black Tuesday on 7 February 1967 causing the largest loss of life and property on any single day in the history of the Australian continent. Pyne described it as, 'an apparition, like some Pleistocene beast, exhumed from the ice, that had come to life in an uncontrollable rampage'. Even as this book was being completed, huge bushfires swept across New South Wales and Victoria, reaching into Sydney and destroying homes. On 2 December 1997, yet another Black Tuesday, two veteran firemen died on Scotsman's Hill overlooking the main street of Lithgow. That night the hills above Lithgow looked like lava flows.

The firing of Australia was no accident. In *The Future Eaters*, Tim Flannery describes an abrupt change, unique in the 700 000-year-old sedimentary history of the Australian continent. Suddenly, the amount of microscopic charcoal fragments—fire residue—increased dramatically. At the same time, almost all fire-sensitive species abruptly vanished. The process of colonisation and domination by the eucalypt had begun. No corresponding climate change accounted for this abrupt change. Flannery describes a self-reinforcing cycle of soil impoverishment, drying and exposure.

I have no doubt that fire has made Australia—originally
the most resource-poor land—an even poorer one.
Fire saw the fat of the land slowly flushed onto the

*floodplains and into the estuaries, where today it sup-
ports swamp and mangrove ...*

*As a result, most of northern Australia is covered with
eucalypt woodlands today. After rain, the water drains
rapidly away, for the plants and thin soil cannot hold it.
The release of moisture to the atmosphere through the
narrow eucalypt leaves is insufficient to form significant
clouds.*

Something dramatic tilted the evolutionary direction. Flannery and Pyne and others have no doubt it was the arrival of
humans and the pervasive use of firestick farming from about
35 000 years ago. Even the climate was remade. By the time
the Europeans arrived in 1788, the structure of the forest
reflected multi-millennia of fire farming.

*Like the eucalypts, Aborigines were uniquely indigenous
to Australia. Genetic marking studies suggest that Aborigines have no close affinities with other human groups
... An entire continent bypassed the Neolithic revolution
which had spread agriculture to the Old World. Unlike
the Americas, no autonomous agricultural centres developed in Australia. None was necessary. Population
remained light, and resources ample. The landscape
could be 'farmed' by fire. The effect was as profound as
a change in climate.*

Firestick farming had created a fragile system that coevolved
with the Aboriginal people. The arrival of a new people from
a different environment quickly dissipated ancient patterns of

conservation. The early European settlers could not know that they were entering the alien realm of a fire-loving species. The ensuing struggle with the eucalypt would define the nation and the national character even more than the struggle with the people displaced by the onrush of a European tide. The bush and its lore have always been the central metaphor of Australian mythology, but the early Australians raped the environment they found. Anyone who has read one of the new generation of environmental histories of Australia—William Lines' 1991 book, *Taming the Great South Land*, is a pioneer of the genre—will have no doubt that rape is the only word for what took place. Only the eucalypt was able to stand up to the onslaught. Lines describes the fate that awaited the continent's only long-lived deciduous tree, the red cedar, which used to grow right along Australia's east coast, until early settlers discovered that it cut easily, warped little, was durable, versatile and grew in a straight bolt up to 45 metres high. Today, not even a stump remains. The pillage extended as far as the new settlers could reach, land and sea. Lines describes the natural cornucopia that was soon swept away.

> *Mariners in the southern seas in those days sailed through an abundance of marine life unimaginable to Australians today. Indeed, the southern oceans served as a vast undisturbed sanctuary for the sperm whale and the right whale ... every beach of the Tasman Sea, each rocky promontory of Bass Strait teemed with rookeries of elephant seals and fur seals.*

At the time of Federation, the pillage was ongoing. Two thousand lyrebird tails were exported in three years. In 1924 two million koala skins were exported. In 1959, the year before native bird exports were banned, 400 000 birds were trapped with only 100 000 surviving for export.

Yet Australians have always paid homage to the bush. The national colours are wattle and green. Gradually we have begun truly to see what we have around us. This maturing clarity shows up in a multitude of ways: from the recognition of native title as a national priority, to the new love of native flowers, to the didgeridoo becoming the unofficial national instrument, to the revival of the classic homestead architecture, to the burgeoning of superb Australian cuisine, to the explosion of popular interest in Aboriginal art and design, to a taste for wattleseed ice cream. The list goes on and on, a mosaic of large and small details. It is a collective, effortless embrace of nativism while also absorbing what the world has to offer, as Australians have always done. It is a recognition that Australia is not Europe, it is not Asia, and it is not California. It is another way in the world.

It helps to leave Australia for a while to fully appreciate the country. During visits home from New York where I lived for a decade, I was struck by how much Australia was *not* America. The scale of Australian culture is less grandiose, more human, more sensual. The new generations are growing colour blind. You see it on the streets, young mixed couples, Asian and European, black and white.

The Australia I returned to is better than the Australia I left and the prodigal eye rejoices in the undulating procession of the seasons, the streets carpeted in mauve as the jacarandas explode and shed, the crimson bottlebrushes and their feeding flocks of rainbow lorikeets, the red December flashes of the flowering gum. The mornings have the visceral thrill of kookaburras' calls. Cockatoos, currawongs, magpies. At night, fruit bats hang upside down in palm trees holding fruit in their claws. They shake the branches of the big Moreton Bay fig trees, and by morning they have left scattered fruit debris on the street below. Beauty is commonplace.

Yet another bit of bush mythology—sheepdog trials—is enjoying a quiet boom. The Australian National Trial Dog Championships are held each March at the Hall Showgrounds outside Canberra, a bumpy oval surrounded by stands of red gums, yellow box and Cootamundra wattle. The old skill of herding with sheepdogs is enjoying a comeback, and the number of dogs competing is rising. The trials have their own laconic drama. In the last run of the 1996 championships, I watched the defending champion, Clyde, with the national title at stake, make a stand, like Horatius, on the bridge.

One of the tests in a sheepdog trial is the bridge, where a dog must direct three sheep up a ramp and over a small bridge before it can move on to the next obstacle. In the last run of the championships all three of Clyde's sheep charged him on the bridge, normally a disaster. Clyde did not flinch. He went chest to chest with the big lead ewe, then bit her on the nose. If this trial had been held in Britain, where sheepdogs have been trialling for more than 120 years, Clyde would have been disqualified immediately. European judges

7

will not tolerate a biting dog. But the Australian merino is much bigger and more aggressive than European sheep. It is almost a free-range beast, used to wide spaces, and some of them can grow powerfully attached to wide spaces unless brought up sharply.

Clyde was not disqualified. He was not even penalised. He received a perfect score on the bridge for showing courage and doing good work. After the confrontation he quickly penned his chastened sheep and won the national championship. Clyde's owner, Greg Prince, the most successful sheepdog trainer of the modern era, explained his victory to me afterwards:

'An Australian dog is allowed to stand up for itself.'

Australia is described as a young country, yet in many ways it is old. It is one of the world's oldest continuous democracies, with political and social structures that have a direct lineage to a thousand years of historical and legal evolution. Australian democracy is so sinewy and instinctive that it is taken for granted, like a gift of nature. (In the United States, supposedly a paragon of democratic virtue, the quadrennial national election campaigns last more than a year and cost several billion dollars. Democracy for sale. In Australia, a national election campaign lasts barely longer than a month and costs less than a single Senate race in California.) Australia's modern culture has evolved over more than two centuries, since before the Industrial Revolution which transformed the world. Australia's physical environment is the most ancient, and the core of its human ecology—the diverse Aboriginal clans—comprises the world's oldest continuous civilisation. Thousands of kilometres of Australian cliffs and rock-faces are daubed and scraped with indigenous rock art older than the millennia of Christianity.

In global ecological terms, the most important people in Australia are the surviving traditional indigenous clans. Some of them are preserving systems of values and laws older than any of the legal systems of Europe and Asia. These islands of vestigial ancient culture also present moral dilemmas for an enlightened, law-based nation like Australia. These dilemmas are all personified in Stephen Barnes Jungarrayi.

Stephen Barnes Jungarrayi did not mean to kill his twenty-three-year-old nephew in March 1996. (The name of the dead nephew has been withheld by the Northern Territory police in accordance with Aboriginal custom not to publicly name the dead.) Both men were drunk at the time. The fight started in the backyard of the home they shared in Darwin, where they were preparing the evening meal. When the argument became heated, Jungarrayi picked up a kitchen knife. His nephew picked up an Aboriginal fighting stick. Jungarrayi later told a court he went for his nephew's leg, but the knife rode up the fighting stick and into the nephew's chest. It sliced the coronary artery. The nephew bled to death within minutes.

Jungarrayi was arrested, charged, and placed in custody. He remained in jail for twenty months, until 29 November 1997, when Justice Dean Mildren of the Northern Territory Supreme Court sentenced Jungarrayi, who by then was twenty-eight and had been an alcoholic since his early twenties, to a four-year prison term for manslaughter. Then the judge let him go. Justice Mildren said Jungarrayi had already served 20 months and was also facing 'payback' punishment in his own community. 'A spearing and a beating is envisaged. I take it into account, as I am obliged to, not because the court approves of payback as a form of punishment but because it is not right that a person should be punished twice, both in his own community and by the courts.'

As soon as he was released, Jungarrayi, a fully initiated member of the Warlpiri clan, travelled the 700 kilometres to his community in Lajamanu to face *yawarra*, a Warlpiri word for blood. Lajamanu, a community of some 1 000 people, is about 200 kilometres from Tennant Creek. It is often isolated during the wet season. Warlpiri is a distinct language and its geographical reach ends at the edge of the Great Sandy Desert, the Gibson Desert, and the Barkly Tableland. It is surrounded by the languages and dialects of the Arrernte, Papunya, Kukatja, Warumungu, Mutpurra, and Gurindji.

Like many other traditional communities, Lajamanu imposes an alcohol ban, enforced by the elders, the same elders who decided that Jungarrayi must face *yawarra*. He was to be speared by close relatives of the dead man, and beaten by members of his own immediate family. *Yawarra* required that he be seriously wounded. Even this punishment was a compromise, a recognition that the traditional clans must live in a nation defined by white law. 'In the old days that Jungarrayi would have been killed, but times have changed and we have to move with the times,' the Lajamanu council president, Martin Johnson Japanangka, told reporter Maria Ceresa. 'We have moved our *yapa* law [Warlpiri clan law] to fit in with *kartiya* [white] law but *yapa* must come first. We are living under *kurruwarri kujarra*—two laws.'

The payback took place within days of Jungarrayi's return. It was done in the traditional way, in a place of ritual. The entire Lajamanu community, including children, was allowed to witness it. Close kinsmen supported Jungarrayi by both arms. Before the first spearing they told him to look away. A relative of the dead nephew plunged a wooden spear into Jungarrayi's leg. The spear tore muscle, glanced off the thigh bone, but avoided the femoral artery. Cutting that artery would cause death. The ritual was repeated five times, each blow tearing deep into Jungarrayi's muscle. His blood poured onto the ground. He was then speared eight more times by other members of the nephew's family. He could no longer stand and was being held up by his kinsmen. But his punishment had not ended. He had to be beaten by members of his own family. His sisters and a woman he called 'mother' used traditional clubs, nulla-nullas. They clubbed him about the head, drawing more blood. He blacked out. When he regained his senses the women hit him again. They hit him four times before it was decided he had suffered enough. Jungarrayi was carried to a waiting air ambulance and flown to Katherine Hospital, 350 kilometres away, to recover from his wounds. He checked himself out after five days, earlier than the doctors advised, and returned to Lajamanu with his legs swathed in bandages. He could barely walk.

The punishment drew divergent reactions. The Katherine

Region Aboriginal Legal Aid Service said Jungarrayi's imprisonment had postponed the proper resolution of the matter. 'Under Aboriginal law, which is community based, the punishment would be meted out as soon as possible,' said Glen Dooley, a spokesman for the service. 'The issue would then be resolved, and the sooner this happens the better. When an offender against tribal law is in prison, this merely postpones the community's resolution. Let the tribal punishment occur first, and then the European court. We would like to see an amendment to the Bail Act allowing release for tribal punishment.' A bail application on those grounds was made, but the judge who heard the application said Jungarrayi was facing the infliction of grievous bodily harm and the law clearly prevented him from allowing the court to be a party to such a crime.

The then Attorney General of the Northern Territory and later Chief Minister, Shane Stone, scoffed at suggestions that the release of Jungarrayi could be a case study in favour of using tribal punishment. 'This custom, under Aboriginal law, is barbaric and will not be condoned by this government. Bashing, beating and stabbing are not condoned by the government. Tribal law is not a substitute for penalties set out in the criminal code. The court can't release people to go through tribal punishment.'

Amnesty International agreed. It described as 'cruel and inhuman' the punishment given to Jungarrayi and drew attention to the International Covenant on Civil and Political Rights. 'To allow such cruel punishment to occur without government response would mean to allow human rights violations to be perpetrated with impunity,' said Amnesty's Dr Heinz Schurmann-Zeggel. 'We cannot accept that the difficult legal and human rights questions involved remain forever in the too-hard basket.'

'Aborigines appeal to the Covenant on Civil and Political Rights when it suits them, but you can't have bits and pieces of the covenant,' the social critic, Terry Lane, wrote, referring to this case. 'Islamic barbarism is "traditional", but that does not make it morally acceptable ... Which brings me to another curious case, the ban on selling alcohol to Aborigines by the Curtin Spring roadhouse in the Northern Territory. It seems that everyone is happy about this ban—the Aborigines, the licensee, the Northern Territory Liquor Commission, and the Human Rights and Equal Opportunity Commission. Well, they are all wrong. Prohibition is wrong ... Discrimination is wrong ... Paternalism is wrong ... How does the licensee at Curtin Springs propose who is fit to drink in his pub and who isn't?'

These are big questions. Lane was right to raise the ancient fundamentalist Islamic traditions of mutilation, which are illegal and unacceptable in Australia. This medieval practice is an *imported* barbarity, one of many imported cultural traditions that Australians have rejected. There is only one group in Australia which could ever consider allowing ritual mutilation as a legal practice, and that is indigenous clans practising traditional law. Genital mutilation does occur among these clans, but it involves men, some of whom must undergo the ghastly ritual of subincision, where the penis is split open from the tip to the urethra.

It is brutal and primitive and unacceptable in the wider society, but if traditional indigenous clans are to have any cultural sovereignty, the elders must have the right to enforce tribal law. This can extend from initiation mutilations to banning the sale of grog, a problem imported from the white world. Terry Lane argued that, 'Men have to learn to discipline themselves. Aborigines are neither barbarians nor children.' They are not white people either, or Asian, or Polynesian. They inhabit a different moral and intellectual universe, and this universe is threatened with extinction. If the larger community can ban Muslim mutilation practices, then indigenous communities can ban the white world's drugs and their shocking toll.

An entire book, *Grog War* by Alexis Wright, has been written about the campaign to ban the sale of alcohol to the Aboriginal community at Tennant Creek, not far from Lajamanu. Wright, an Aborigine, provides plenty of grit from the front-line of this little cultural war, quoting the women who bear the brunt of the problem.

> *'Wife get bashed all the time.'*

> *'Parents saying, "if we smash your drink", they saying they will go up the road and commit suicide.'*

> *'That five-litre cask killed a lot of people. Some not even old.'*

> *'Go around stabbing people when drunk and sniffing petrol.'*

'That's why they buy that long neck wine, port wine, for a weapon. They can buy it and smash it. And hurt each other proper hard.'

'They cut themselves all over. He got habit of taking pocket knife in his pocket. When someone else steal grog that person take a knife or a glass and start cutting themselves. They got scars everywhere.'

Paternalism has its limits. Indigenous problems need indigenous solutions. You have to be there, under the skin, to really understand. Yet even the issue of cultural sovereignty shrinks compared with the larger question of indigenous identity. Who is an Aborigine? About forty percent of the indigenous population is now made up of uninitiated, nontraditional people of mixed race living in cities, and their number is exploding. In the 1996 census, 352 970 people described themselves as indigenous Australians, an increase of thirty-three percent in just five years. This explosion in numbers, surely a positive sign, has its own problems. A cultural ocean exists between communities such as the Warlpiri at Lajamanu and nontraditional urban blacks. Yet a myth has grown up among white Australians that the indigenous populations are somehow a homogeneous group. This is ridiculous. Later on this book will be looking at this and other myths as we travel among the barbarians. But right now we are looking at just one Australian, Stephen Barnes Jungarrayi, and he is difficult enough.

Jungarrayi is a drunk who has killed someone. He has

never held a steady job. The system of justice that freed him has also sometimes been abused in the past by being used merely to avoid incarceration. Violence against women in the indigenous communities is endemic, appalling by the standards of the wider society. The people on both sides of the Jungarrayi case have powerful moral arguments, which is why these issues are so difficult.

Despite all the problems, I'm going with Jungarrayi and the Warlpiri elders. Justice Mildren was right to free him for traditional punishment. The law is already winking in this direction. Those who administered the bloody ritual punishment to Jungarrayi are liable to punishment of up to life imprisonment if a court were to find they had inflicted premeditated grievous bodily harm, which certainly was the case. But no-one, before or after the payback, has ever suggested that any legal action be taken against those Warlpiri people who exacted ritual retribution. What happened to Jungarrayi was not unusual. There is still plenty of tribal punishment and payback meted out in the traditional clans, below the sight and reach of *kartiya*, white law. No matter what the Chief Minister and the judge say, there is *kurruwarri kujarra*, two laws, in the Northern Territory.

The jargon about 'human rights violations' from Heinz Schurmann-Zeggel of Amnesty International is sanctimonious. His comments about crimes 'perpetrated with impunity' is typical of the imperial thinking that still afflicts Europeans in their dealings with other parts of the world. Stephen Barnes Jungarrayi went to his own brutal punishment willingly. The enactment of the punishment was difficult for everyone and was carried out according to custom. The punishment itself was modified by the wider context of white law. Moral and emotional issues were resolved by the people most directly involved. Until Dr Schurmann-Zeggel has sat down and talked to Martin Johnson Japanangka and the other elders who are trying to save an ancient culture, he can hold his punctilious advice.

I know a white man, exactly my own age, also from Sydney, who while the rest of us went to university, or began careers, or travelled the hippie trail looking for enlightenment, went up to the centre, out of curiosity, and stayed twenty-two years. He learned Warlpiri and developed skin relationships and learned the complex skin systems. After he had been abused enough times by drunken Warlpiri men who called him less than a man because he wasn't initiated, he became fully initiated. The Warlpiri are subincision people, so they opened him up all the way. He married a Warlpiri woman with the right skin relationship and they had three children. He has always worked hard, but when I saw him in February 1998, he had moved to Alice Springs. He was worn out. Twenty-two years as a human bridge across the chasm between two worlds had finally washed his family out of the bush. How many of us really understand the distance he had travelled? Very few.

We'll leave the last word to Stephen Barnes Jungarrayi.

'The courts should realise we are still living traditional around here. I was really glad I was able to face my family in the traditional way. My family has accepted me back, started talking to me again, and things are starting to get back to normal … After what I have been through, bad times, bad experiences, I will try to teach the young people in this community both ways, traditional and reading and writing.'

Asked if, prior to the attacks, he had thought of returning to jail and Australian law, Jungarrayi said: 'No … Sometimes [in prison] I considered doing something to myself or hanging myself. I knew what was coming to me. It's always been the way … I had to face it.'

2
IT WASN'T LUCK

CHARLES DARWIN DESCRIBED NEW South Wales as 'a very paradise to the worshippers of Mammon' after he visited the colony in January 1836 during his now legendary journey aboard HMS *Beagle*. He was struck by the wealth and energy of the young colony. In a letter to his wife, Susan, he wrote of Sydney:

Ancient Rome in her imperial grandeur, would not be ashamed of such an offspring ... Can better proof of the extraordinary prosperity of this country be conceived than the fact that 7/8th of an acre of land in the town sold by auction for 12,000 pounds sterling? There are now men living, who came out as convicts (and one of whom has since been flogged at the Cart's tail round the town) who are said to possess without doubt an income from 12 to 15,000 pounds per annum ...

It is an admirable country to grow rich in; turn sheep herd and I believe with common care, you must grow wealthy.

This was just two generations after the arrival of the First Fleet. The colony's almost instantaneous distinctiveness and progressiveness is described in Alan Atkinson's ground-breaking and award-winning 1997 history, *The Europeans in Australia, Volume One.*

> *From the very beginning, Australian political culture ... was remarkably original, especially when we take into account the remoteness and smallness of early European settlement ...*
>
> *White settlement began here during the 1780s, a decade of extraordinary creativity, the climax of the European Enlightenment ... A century whose climax was marked by great political revolutions in North America and France, and by vast and unprecedented demographic and industrial change, especially in Britain, was not 'a static time'...*
>
> *The First Fleet sailed from England two years before the outbreak of revolution in Europe, and for many years in this remote corner of the globe the eighteenth century stood still. For an entire generation, European order was worked out in Australia as if all the exquisite promises of the Enlightenment might still come true.*

Throughout the crucial first fifty years of modern settlement when the enduring core of Australia's character was set in place, Britain was at the height of its military strength, administrative reach, and cultural certainty. It had developed a vigorous bureaucracy to run an empire, with the services of superbly trained officers from the Royal Navy and the British army. Australia was administered with relative efficiency, probity and equity, especially when measured against the standards of the time and the brutish behaviour of the other imperial powers of Europe. Above all, Australia was meant to be an egalitarian society. This point is central to Atkinson's history. He describes 'the chemistry which created social order' in which leading ex-convicts were central to the management of the economy from an early stage. 'The original British plan [was] for a "community of peasant proprietors" in the Antipodes,' Atkinson explains. He challenges the argument, put most famously by Robert Hughes in *The Fatal Shore*, that formative colonial Australia was designed as the world's first concentration camp:

> *Botany Bay, it has been argued, was meant as a Gulag*
> *before Gulag ... Nothing could be further from the truth.*
> *In autumn 1786, if not later, New South Wales was envis-*
> *aged as a land of Englishmen where the rights inherent*
> *in living conversation, the rights admired by the more*
> *old-fashioned advocates of liberty, would prevail ...*
> *At Botany Bay, so it was thought, the convicts would be*
> *peasants in a country of their own ... It was not, so*
> *[Lord] Sydney hoped, to be a place where the Crown*
> *might tighten its hold on humble, helpless Englishmen.*
> *So Sydney hoped.*

Atkinson's work builds on the myth-demolishing work of Professor Alan Frost, who has challenged and largely dispelled some of the mythologies in popular history surrounding the First Fleet.

That Aborigines were devastated by smallpox contracted

from the settlers of the First Fleet. This is one of the grim cornerstones of the thesis of Australian genocide against the indigenous people, so the facts are crucial. Frost argues that the documentary evidence does not support the speculative contention of smallpox transmitted to the Aborigines by the settlers. He has written that none of the Europeans on the First Fleet contracted smallpox, and that any contaminated materials, such as blankets, which may have left England between 1786–87 would have lost potency during such a long sea voyage. He has also found that the pattern of smallpox in the Pacific region at that time points to the disease travelling south through Australia, from Asia, rather than from the new settlers.

Frost's work is supported in the *Medical History Australia 1997*, which states: 'The gruesome spectre of the smallpox epidemic of 1789, that extraordinary calamity which struck the aborigines about Port Jackson, has haunted the medical history of the early settlement of New South Wales. Its origin is a conundrum that historians have tended to solve by intuition and bias. The most judicious survey of this phenomenon and the most reasonable and carefully reasoned explanation of the disease's origin is to be found in chapter 10, "The Curse of Cain?", of Alan Frost's book, *Botany Bay Mirages: Illusions of Australia's Convict Beginnings.*'

That New South Wales was conceived solely as a colony of exile. Wrong. The Pitt government also wanted to expand British commercial trading, pre-empt French expansionism, and find a new source of naval materials.

That the First Fleet was so incompetently assembled that

it lacked such basics as ploughs, seed potatoes and adequate clothing for the convicts. Wrong. All these items were included. Among many examples of good planning cited by Frost, scurvy did not afflict the fleet, and the fertility of the women suggested they were in good health.

Thus, the enterprise of penal servitude was not the only element that forged Australia. Early Australia was not built by convicts, but largely by *ex*-convicts. Nearly all convicts had only seven-year sentences and all had served at least a year by the time they landed in New South Wales, and some three or four years. They could not be kept in bondage once their time was up. Hope and optimism were also strong. Watkin Tench and David Collins saw bright hope on the faces of those setting out in the first journeys to New South Wales. Collins wrote that 'joy sparkled in every countenance' as the fleet sailed.

These first arrivals could not know how hard the eucalyptus domain would be. By the time of Federation a century later, ecological and economic crisis was the backdrop of Australian history. The long depression of the 1890s overlapped exactly with the Long Drought. A bank collapse in 1891 fed into the global depression of 1893 and forty percent of Australia's export income went to service British debts. Cropfields and pastures were left to return to bush. Overstocked herds were culled. Tracts of farmed land blew away in clouds of dust. The rabbit plague reached catastrophic proportions. The Red Centre expanded. Society was retreating from the hinterland. The years following Federation saw Australia lose population. The eucalyptus forests burned.

This environment demanded egalitarianism. A European population spread thinly through the fire forests of the continent could not sustain the social hierarchies of Europe. Even by independence on 1 January 1901, Australia's population was barely three million. The full extent of colonial Australia's defining battle with the environment is only now being truly understood. It has been fashionable in recent decades for historians to trivialise the process of nation-forming for ideological purposes. That fashion is now under assault from the weight of later histories not deformed by the requirements of ideology. Among the new histories, Robert Birrell's *A Nation Of Our Own* (1995) confronts the distortions of ideology head-on.

Two decades of revisionist writing have diminished the reputation of the early nationalist leaders and the institutions they created. This soiling of the early years of our national experience has helped to undermine Australians' faith that there is anything in their heritage worthy of inspiration ...

There is a widely held view that the achievement of Australian nationhood in 1901 was little more than a shabby administrative deal between colonial leaders, motivated in large part by a desire to remove impediments to inter-colonial trade. According to this perspective, nationalism was not a crucial factor ... Thus Manning Clark's devastating comment that federation was 'one of those constitutional devices recommended by apologists for bourgeois democracy for containing political equality'.

What was the historical basis of Manning Clark's claim? Helen Irving's 1997 history of the Australian constitution, *To Constitute a Nation*, looked for evidence and couldn't find any. The claim that there was a conscious conservative strategy, even conspiracy, has been subjected to scrutiny by several historians and has been found to be without corroboration, Irving writes. 'The fact [is] that almost no direct evidence exists of conservative opinion or advice along such lines, and that many of the most conservative also opposed Federation ... '

The nonchalant and cynical dismissal of the struggle to create Federation is now being challenged by scholars undeformed by outdated Marxist analysis. 'Australian nationhood cannot be explained in these terms,' writes Birrell. There were too many obstacles to be overcome in the form of intercolonial jealousies and too little in the way of shared grievances against British control. Each Australian colony had pursued its own development independent of the others. Their main external links were with Britain, not the other colonies. Each colony had developed its own railway system in order to prevent neighbouring colonies from attracting cross-border traffic. Each colony had its own well-developed sense of identity. In Victoria at the time of Federation, seventy-nine percent of residents were Australian-born, but only six percent were natives of other States. In New South Wales, 80 percent were native-born, but only eight percent were from other States. To win Federation required incumbent politicians not only to give up powers and privileges to an unknown federal authority. The anchor of political inertia was heavy.

But the sheer scale of the problems facing Australia in the 1890s overmatched the ability of the colonies to deal with them individually. The sense of siege helped create a collectivist response. The experience of the United States, far from serving as a beacon, served as a warning of a racially divided society. Helen Irving points out what many people have missed: that the Civil War, so historically distant from us now, was a matter of living memory for even the youngest of the delegates to the federation conferences in the 1890s. Even as late as 1898, debate was continuing in Australian newspapers over the causes of the Civil War and its lesson for Australia.

Out of all this came a mood from which to create a new nation, a new constitution and a new government, despite the fears of the small States that any national parliament would be dominated by New South Wales and Victoria. The success depended on the ability to mobilise support across the class spectrum, and from both city and country. Alfred Deakin and his federation supporters expressed their ideas around the theme that Australia was to become a 'new world' free of 'old world' social divisions. This ideal was the rallying point for the diverse electoral coalition the federationists constructed. 'An emotional commitment to the establishment of an Australian nation, primarily among native-born colonists, was a crucial factor in overcoming obstacles,' writes Birrell.

Helen Irving, too, debunks the cynical view. She points out that the framers of the Constitution were working with the conceptual tools they had at hand. After scouring the history of the Australian Constitution, she does not dismiss the collective idealism of the people. Australians were capable of both pragmatism and romanticism, writes Irving, and this practical blend made Federation possible. It was certainly not the work of British imperialism, which by the 1890s had been reduced to a mainly ceremonial role in the governance of the colonies.

When Federation passed overwhelmingly in 1899 (though only narrowly in New South Wales) with sixty percent of adult males voting, independence unleashed a sequence of egalitarian social legislation that was unprecedented anywhere in the world. State funding for free State education was extended to secondary school. Women won the vote. Maternity benefits, creches, kindergartens and playgrounds, nursing services, pure food and milk supplies were all funded by the State. By 1910 the infant mortality rate in Australia had fallen to 71.7 per thousand while in Britain the rate was 105 and in France 111. In 1908 an Old Age and Invalid Pension Bill was enacted, paying double the value of the pension paid in Britain.

Australian nativism was active across the full range of culture. Artists such as Streeton, McCubbin and Roberts fed off the bush to create a distinctive Australian art. The Australian Football League was a response to the popularity of soccer among British immigrants. Australian labour was protected by a tariff wall, and government imposed itself in the setting of wages, hours, conditions, demarcations and collective bargaining. A protective wall also went up around Australian industry. Neither protective wall would come down for seventy-five years. The sense of self-reliance extended to military spending. By 1911–12, writes Birrell, Australia was approaching the per capita defence expenditure of Britain and substantially exceeding that of Canada, the United States and even Germany. Through the period between 1901 and 1909, when legislation was passed to establish a civilian militia based on compulsory training, the British military authorities advised it would be more appropriate to develop a field force which could be integrated with the Imperial defence forces. This advice was rejected.

Australia's military commitment would be tested soon enough. By the end of 1914, just months after the outbreak of World War I, 52 561 men had enlisted, from about 820 000 eligible for service. Patriotism and adventure were the greatest factors, but drought and hardship were also important. In 1914 the wheat crop had been reduced by two-thirds, and unemployment in the bush was high. The collective character of the young Australians who went to war is captured in their letters, used by Bill Gammage in his brilliant 1974 book, *The Broken Years*. Ellis Silas, of the 16th Battalion, wrote these words in 1915 just before the first Australian wave landed at Gallipoli:

> *We have been told of the impossible task before us, of probably annihilation; yet we are eager to get to it; we joke with each other about getting cold feet, but deep down in our hearts we know when we get to it we will not be found wanting ... for the last time in this world*

many of us stand shoulder to shoulder. As I look down
the ranks of my comrades I wonder which of us is
marked for the land beyond.

The disaster of Gallipoli did not prevent the Australian army from prodigious achievement over the course of the war. During the final nine months of the war in 1918, the Australian army opposed thirty-nine divisions and defeated them all. They took 29 144 prisoners (twenty-three percent of the British total), 338 guns (23.5 percent), and forty miles of ground (21.5 percent), and made possible the gaining of much more. Yet they made up less than ten percent of the British army.

These achievements were also made in inimitable style. In 1917 three Australian divisions recorded twelve times the number of absence without leave convictions than the twenty-two other divisions of the Third Army. In March 1918, 9000 Australians were in field prisons, compared with fewer than 2000 in every other British or colonial force. Bill Gammage wrote that Australian forces received some visits by the King in stolid silence. He also described, 'the fierce individualism with which he fought Turks, Arabs and English staff officers'. Gammage describes the Australian light-horseman as laconic, practical, with the equanimity and resourcefulness of the bushman. 'Probably his kind will not be seen again for the conditions of war and romance that produced him have almost entirely disappeared.' The words of an Australian soldier, writing in his diary in 1917, would reverberate through the nation:

Adieu, the years are a broken song,
And the right grows weak in the strife with wrong,
The lilies of love have a crimson stain,
And the old days never will come again.

Australians' character would soon be tested again on an even greater scale in a war of national survival. Gavan Daws in *Prisoners of the Japanese*, a history of the allied prisoners in the Pacific theatre of World War II, describes cultures stripped down to their most elemental basics.

> *I started coming across national differences in behaviour from the very first days of my research, and the evidence kept piling up. When I tried to think of simple expressions to describe what I was finding, the words that came to mind were* tribes *and* tribalism ... *Tribalism has always had enormous power: it still does. And certainly it did in the prisoner of war camps.*
>
> *I would go so far as to say that it was nationality above all that determined, for good or ill, the way POWs lived and died, often* whether *they lived or died.*

In the camps Australians discarded their differences (the biggest was the suspicion between Catholics and Masons which even showed up in the camps until crushed by the conditions) and became a tribe, a tribe which was always the most successful group. The core of this success was an ethos of mateship and egalitarianism which not only survived the ultimate dehumanising duress of the death camps, but shone through as the dominant Australian characteristic.

The juices crushed out of the POWs were of course human in the most fundamental sense. But at the same time, all the way down to starvation rations, to a hundred pounds of body weight and less, to the extremities of degradation—all the way to death—the prisoners of the Japanese remained inextinguishably American, Australian, British, Dutch ...

The Americans were the great individualists of the camps, the capitalists, the cowboys, the gangsters. The British hung on to their class structure like bulldogs, for grim death. The Australians kept trying to construct little male-bonded welfare states ...

[Unlike Americans] Australians could not imagine doing men to death by charging interest on something as basic to life as rice. That was bloodsucking; it was murder. Within little tribes of Australian enlisted men, rice went back and forth all the time, but this was not trading in commodities futures, it was sharing, it was Australian tribalism.

One of the most memorable passages in *Prisoners of the Japanese* is a survivor's description of what happened after the sinking of a Japanese freighter, the *Rakuyo Maru*, filled with prisoners of war:

When the Rakuyo Maru *went down with seven hundred Australians and six hundred British aboard, it was the Australians who tried to preserve the biggest prisoner*

*tribe. On the third day in the water, some Englishmen
who were almost finished sighted a mass of black shapes.*

*As we drew nearer we saw there were about two to
three hundred men gathered on a huge pontoon of rafts.
They had erected a couple of lofty distress signals,
coloured shorts and other bits of clothing fixed to spars
of wood. As we paddled up we saw there was a large
outer ring of rafts linked to each other with pieces of
rope. Inside the circle were other rafts, unattached but
safely harboured. They seemed organized compared with
the disintegrated rabble we had become during those last
two days. They may have been drifting aimlessly as we
had; but at least they all drifted together. A lot of them
still wore those familiar slouch hats—we had caught up
with the Aussie contingent. One of them looped us in
with a dangling end of rope. "Cheers, mate," came the
friendly voice. 'This is no place to be on your lonesome'.*

It is important to remember the privations of these wars, and
the pervasive sense of dread for the millions of Australians
who lived through them. The world wars are rapidly receding into historical abstractions, and as they fade from the
collective experience it is becoming discreditable in universities to invoke the memory of these struggles. It is almost as
if the past is now mainly invoked for what was lost, not won.
But the red stain across Australian history was not left only
by the receding Aboriginal tribes. Stoicism in the face of pain
was ingrained in the evolving Australian character from the
earliest days, a characteristic duly noted by Robert Hughes in
The Fatal Shore.

*The scarred back became an emblem of rank. So did
silence. Convicts called a man who blubbered and
screamed at the triangles a* crawler *or a* sandstone.
*(Sandstone is a common rock around Sydney; it is soft
and crumbles easily.) By contrast, the convict who stood
up to it in silence was admired as a* pebble *or an* iron
man.

Something happened to Australian stoicism and nativism
during the comfort and success of the boom after World War
II. A key record of this change was Donald Horne's *The
Lucky Country*, first published in 1964. It was a huge best-
seller, reprinted for many years thereafter, and became a
formative document. *The Lucky Country* is a lucid book but
also an extremely patronising book. More than any other
postwar work, it created and legitimised the practice of sneering at Australian culture. Again and again, Horne's tone is
one of unambiguous embarrassment, the embarrassment of a
provincial intellectual.

*The possibility that the world should become like Aus-
tralia would profoundly alarm most cultivated people in
the world ...*

*Australia is a lucky country run mainly by second-rate
people who share its luck. It lives on other people's ideas
and, although its ordinary people are adaptable, most of
its leaders (in all fields) so lack curiosity about the
events that surround them that they are often taken by
surprise. A nation more concerned with styles of life than*

with achievement has managed to achieve what may be the most evenly prosperous society in the world ...

It is usually not possible to conduct in Australia the kind of conversation that would be immediately acceptable among intellectuals in Europe, or New York ...

Intellectual life exists but it is still fugitive. Emergent and uncomfortable, it has no established relation to practical life. The upper levels of society give an impression of mindlessness triumphant ... at the top the tone is so banal that to a sophisticated observer the flavour of democratic life in Australia might seem depraved, a victory of the anti-mind ...

In Australia people get away with things that would be exposed in a more sophisticated nation ...

But the tiredness and cliche-thinking of opinion-makers is unable to capture the skepticism of the people. It is almost a conspiracy of tiredness of the spirit ...

Australia has not the resources to play Lady Bountiful to all Asia but per capita national income in Australia is sixteen times that of Asia. Despite its internal democracy, Australia plays an aristocratic role in the society of Asia—rich, self-centred, frivolous, blind ...

Australia did not 'earn' nationhood by struggle against the oppressor or civil war. It could have become a nation earlier than it did, if it had wanted to. At the end of the 19th Century there was a desultory debate for 20 years as the six separate Colonies began to talk about federating. Finally there was a referendum. Sixty per cent of Australians voted in it; altogether 43 per cent of all electors voted 'yes'.

The Lucky Country must be judged in the context of its time, and in this context Horne's comments were intelligent and forward-looking. His book was a resounding success in the marketplace of ideas. The social context of his arguments was the provincialism of the 1950s and 1960s (though similar provincialism existed in most places around the world if one cared to look). Taste-makers like Horne, in helping to shed the narrowness of postwar Australia, also laid the foundation for a much more destructive and methodical assault on Australian history in the 1970s and 1980s—fuelled partly by the idealistic folly of the Vietnam War—an assault led first by academic Marxism and then by the multicultural industry.

'Advocates of multiculturalism tend to resist arguments that a unique Australian society and identity emerged with Federation, and especially the expectation that this identity should be the basis of immigrant assimilation,' says Bob Birrell, the Monash University demographer and historian. 'One way to discredit such expectations is to argue that the early Australian nationalists did not in fact create a society or culture which can be regarded as distinctly "Australian" ... In response to those who insist that Australia is distinctive, people like Stephen Castles argue that much of this is mythical, or worse, a cover-up of a rather seamy historical reality.'

Australia grew up as part of the British Empire. Unlike

> *the USA, India or Britain's other far-flung possessions,*
> *Australia never managed a decent independence move-*
> *ment, let alone a liberation struggle. Australia was made*
> *a nation by an Act of the British Parliament in 1901. The*
> *creation of a nation in a struggle for independence is*
> *usually the pre-eminent moment for the definition of*
> *national character, language, culture and myths. Aus-*
> *tralia has missed out on this.*

The authors of this summation, an echo of Donald Horne, were Stephen Castles, Mary Kalantzis, Bill Cope and M Morrissey, writing in *Mistaken Identity, Multiculturalism and the Demise of Nationalism in Australia* (1990), a work typical of the genre. During the years of Labor's ascendancy in Canberra, Castles, Kalantzis and Cope were key players for the ideology of multiculturalism. Their ideology was, and remains, hostile to the mythology of Australia's egalitarian tradition.

> *It has been racist, justifying genocide and exclusionism,*
> *and denying the role of non-British migrants. It has been*
> *sexist, ignoring the role of women in national develop-*
> *ment, and justifying their subordinate position. It has*
> *idealised the role of the 'common man' in a situation of*
> *growing inequality and increasingly rigid class divisions.*

This hatred of Australia's past manages to turn success into failure. Since World War II no other nation in the world has remade itself so comprehensively and so seamlessly as Australia, absorbing and adapting a wide range of cultural influences and immigrants. In 1964, the year *The Lucky Country* was published, Australia's population was 11.25 million. In the year 2000, the population will be nineteen million, an increase of two-thirds in little more than a generation. This transformative thrust was not the vision of a self-satisfied, narrow nation.

David Malouf, in his foreword to the third edition of the *Macquarie Dictionary* (1997), the superb and now ubiquitous cultural reference point which did not exist when Donald Horne produced *The Lucky Country*, wrote of his changing country and its changing language:

> *For a long time we tended to see our local world, for all*
> *its vastness and the variety of its landscape, as uniform,*
> *not because it was, but because we had not yet found a*
> *use for variety and for that reason had no eye for it.*

'It's miraculous!' another acute Australian writer, Clive James, said in 1997. 'It is so striking after you come home after a long time away because back in the 1950s I can remember how short of culture we felt we were. And now there's no question of shortage. For a long, long time, people were spending a lot of time talking about what Australian culture should be, and not realising that culture grows like a coral reef, through accumulations, through accretions, often through the deaths of a lot of little anonymous creatures.'

Success and solidity has been built over the long-haul. The wealth which so amazed Charles Darwin in 1836 has not, as in so many other naturally wealthy countries, been dissipated. Australians are, on average, almost five times richer than they were at the start of the twentieth century, according to a 1997 study by the CSIRO. The average life has increased between the 1890s and the 1990s from forty-nine to seventy-eight. The adult life of the average Australian has almost doubled in a century.

The World Bank, which now uses a complex formula to measure the relative wealth of nations, including 'natural capital' and environmental stewardship, rates Australia the sixth wealthiest nation in the world after the United States, Switzerland, Canada, Japan and Norway. 'Australia's quality of life looks even better than the purely economic index,' Professor Fred Gruen told me in 1996. 'Japan, for example, appears much wealthier than Australia. But if you look at Japan by other, more subtle measures the standard of living is worse than Australia's. The Japanese work much longer hours, commute much longer and live in much smaller homes.'

Australia is still called the lucky country, and the description is still not a kind one. It implies a nation that lives off an inheritance. But Australia, distant from its markets, sparse in its population, living off a largely threadbare continent, has taken what was available and used its advantages, despite mistakes, logically and efficiently. It wasn't luck.

In *The Lucky Country* Donald Horne looked back and quoted Vance Palmer who, beneath the shadow of social annihilation in 1942, with everything at stake, wrote:

The next few months may decide not only whether we are to survive as a nation, but whether we deserve to survive

*... If Australia had no more character than could be seen
on its surface, it would be annihilated as surely and
swiftly as those colonial outposts white men built for
their commercial profit in the East—pretentious facades
of stucco that looked imposing as long as the wind kept
from blowing. But there is an Australia of the spirit, sub-
merged and not very articulate, that is quite different
from these bubbles of old-world imperialism ... sardonic,
idealist, tongue-tied perhaps, it is the Australia of all
who truly belong here ... And it has something to contribute to the world. Not emphatically in the arts as yet,
but in arenas of action, and in ideas for the creation of
that egalitarian democracy that will have to be the basis
for all civilized societies in the future. That is the Australia we are called upon to save.*

That is exactly what has happened. The half century
1947–1997 saw a social revolution in Australia that was
bloodless, gradualist, democratic and open-minded. In 1947,
the Australian population was just 7.5 million; it was ninety
percent Anglo-Celtic; it was ninety-nine percent European;
the Aboriginal and Asian populations combined were less
than one percent of the overall population; public policy still
enshrined White Australia, which had helped define the
nation since independence; links with Asia were minimal; the
British Privy Council was still the ultimate court of appeal;
Aborigines did not have citizenship, and had barely any role
in society. There were no computers. There was not even
television. There was no gaping hole in the ozone layer, or

global warming. The nation had just fought a monumental struggle for survival against a powerful and ruthless Asian invader.

Fifty years later, no other nation in the world, not even the United States, had remade itself so comprehensively, so equitably, and with such unselfconscious ambition, as Australia in the era after World War II. The overt culture of the nation— its language, cuisine, music, writings, film, dance, architecture, design, sport—all, at their highest expression, have become sophisticated, exuberant, worldly and distinct.

The myth of the lucky country is dispelled by dozens of countries with abundant natural wealth that have failed in those fifty years. It is dispelled by the many countries, the great majority of nations, that have not matched the dexterous, adaptable, democratic joy of Australian culture, and by the many countries where ethnic divisions have led to violence. The myth is dispelled by all the blood in the pages of Australian history. The myth of the lucky country needs to die. The truly lucky ones have been the perpetrators of this myth. It's time their luck ran out.

3
BLACK RAIN

AN ENTIRE ECONOMY DISAPPEARED in 1997. Seven hundred billion dollars. Gone. The twelfth largest economy in the world, much bigger than the gross national product of Australia.

Evaporated.

The crisis took physical shape in August when thick smoke rolled over the green hills and grey cities of South-East Asia and the sky disappeared. Fires burned, thousands of people became sick, millions hid indoors, and in Papua New Guinea hundreds died and half a million people went starving. The dense haze drifted from New Guinea to Malaysia, a distance wider than Australia. Something was badly wrong in Asia.

Even the once impregnable rainforest of Borneo, a forest canopy so large it appeared from the air like an enormous rolling lawn, has been so gashed by decades of logging that when the monsoon failed and the land dried, tens of thousands of hectares of rainforest peat caught fire and burned through July, August, September, October and into November. Twenty million Indonesians were exposed to chronic pollution, and millions more around the region. Airports were closed, flights cancelled, travel and trade disrupted. In the evergreen forests, poorly adapted to fire, trees were dying. By the time the monsoon finally came in November, the crisis had taken a different form. An electronic, computerised deluge—a black rain—had engulfed the entire region, reaching Japan, South Korea and Hong Kong as well.

On 30 June 1997 the combined value of the dynamic stock markets of Asia—Japan, South Korea, Taiwan, Hong Kong, Malaysia, Indonesia, Singapore, Thailand and the Philippines—had been almost exactly 3000 billion dollars, according to the American bank Morgan Stanley. Six months later, after fires, bank failures, property market collapses, currency shocks and stock market meltdowns, the combined value of those same nine stock markets had dropped to around 2300 billion dollars. Seven hundred billion dollars carried away in an electronic typhoon.

Estimates of the total market/currency losses in Asia in 1997 settle at well over US$1 trillion. By comparison, the entire net worth of all Australians' homes, savings and assets in 1997 were estimated at around A$1.9 trillion. Add to the market crash the Asian property crash, the tens of billions in unrecoverable loans from Japan to Indonesia, and the debased value of some currencies, and the total losses created in 1997–98 were much more than twice the size of the Australian economy—the disappearance from the global balance sheets of one of the world's ten largest economies.

Flimsy banking structures exposed flimsy political structures. Factories were burned down in Thailand amid rioting. There were more riots in Indonesia, where unemployment rose, prices soared, panic buying stripped supermarkets of food, and people began hoarding. Indonesia's debt was downgraded to 'junk bond' status. Jakarta was alive with skittish rumours about the aging President Soeharto. The International Monetary Fund had to bail out a bankrupt system. The plutocracy looked frail. In strict accounting terms, Indonesia was insolvent. The value of the stock market was much less than its debts and its capacity to pay those debts, many of them in now extremely expensive foreign currencies. South Korea was also technically insolvent, amid mass demonstrations, bankruptcies, a currency free-fall, a market collapse and a blow-out of foreign debt. The IMF had to provide more than 100 billion dollars in loans to prop up South Korea, Indonesia and Thailand, the largest bail-out in the IMF's history.

Malaysia refused to go to the IMF, but its problems were among the worst. Cracks began to appear in the economy as early as July, and they were made worse when the Prime Minister, Dr Mahathir Mohamad singled out the world's leading individual financial trader, New York based George Soros, describing him as a 'self-serving rogue'. The government-controlled media suggested Soros had been a Nazi sympathiser—even though he is Jewish—and also had links to 'the international Zionist conspiracy'. Mahathir then made another attack on Soros, describing him as a 'moron' and a 'criminal'. Months earlier, Mahathir had already banned the movie *Schindler's List*, with its portrayal of the Jewish Holocaust.

On 4 September 1997 the Malaysian government attempted to stare down the international currency market by backing the ringgit. The government lost thirty billion dollars in a single day. This sent the Malaysian stock market plunging. By then the Malaysian capital, Kuala Lumpur, was draped in the thick smoke haze that clung throughout the region. In the midst of all this, Mahathir travelled to Cuba to receive a prize from the Cuban government. At a state dinner in Havana, he praised his host, Fidel Castro. 'Nations need politicians like yourself,' he told the world's longest-serving dictator. Then he harangued the 'rich and powerful' nations who continued to give orders to the rest of the world. The Malaysian currency and stock markets continued to fall.

Like a gambler digging a deeper hole to recoup his losses, Mahathir told supporters at a regional political rally on 11 October: 'We may suspect that they, the Jews, have an agenda, but we do not want to accuse.'

He accused George Soros of conspiring against the ringgit, pointing out that he was Jewish. 'Incidentally, we are Muslims, and the Jews are not happy to see the Muslims progress … The Jews robbed the Palestinians of everything, but in Malaysia they could not do so, hence they do this, depress the ringgit.'

Pushed into a corner with the economy tumbling around him, the seventy-one-year-old Dr Mahathir, in his sixteenth year as Prime Minister, exacerbated the country's problems with a series of disastrous government interventions, ordering a trading curb on 100 blue-chip stocks on the Kuala Lumpur stock exchange, announcing a 200 billion dollar fund to defend the stock market—bigger than half Malaysia's GNP—to be financed by higher taxes and special bonds, and restricting foreigners trading in Malaysian stocks and currency.

The market continued to crash and the currency continued to fall. By the end of 1997 the value of the Malaysian stock market had plummeted seventy-six percent in US dollar terms. Mahathir's grand national building schemes collapsed. The Multimedia Super Corridor, Cyber Jaya and Linear City were scrapped. His international media coverage included the phrases 'staggeringly inept', 'ridiculous', 'xenophobic' and 'racist'.

Asia's speculative excesses were the cause of the Tiger crisis, and the overheated economies were engulfed by an existential deluge. It came out of the future, not the past. It was an electronic black rain of volatile trading that dwarfed all the economic structures of the world. Money and value were being reinvented, redefined, repackaged and resold in multiplying combinations. Markets were being made not just in common stocks, but in preferred, participating preferred, second-preferred, prior-preferred, cumulative preferred, bond convertible, treasury, DARTS, ARPS, warrants (put, instalment, endowment, capital plus, subscription), subscription rights, debenture stocks, SCOREs, PRIMEs, stock options (naked and covered), ADRs, PIKs, index funds, bond index baskets, futures (stock, commodity, currency, index) and futures options. Bonds: junk, savings, dollar, euro, eurodollar, Yankee, yen, Aussie, gold, CTBs, CBBs, baby, put, convertibles, convertible preferred, coupons (zero, liquid yield, current, short, long, full and registered), MIGs-1, -2, -3 and -4; pass-throughs, pickups, citizens, cushions, flowers, obligations, adjustments, resets, perpetuals, super sinkers, IDBs, MITs, ARMs, ARM fixers, LYONS, REDs, HITs, BAN's, RTCs, CMOs, RANs, RAMs, TABs, TANs, REITs, REMICs, PRIMES, SCORES, GAINS, FIGS, FEARS, STRIPS, TIGERs, CATs and LIONs. In the midst of the electronic deluge Wall Street traders were inventing new securities, derivatives of derivatives, and calling them REPS and Mopprs.

These multiplying products didn't exist except on computer screens, traders' receipts and owners' accounts, but they had real meanings and real consequences. In nominal value the derivatives trade towered over the global equity and bond and commodity markets. The value of interest-rate swaps alone was more than twenty-five *trillion* dollars a year. More than ninety percent of the stupendous multi-trillion global electronic money flow was speculative. Less than ten percent was for trade or investment or travel.

The losses in Asia in this global financial casino were staggering. Expressed in US dollar terms, which combines plummeting markets with crashing currencies, the Thai stock market fell seventy-six percent in 1997; South Korea also fell seventy-six percent; Indonesia seventy-four percent; Malaysia seventy percent; the Philippines sixty-one percent, Singapore forty percent and Hong Kong 22.6 percent. Imagine the Australian stock market falling from 2600 to 1600, or your retirement nest egg from $100 000 to $40 000, and you get a sense of what it was like to be a Tiger in 1997. Imagine your bank is technically insolvent.

One of Australia's finest economic writers, the late

TM Fitzgerald, warned in 1990 about the increasing velocity of global currency flows.

The economic situation that we have to address now is more difficult than anything that I have ever seen because so many things are now beyond our control. Australia is now on sufferance to foreign lenders of huge amounts of volatile short-term funds. In the past ten years the transformation has been total: an overwhelming preponderance of a vastly bloated capital inflow on very short term ... Naturally, that locust plague has tended to drive away most of the traditional bedding-down kind of capital, apart from money to effect takeovers of existing Australian enterprise by foreigners.

Dr Doom had also warned us. In a major speech in New York on Anzac Day 1994, Dr Henry Kaufman, known as Dr Doom on Wall Street, had predicted much of what came to pass in 1997, blaming what he called 'the Americanisation of finance' for the roiling mountains of financial turbulence.

The technology is in place for a cascade of selling by investors ... The market is driven by an expanding group of high-octane portfolio managers using new trading techniques, especially derivatives, who are free to roam throughout the financial sphere, in and out of currencies, equities, bonds, commodities, derivative instruments, with primarily a near-term focus, and no particular loyalty to any national marketplace.

Dr Doom correctly predicted the emergence of traders commanding portfolios worth around 500 billion dollars roaming the world. The most famous of these was George Soros, the ultimate black rainmaker, the man so reviled by Dr Mahathir Mohamad. George Soros was worried. He saw great potential danger in the markets he had ridden to such wealth and influence. Prior to the 1997 currency shock, he wrote:

> *Although I have made a fortune in the financial markets, I now fear that the untrammelled intensification of laissez-faire capitalism and the spread of market values into all areas of life is endangering our open and democratic society. The main enemy of the open society, I believe, is no longer the communist but the capitalist threat ... The present situation is comparable to that at the turn of the past century. It was a golden age of capitalism, characterized by the principle of laissez faire: so is the present. The earlier period was in some ways more stable ... The earlier period had the gold standard; today the main currencies float and crush against each other like continental plates. Yet the free market regime that prevailed 100 years ago was destroyed by World War I. Totalitarian ideologies came to the fore and, by the end of World War II, there was practically no movement of capital between countries. How much more likely the present regime is to break down unless we learn from experience!*

After the crash of 1997, Soros's urgency became pronounced.

I cannot believe that the present global boom will not be followed by a bust ... The recent turmoil in Asian markets raises difficult questions about currency pegs, asset bubbles, inadequate banking supervision, and the lack of financial information ... There is no international regulatory authority for financial markets, and there is not enough international cooperation for the taxation of capital ... What started out as a minor imbalance has become a much bigger one that threatens to engulf not only international credit but international trade.

China, with its huge foreign reserves, big trade surplus, strong currency, and growing local economy, rode out the Tiger crisis. But Soros warned that China, too, could suffer its own meltdown.

From now on, whatever China does will have large-scale repercussions for all of Asia, including Australia. The economic emergence of China is one of the reasons why the Tiger economies suffered a meltdown in 1997. Ten years earlier, Indonesia, South Korea, Malaysia, Thailand and the Philippines had all enjoyed large trade surpluses. By 1997, they all had trade deficits. Professor Lester Thurow explains why: 'Their swing from surplus to deficit is directly traceable to China's decision to concentrate on increasing exports as its engine of growth. Since China could offer better educated but cheaper workers than Southeast Asia, and since it has a much bigger internal market for its own products, it quickly gained a US$40 billion trade surplus, taking export trade away from other Asian countries.'

Behind this economic surge was a much darker phenomenon—runaway pollution—as China despoiled its environment in the cause of economic growth. Because of the huge pool of underemployed workers built up during the decades of Communism, China, unlike Australia, must maintain high levels of economic growth just to maintain the status quo. Even the official *Chinese Daily* estimates that the cost of China's environmental degradation caused by unrestrained development is equal to about seven percent of the gross domestic product each year. This is an understatement. An expert on China's economic geography, Canada's Vaclav Smil, wrote that the real long-term cost of pollution in China is between 10 and 15 percent of GNP per annum, a level of despoliation that, unchecked, will eventually lead to an environmental crisis.

China is also exporting its pollution problems. Chinese plants making the CFC chemicals which destroy the ozone layer are engaged in large-scale smuggling of illegal CFCs to overseas markets.

'In China', wrote the international environmental law experts, Andre Dua and Daniel Esty, 'provincial governments and local entrepreneurs often conspire to build stripped-down, low-cost, and thus highly polluting, power plants which generate the maximum amount of electricity per dollar of capital invested. American companies that have included pollution control technologies in their proposals for electricity-generating facilities have been told to eliminate these features, and cut the cost of their bids accordingly, or lose the chance to be chosen for the project.'

China plans to build more than a hundred new power stations during the first decade of the new century.

Dirty plants pour acid rain not only onto China but onto neighbouring Japan and Korea. The Chinese deny claims that clouds of acid rain flow across Japan. And the only action the Chinese will take is if the Japanese pay to install the scrubbers to dirty plants, which the Japanese are having to do. The American reporter Mark Hertsgaard travelled through China in 1996 to study China's ecology. He would go for days in a country where, 'the land had been scalped, the water poisoned, the air made toxic and dark'. He found places like the Chongqing Paper Factory, perched near the intersection of the Jialin River and the mighty Yangtze, the artery of central China, which Hertsgaard described in the *Atlantic Monthly* in November 1997.

> *The astringent odor of chlorine attacked our nostrils, and once we reached the stream's edge, the smell was so powerful that we immediately backed away. Below us, where the discharge emptied into the Jialin, a frothy white plume was spreading across the slow-moving river … a vast, roaring torrent of white, easily thirty [metres] wide, splashing down the hillside like a waterfall of boiling milk.*

There are at least 100 000 raw polluters like the Chongqing Paper Factory. Acid rain is endemic in China. Five Chinese cities, including Beijing, are ranked in the world's top ten cities with the worst air pollution. Most petrol sold in China is still leaded. Most coal is not 'washed' before it is burned, and coal remains China's only abundant and affordable energy resource. In Beijing the level of nitrogen oxide in the air is 250 percent the international standard of acceptable air quality. In major Chinese cities, the levels of total suspended particulates in the air—soot, dust and fecal matter—are more than ten times greater than in Sydney.

Fertile cropland lost in China since 1950 is greater than all the arable land in Australia and equivalent to all the farmland in the United Kingdom, Germany and France. China's population is growing each year by sixteen million, almost the population of Australia. China is bursting with excess workers. Rural underemployment is estimated at about thirty-five percent, or 175 million people. Underemployment in the bloated state sector, which employs 110 million workers, is also chronic. The huge steel and textile industries will shed at least twenty percent of their workforce as they modernise to compete on the world market.

Official rhetoric from Beijing about closing 60 000 heavily polluting factories sounds impressive until it is realised that these factories represent only one percent of total output, and they are bankrupt anyway. 'China's estimated economic growth will turn the country into an environmental nightmare,' the Regional Institute of Environmental Technology, based in Singapore, warned in 1997. Its report said about eighty percent of China's urban river systems are polluted, commonly with ammonium, nitrate, volatile phenol and oxygen-consuming organic materials. The Institute estimated that fifty billion dollars would need to be spent to protect the nation from acid rain, smog and polluted drinking water. Mark Hertsgaard, after his trip through the country:

> *China is a greenhouse giant. It has already surpassed the former Soviet Union to become the world's second largest producer of greenhouse gases, trailing only the United States. With its immense coal reserves, huge population, and booming economic growth, China is very likely to triple its greenhouse emissions by 2020.*

The rest of the world, especially Japan, will have to pay a price, though most of the costs will fall to the people of the People's Republic of China. One of every four deaths in China is caused by lung disease. The rate of lung cancer has increased by 18.5 percent per year for the past decade, the number of cases doubling every four years. China also carries a mountain of bad loans piled up by the four big state-owned banks, estimated at about twenty percent of the loans outstanding in the Chinese financial system. The state banks will not be able to survive without massive injections of China's foreign reserves. Thousands of state enterprises are zombie companies kept alive by government subsidy. China's political system is also one of the world's most corrupt.

When all the elements are factored into the reality of modern China—despoliation, vandalism, poor health, increasing fertility, high debt and high corruption—the Chinese miracle becomes in part the Chinese mirage.

Where does all this leave Australia? Amid all the problems of Asia, Australia proved something during the 1997 Asian meltdown. It proved to have a political, financial and social system that could weather a storm. It proved that economic wealth and rapid growth are not enough. A nation needs rigorous institutions and financial transparency. While the East Asian stock market (except China and Taiwan) saw 40 per cent of its market value wiped out, the Australian stock market rode out the crash. The Australian dollar was like an innocent bystander, knocked down by a car out of control, yet it staged an orderly retreat against the US dollar as commodity prices declined, several major Australian export markets went into free-fall and tourism from the wounded economies fell off a cliff. The Australian property market grew while Asian property bubbles burst. Jobs increased. Unemployment held steady. Interest rates stayed near historic lows. Bankruptcies were at their lowest level in a generation. The federal budget was close to balance. The Australian dollar rose against most Asian currencies. Politically, the country was as steady as a rock.

'Australia was remarkably resilient, and it has been resilient and adaptable over a long time,' said the economist and columnist Max Walsh. 'And unlike most of Asia, it has built a clean financial system.'

Australia firmly weathered the region's crisis, but the Tiger meltdown of 1997 was the harbinger of further volatility. As this book was going to the publishers, the newspaper headlines in 1998 foreshadowed more black rain.

SEOUL FIGHTS OFF COLLAPSE, THAIS BEG FOR
MERCY

INDONESIA: TOUGH TIMES SPARK MARKET
RIOTS

CHINA: MIGHTY YUAN STARTS TO CRACK ON
BLACK MARKET

CHAOS FEARED AS MIGRANT MILLIONS FACE
EXPULSION

INDONESIAN ECONOMY CRASHES

RIOTERS KILLED IN INDONESIAN RACE-HATE
RAMPAGE

Indonesia was rated as the most corrupt country in Asia in
a 1997 survey by the Political and Economic Risk Consultancy, based in Hong Kong. A 1996 ranking of corruption by
the *New York Times*, using seven indexes and surveys, rated
Indonesia the most corrupt system, followed by China. Also
in the top ten ranking were the Philippines, and Thailand.

We are in for a rough ride. The vision of Asian splendour
which so intoxicated many Australian public intellectuals
will be a more arduous road than expected. Australia's stability in the 1997 crisis was the second time in three years the

nation had been challenged by the formidable new realities of Asia. In 1995 China had competed directly and aggressively against Australia when it sought the glittering prize of hosting the first Olympics of the new millennium. China built Olympic facilities. It held huge rallies for the International Olympic Committee. It called in diplomatic debts. It mobilised political power. China was the giant in this contest. Beijing the great imperial capital. Its only serious rival was Sydney. Almost one in every five persons in the world lived in China, while Australia had just 0.25 percent of the world's population. China represented the next frontier of international markets, while Australia was an important yet mature and secondary market.

It seemed an unequal contest. It was not. While Australia had only 1.5 percent of China's population, its gross national product was one-third the size of China's. Australia, not China, had a long and distinguished Olympic tradition. Australia, not China, had long-term political stability and commitment to democracy, the rule of law, and individual freedom. Australia, not China, had superb communications infrastructure and a professional, worldly and untainted public sector. Australia, not China, was untroubled by endemic corruption. Australia, not China, had a globally-traded currency, open equity markets and a transparent and efficient financial system. Australia, not China, was integrated into the greatest economic and cultural force in history—the alliance of English-speaking nations led by the United States.

China's Olympic city, Beijing, was coated in the squalor of its own lungs, a permanent brown haze so foul it made the normal metropolitan pollution problems of rival Sydney appear inconsequential. When the International Olympic Committee made the long trip to Sydney, they found a team that was ready and a city built around one of the great visions of the world, a place where, as a former Sydney boy Clive James once wrote: 'In Sydney Harbour the yachts will be racing on the crushed diamond water under a sky the texture of powdered sapphires.'

China lost.

4
AMONG THE BARBARIANS

IN HIS ESSAY 'TO SCREW Foreigners is Patriotic', China scholar Geremie Barmé points out that Beijing's pride was deeply offended when Australia defeated China in the international contest for the 2000 Olympics:

> *The internal propaganda campaign for a Beijing*
> *Olympics emphasised the primacy of a unique Chinese*
> *national spirit and the ability of the people to 'move*
> *mountains and drain the oceans' ... The eventual failure*
> *of the Chinese bid was deemed to have been orchestrated*
> *by Western bullies, and the Olympic Committee's deci-*
> *sion to give the 2000 Olympics to Sydney was seen as an*
> *affront to Chinese national sentiment ...*

The Chinese government's attitude to the Games has not exactly been in the spirit envisaged by the Olympic organisers. On 8 January 1998, after years of controversy and accusations and improbable performances by Chinese athletes, Australian customs officers seized a drug growth hormone from the bag of a member of the Chinese swimming team as the squad arrived to take part in the World Swimming Championships in Perth. Officers found thirteen vials of a substance labelled Somatropin, a synthetic human growth hormone which can be used as a substitute for anabolic steroids and is undetectable. They also seized thirteen vials of saline solution, used to dilute the Somatropin before injection. The twenty-six vials were discovered packed in ice in a vacuum flask, wrapped in a plastic bag, inside the luggage of a female swimmer, Yuan Yuan. Australian officials said there was more than enough Somatropin, which is banned by the International Olympic Committee, to inject the entire Chinese squad over a period of three weeks. The swimmer and her coach were sent home.

The following week, four more Chinese swimmers failed drug tests. All tested positive for a banned diuretic called Triamterene, used to dilute the urine and thus mask the effects of steroids or illegal hormone treatments. The swimmers, like most other swimmers arriving for the championship, had been tested soon after they arrived in the country and it may have been earlier than they were expecting. The International Olympic Committee treats diuretics as if they were the same as steroids, and strictly bans them, unlike the international swimming body, FINA.

All four Chinese swimmers were from the Shanghai club, coached by Zhou Ming, who had been previously suspended for drug involvement when seven of his swimmers were caught using steroids in 1994. Chinese athletes had already been involved in twenty-three positive steroid tests since 1990, and innumerable accusations. In the previous world championships in Rome in 1994, China, having never been a swimming force in previous decades, won twelve of the sixteen titles. Seven of the swimmers, including two of the

new world champions, tested positive for steroids at the
Asian Games a month later. In the midst of the debacle at the
1998 World Swimming Championships in Perth, the veteran
Australian national swim coach, Don Talbot, described Chinese swimming officials, who expressed shock at the positive
drug tests, as 'bloody liars.'

In 1995 the journalist and oral historian Sang Ye, an Australian citizen who had immigrated from China, interviewed
a member of the Chinese national athletics team. The interview, published in the literary journal *Heat* in 1997,
suggested the problem was even worse than it appeared.

> *I've taken part in three major competitions: two world
> championships and one Olympics. I wasn't in very good
> form, so I didn't win any medals. But it's not a matter of
> pitting athletes against each other in competition. What
> you're really doing is comparing drugs. If the drugs
> we're using aren't any good, you don't have a hope. We
> Orientals are biologically different from foreigners;
> we've got the skills and quick enough reflexes, but we
> just don't have the stamina. Relatively speaking we need
> to use drugs, and they're pretty effective ... Whether it's
> track events or swimming, it's the same deal. Even
> sharpshooters use them.*

The improbable performances of Chinese swimmers and athletes appeared to be as systematic and blatant as the illegal
drug regime of East Germany, a national sports system
which, after the collapse of the East German communist
regime was exposed as rotten from top to bottom. A German

historian who has specialised in the East German drug sport era, Dr Gisether Spitzer, has unearthed evidence that more than 10 000 athletes across a range of sports had been given performance-enhancing drugs.

Sang Ye's Olympian also added something uglier to the mix:

> *When [we] take part in an international competition ...*
> *We've got our backs to the wall. 'The Motherland and*
> *the People are waiting for you to fight a victorious war.*
> *You must achieve glory for the nation!' And it's just like*
> *going to war, too. The pressure is intense ... I bummed*
> *out in the Olympics and didn't get a place, and so people*
> *back home started abusing my mum and dad for having*
> *produced a birth defect like me, one that had lost face*
> *for the nation. Someone slashed my dad's bike tyres too,*
> *and my younger brother was beaten up ...*

Rampant nationalism was not merely the providence of the mainland Chinese. The Olympian found the overseas Chinese even worse:

> *They* [the overseas Chinese] *have it pretty good but they*
> *always have this inferiority complex thing going. They*
> *hate foreigners and see us as representing China in their*
> *own war with whitey.*

The year that Beijing lost the Olympics to Sydney, the most popular tele-series in China was 'A Beijing Man in New York'. It told the story of a Chinese hero making his way through an avaricious, amoral America. In an especially popular scene, the Beijing man hires a busty blonde prostitute and, while showering her with dollars, orders her to cry out repeatedly, 'I love you, I love you.'

> 'A Beijing Man in New York', writes Barmé, *was broadcast at a time when both the Chinese authorities and segments of the population were becoming increasingly irate about their (perceived) position in the New World Order and the attitude of the United States towards China. It also represented, perhaps, the coming of age of Chinese narcissism, and bespoke a desire for revenge for all the real and perceived slights of the past century.*

Plenty of Chinese resentments can be found about Australians, too. This is not surprising given the dynamic chauvinism at the core of Chinese culture. Yet Australia's national debate is dominated by the view that the only racism which matters is white racism. This extraordinary attitude is not only myopic, self-absorbed and neocolonial, it is also dangerously naive. In *The Year the Dragon Came*, a 1996 book by Sang Ye about Chinese immigrants to Australia, especially the so-called Bob Hawke Tiananmen Square immigrants, it does not take long before the insults against Australians start flying.

> 'You can only speak like this to Chinese, you know. The Australians are dogs. Can't expect them to understand.'

That's on page 2.

So many insults flow through the book that Sang Ye, who

interviewed more than 100 Chinese immigrants, warned
readers in the introduction:

> *China is a country with a strong xenophobic, isolationist
> tradition; a place where deeply racist sentiments are not
> uncommon ... Nearly all of the interviewees here referred
> to Australians as 'devils'* (guizi) *or foreign devils* (yang
> guizi) *or the slightly more polite 'foreigners'* (laowai or
> waiguoren), *apparently oblivious to the fact that in Aus-
> tralia, it's they who are foreigners.*

Sang Ye, a delightfully friendly man, says he didn't choose
the most provocative interviews for his book, merely the
most interesting. He believes they represent an accurate
reflection of what he heard. It isn't good. After being called
'dogs' in the first chapter, things don't improve much for
Australians thereafter. China scholar Jamie Mackie, in a
review of *The Year the Dragon Came*, wrote: 'Read this book
to rid yourself of stereotypes and illusions about Chinese
immigrants. And ponder whether (and how) Australian society or culture has been either enriched by the presence of
these immigrants or put under strain.' Neil James, writing in
the *Australian's Review of Books*, said of *Dragon*: 'The por-
traits do not make for comfortable reading. Above all else,
the voice of self-interest sets the tone.'

Chinese self-interest and cynicism in Australia is not
exactly hard to find. It can be found in official pronounce-
ments from Beijing, in the Chinese-language news media,
and in books such as *I Married a Foreign Woman*, *My Fortune in Australia*, and *Australia—Beautiful Lies*, the last two

published in Australia under the title, *Bitter Peaches and Plums: Two Chinese Novellas on the Recent Chinese Student Experience in Australia.* Professor Bruce Jacobs and Dr Ouyang Yu, in their introduction to *Bitter Peaches and Plums*, write:

> *The image of Australia presented in these novellas is quite limited ... [They] concentrate on the Chinese student communities, communities which are basically inward-looking and which have very little interaction with Australian society as a whole ... They lived extremely frugally and, as shown in* Beautiful Lives, *developed numerous illegal tactics to save money. Most had borrowed money in China and had heavy debts to repay.*

'It is common knowledge there are all kinds of immigration schemes among Chinese immigrants,' says the head of the anthropology department at the University of Sydney, Dr Richard Basham. 'A lot of so-called students from the PRC arrive with big debts to pay back.' Also common knowledge is the booming racket in phoney marriages. A remarkably high percentage of Australian marriages—30 percent—currently involve offshore spouses, says Bob Birrell of Monash University, and ethnic Chinese immigrants provide the largest flow. The final passage of *Australia—Beautiful Lies*, contains sentiments that are common in Chinese writing about Australia, and are not exactly grist for romantics.

> *It can be said that Chinese students who went to*

Australia have varying degrees of hatred towards this
kangaroo kingdom. But did the Australian government or
people commit any crimes? How can the present situa-
tion of Chinese students in Australia compare with
China's modern history, replete with servility and
humiliation?

The beauty of immigration is that most of the children of the
Chinese wayfarers who stay in Australia will not share this
alienation. Although there is widespread grumbling among
Australian-born students and parents that Chinese students
prefer to mix with each other, the historical experience of
immigration shows that the intense peer pressures of adoles-
cence is more powerful than cultural insularity and by the
second generation the children of all immigrant groups walk,
talk and think like Australians. School is the fulcrum of
social formation. The Chinese students now in Australia,
already distinguished academically, will add to that long,
tough, durable, creative seam of Chinese history in Australia,
which began on the goldfields of the nineteenth century.

The imponderable ingredient in this new mix, and the big
difference between the new generations of Chinese-
Australians and the previous waves of post-war immigrant
Australians, is that the bristling chauvinistic bulk of China
will dominate the politics of Australia's hemisphere in the
future. China has shown it is a superpower with a chip on its
shoulder and the Chinese have an enormously long cultural
history of regarding non-Chinese as lesser beings. This feeling was mutual among the generations of settlers who formed

Australia. White Australians feared the Chinese and excluded them (just as some still fear them and wish to exclude them). Helen Irving, in her history of the Australian Constitution, *To Constitute a Nation*, wrote that the small Australian population at the time of Federation was shaped by the alien magnitude of China:

> *While every other question raised during the Federation campaigns and debated in the Conventions produced several lines of major disagreement, no significant group of opinion favourable to Chinese immigration existed in Australia by the 1890s...*

> *With racial divisions came the risk of civil war. To Australians the Chinese appearance, language, script, way of working, dressing, worshipping, relaxing and eating were all utterly unlike anything they understood.*

A century later, in a world run by an international middle class, most Australians can see that Chinese drive and intelligence can be a national asset and a trading bridge. In *The Tyranny of Fortune*, two Australian Asia experts, Reg Little and Warren Reed, urge Australians to show a greater respect for the emerging forces in Asia.

> *Australia is in the process of becoming the plaything of forces, possibly tyrannical, outside the control of its people ... '*

> *East Asian organisational skill, which is today arguably the world's most effective and competitive, is the product*

of a rich and powerful civilisation which is understood
by few Australians. The people of that tradition of civili-
sation often look on Australian individuality, for example,
as a form of simple-mindedness, bordering on barbarism.

Ouch! Geremie Barmé, a senior Fellow at the Australian
National University, is one of the scholars watching the resur-
gent nationalism of China. What strikes him, and other China
watchers, is how this new nationalism transcends political
divisions. The racial nationalism of emerging China extends
to the overseas Chinese. The young Chinese Olympian interviewed by Sang Ye was positively scathing about the
chauvinism of many of the ethnic Chinese who live outside
China.

When people back home insult you after you've lost a
competition overseas it's not that big a deal ... But the
overseas Chinese! If we win we're national heroes; if we
lose we're nothing more than traitors and scum ...

If you can't get the five-star flag of the People's Republic
up there fluttering, if you don't make them feel like
bigshots in front of all the foreigners, then you're nothing
more than a big traitor.

Barmé speculates that a strain of self-loathing lies beneath
Chinese self-aggrandisement. So do other China scholars. So
does Sang Ye. So does the Chinese Olympian. It doesn't
really matter what motivates this chauvinism, it will have to
be dealt with. In an essay called 'Computer Insect', Sang Ye
describes a brilliant young computer hacker in Beijing who

personifies what he calls the 'in-your-face China' that will be much more common in the future:

The way I see it, pirating software is no big deal. The four Little Dragons [Hong Kong, Taiwan, Korea and Singapore] *created the wealth and prosperity they enjoy today by pirating. You tell me what those little shits in Hong Kong have ever discovered? Zilch. They're a pack of pseudo foreign devils who started out as tailors and cobblers ... Foreign devils* [Americans] *are just plain unreasonable. To be honest, they've been getting away with ripping off the Chinese for ages. What's all this stuff about intellectual property? Whose ancestors got it all going in the first place?*

For more than a hundred years China has been abused, exploited and lectured to by Western powers. Australia has done its share of misreading China. Australians still tend to regard Chinese as one-dimensional abstractions, oblivious to the deep ocean of Chinese culture. Australia has never had a revolution. China endured three cultural revolutions in three successive generations and yet continued to grow as a great nation. In Australia even minor structural change provokes fits of outrage from vested interests. Australia's softness compared with China, its naivety, its sometimes second-rate diplomatic and trade performances, its failure to understand the central place of China and the overseas Chinese in the culture and business practices of the hemisphere, have been pointed out by a number of Australian experts on Asia.

Australia has, however, embraced large-scale immigration

by ethnic Chinese. The Department of Sociology at Monash University studied the 14 750 citizens of the People's Republic of China present in Australia in 1989, the year of the Tiananmen massacre, and found that by 1993 they had brought an additional 13 900 spouses and dependents to Australia, none of whom were subject to skill, asset or English proficiency tests. The 14 750 had thus grown to 28 150, and the study projected, accurately, that the Bob Hawke immigrant stream would increase to 40 000 by the mid-1990s, pushing the number of ethnic Chinese in Australia to more than 300 000.

The reactions to the new nationalism in China among those 300 000 ethnic Chinese in Australia ranges across the spectrum from those who despise anything that comes out of official Beijing to those who mimic the Beijing line. After the pastor of the Ashfield Uniting Church, which has a partly Chinese congregation, flew the Tibetan flag on Tibetan National Day in 1996, Councillor Spencer Wu, a member of Ashfield Council, wrote an angry letter to the press.

*The Tibetan flag raised at the Uniting Church did not
escape the notice of the Chinese population of Ashfield.
They were outraged enough to [be] ready to storm the
church ... Without my timely intervention dozens of eggs
would have landed on the ground. The Chinese population now believes [the] Uniting Church is an
anti-Chinese political organisation ...*

There is a strong resemblance between the logic of this micro-rhetoric and the big rhetoric coming out of Beijing.

When Prime Minister Howard met the spiritual leader of Tibet, the Dalai Lama, during Howard's first year in office, the official organ of Beijing, the *People's Daily*, frothed: 'What is really inconceivable is the absurd philosophy of this Australian politician. If it is not out of his ignorance about Chinese and Tibetan history, it is because he deliberately wants to rudely interfere in China's internal affairs.'

The New China News Agency was even more splenetic when the US government issued reports about China's success in suppressing domestic dissent. This is a typical outburst: 'Enough is enough. What qualifications do you have to talk about these issues in front of the Chinese people who have a 5000-year-old civilisation?'

Despite these intemperate outbursts, recent Australian governments have managed to handle the relationship with China quite well. They have not fallen into line with the United States. They have not lectured the Chinese on human rights, thus throwing away the relationship for no gain. They have sought to build trade ties with painstaking patience. Above all, they have opened Australia to immigration by ethnic Chinese.

China, in turn, has treated Australia as a nation it can do business with, and has made Australia an official tourist destination, a freedom the government has not extended to most countries. Hopefully the relationship will flower. Australia's prudence is wise. Modern China is increasingly in a position to back its rhetoric with action. After the show of American military power in the Gulf War, defence spending in China began rising even faster than its double-digit economic growth. China has also become the biggest buyer and holder of US debt, overtaking Japan. Chinese investments have become important to the stability of the US bond market. During the 1997 Asian currency and market meltdowns, China's stock market and currency held steady, with the Chinese market even rising amid the surrounding turmoil. China also absorbed Hong Kong with smooth efficiency.

Chinese irritation with lectures from Western governments is reflected in Beijing's failure to censor ultranationalist books such as *China Through the Third Eye*, and *Winds in the Wilderness*, and the best-selling, *China, Just Say No!*, which mimics the anti-American Japanese bestseller, *Japan Can Say No*, with chapters such as 'Burn Down Hollywood' and 'Don't Fear Declaring, Prepare For War'.

In Australia, when the Howard government began making changes to the immigration system, the Independent Council for Refugee Advocacy, a lobby group for Chinese immigrants, informed the Minister for Immigration that the plan to impose English-language tests on immigrants was 'racist' and 'based on a false premise that English speakers are superior'.

When the Haymarket Property Owners Association, made up of ethnic Chinese property owners in Sydney's Chinatown, was denied a development permit by the Sydney City Council, the president of the association, Tony Ma, accused the City Council of race discrimination and threatened action under the Race Discrimination Act. The Lord Mayor of Sydney, Frank Sartor, dismissed the accusation as 'nonsense'.

When Councillor Ted Seng, Deputy Mayor of Randwick

in Sydney, an ethnic Chinese who immigrated from Malaysia, called for a three-year moratorium on immigration from Asia because of the social stresses it was causing, he was attacked in the local Chinese-language media. 'My view is that Asian migrants should adopt what I describe as core Australian values, whilst at the same time retaining their cultural heritage,' Seng told me. 'Some of those core Australian values include a fair go for all, free speech, real environmental consciousness, and maintaining the fight against corruption.' This is not quite how his views appeared in some local Chinese-language reports. One headline proclaimed: THE EMERGENCE OF THE FIRST CHINESE WHO IS IN AGREEMENT WITH HANSON'S VIEWS. An insulting photo caption depicted Ted Seng as, 'The Deputy Mayor Who Can't Write His Own Name in Chinese.'

The issue of cultural insularity among overseas Chinese has been raised by a number of Australian scholars, most elegantly by Nicholas Jose in a 1996 essay for the *Australian Book Review*.

China has the numbers. Further, Chinese culture has proved adept at absorbing useful elements of other cultures while remaining relatively impervious to being absorbed in return—particularly in the encounter with the West, which has been regarded as a source of specific modernising ideas rather than posing a wholesale cultural alternative. Then, since Chinese culture exists most strongly in intangible things, customs, thoughts and attitudes can be transferred even when the outward and

visible signs are excluded or rejected. Chinese culture is
disposed to survive, even in a hostile environment.

When I asked one China scholar why complaining about
Australia was so prevalent in the local Chinese community,
he replied: 'It's a technique.' If so, the technique has worked.
Criticism of ethnic Chinese is treated as racist. Thus, the prevailing myopia of an obsession with any hint of white racism,
while excusing or ignoring Chinese cultural chauvinism. This
myopia is the result of several factors: the arrogance that the
only morality that matters is white morality, the lingering
presence of Australia's outdated cultural cringe, the residue
of guilt over the old White Australia policy, and the willingness of Chinese lobby groups in portraying Chinese in
Australia as victims.

The Chinese immigrant as 'sojourner', never completely
at home in the new country, is a portrait built by the work of
the Australia-based China scholar Wang Gung-Wu, who has
traced the patterns of Chinese leaving the homeland but
remitting money to the homeland and operating among the
overseas Chinese network. Sterling Seagrave, in *Lords of the
Rim*, portrays an immensely successful overseas Chinese
community transcending national borders.

Offshore China is an empire of fifty-five million people,
intricately interlaced by systems of guilds, benevolent
societies, tongs, triads, kongsi *and name-and-place asso-*
ciations, which, individually and together, supply the
personal connections and financial linkages that make
the Overseas Chinese such a potent force. It is an empire

> *without borders, national government or flag. It is delib-*
> *erately opaque—an invisible empire of conglomerates ...*

All these strings of Chinese power and cultural insularity were drawn together in *The Tyranny of Fortune* to portray an international Chinese community of great influence.

> *Japan has over a dozen trading companies with overseas*
> *networks which are more substantial and better trained*
> *... than Australia's Department of Foreign Affairs and*
> *Trade. [Yet] even Japan's extraordinary reach is prob-*
> *ably not competitive with the vast, informal,*
> *international information networks controlled by the*
> *overseas Chinese, who are beginning to replace the*
> *Japanese as the dominant force driving economic trans-*
> *formation in Australia's region, if not the world more*
> *broadly.*

The extent of China's political influence and intelligence-gathering through the global ethnic Chinese diaspora may have been glimpsed in a 1998 draft Senate committee report which said that several Chinese-American businessmen who had contributed heavily to the re-election campaign of President Bill Clinton also had long-term relationships with Chinese intelligence.

Anyone who studies the history of China's mendacity in Tibet (and books such as *Fire Under the Snow*, published in 1998, are finally revealing the full extent of that mendacity) can only be appalled by the brutal and methodical suppression of Tibet's 2000-year-old culture and language since

China's invasion in 1950. It follows that one can only be shocked by the open support or, at the least, the blind eye turned by Chinese nationalists in Australia toward China's continuing ethnocide in Tibet.

But history is written by the victors, and China is beginning to shape the history of Australia's region. The rise to power and influence of the Chinese people in the twentieth century is embodied by Lee Kuan Yew who, more than any other individual, helped show the world the enormity of Chinese potential. In 1993 I interviewed Lee in his office in the Istana complex, a white colonial palace with Gurkha guards, set in lush quiet grounds near the heart of Singapore. Only two people have offices in the palace—Lee on the second floor and the Prime Minister of Singapore on the third. Lee, who gained one of the most brilliant passes in the history of Cambridge University, became Singapore's founding father at the age of thirty-five and ruled the country for another thirty-five years. Although he stepped down as Prime Minister in 1990 at the age of sixty-eight, he remained for a time the de facto head of state and in retirement he continued to personify the Confucian ideal of hard work and civic service, working six days a week, ten hours a day. If four decades of power had left their mark on him, it was only lightly.

It did not take long for the bemused attitude felt by many educated Chinese towards Australians to reveal itself in Lee Kuan Yew. 'I've had innumerable anecdotal accounts of Asians [in Australia] who just give up and begin to work at the pace of Australians ... That's okay if you're selling your services only to Australia, but not when you're selling your services to the world …

'I think you will have to take your unionists and your educationists on a tour of East Asia and see how other societies start from kindergarten: the intensity and the dedication, not only of the child, but of the parents and the siblings and of the school, the teachers, the class monitors, in getting every student to put in his best.'

His words echoed the brilliant record of success by Chinese students in Australia.

Lee Kuan Yew is the world's most famous employer of Confucian values, which he used to justify political and social repression as he built the dazzling economic success, stability and efficiency of his Singapore city-state. But Chiam Yau-ming of La Trobe University has critiqued Lee's selective Confucianism. 'Lee's party, the People's Action Party … does not tolerate criticism or even mini electoral losses. PAP leaders have openly threatened that constituencies that vote for non-PAP candidates risk losing public infrastructure development. It is doubtful whether Confucius would have applauded.'

During my interview with him, Lee broke taboos observed by Western politicians. He is one of the few leaders secure enough to venture into discussions of racial characteristics and the differences in national character, although this habit finally caught up with him in 1997 when he managed to sour Singapore's tender relations with Malays with comments about the level of crime committed by Malaysians. He was just as blunt with me, citing his experiences with the British

military officers who built Singapore to describe the tough-
ness of the Chinese:

> *When doing a project they would put the Chinese in the
> middle and put the Indians at the side, and the Indians
> were expected to keep the pace of the Chinese. And there
> was a hell of a problem, because one Chinese would
> carry one pole with two wicker baskets of earth, whereas
> two Indians would carry one pole with one wicker basket
> between them. So it's one quarter. Now that's culture.
> Maybe it has to do also with genetic characteristics, I'm
> not sure. But any doctor will tell you in our hospitals,
> that even if you just touch an Indian with an injection he
> is howling. The Chinaman isn't. He has got a very high
> level of tolerance for pain.*

Listening to this tough little parable it is easy to see the guid-
ing hand behind the housing laws in Singapore which
effectively prevent the formation of ethnic enclaves of Indi-
ans and Malays. Most housing clusters must have ethnic
occupancy in the same ratio as the general population, which
guarantees a dominant ethnic Chinese majority and the dispersal of the non-Chinese population. And although
Singapore wants to boost its population, it is not turning to
immigration to do the job. Lee did not speak of Singapore as
a new culture. He spoke of '4000 years of folk memory'. So
I asked him if 4000 years of tradition of centralised, mono-
lithic, autocratic power meant it was naive for the West to
believe that China would ever change.

'Four thousand or 5000 years of centralised government

and hierarchy also have to adjust to the conditions of the world today. A modern industrial society requires large numbers of educated people, managers, engineers, technicians, accountants, entrepreneurs, who are in constant touch with their counterparts throughout the world via fax, via satellite, and who will travel freely. Therefore, there is bound to be some osmosis and the forms cannot remain unchanged ... I think it will evolve, but it will still be, in my view, a hierarchical society.'

Given Australia's commitments to democracy, individualism, egalitarianism, environmentalism and the blending of sport and play into the texture of life, I suggested Australians could not compete in the world on Chinese terms nor were even interested in doing so.

Lee smiled, paused, then replied: 'I'm not sure you will lose every time. There are certain areas where you have natural advantages. Look, I don't believe, however hard they try, Singaporeans will make world-class tennis players.'

5
AN EMPIRE OF THE SOUL

THE GIGANTIC BREATHING SPREAD of Australia's desert, mountain, forest, farmland, scrub, cities, towns, coasts, reefs, continental shelf, islands, rivers, deepwater ocean, seamounts and Antarctic icecap is as large and as real as any empire built by conquest. In sheer size, it is the third-largest legal entity in the world.

It is also no longer the same country built by the time-travellers of the eighteenth century who colonised Australia.

Until the late eighteenth century no European had ever seen a eucalypt, and very strange they must have looked, with their strings of hanging, half-shed bark, their smooth wrinkling joints (like armpits, elbows and crotches), their fluent gesticulations and haze of peren-nial foliage. Not evergreens, but evergreys: the soft, spatially deceitful background colour of the Australian bush, monotonous-looking at first sight but rippling with nuance to the acclimatised eye.

Robert Hughes, writing in *The Fatal Shore*, understood the magnitude of the alienation that these Europeans faced, even if they did not fully understand it themselves at the time. Another superb historian, Simon Schama, saw how much

Australians were formed by their environment rather than the other way round. 'Australia has never had a sense of omnipotence in the way the Calvinists had when they first arrived in America, or the generation who opened up the American West, who thought the whole continent was a Christmas present given to them by God,' Schama told me. 'For Australia, it was bloody hard to just survive on the fringe of the continent.'

Australia's ingrained cultural modesty was imposed by fire, drought, ironbark, distance and isolation. Still, the nation has been growing and thriving in an age that has been hard on the old imperial vanities, when the maps we grew up with have been redrawn along the true dividing lines of history—geography and blood. On 16 November 1994 a whole new set of lines came quietly into force around the world when the United Nations Convention on the Law of the Sea redrew the world's sovereign boundaries. No nation gained more under this law than Australia, which now has legal stewardship and exclusive economic rights over a prodigious expanse of land, coastal sea and continental shelf. It is one of the three largest claims, though the final legal boundaries are still years from being resolved. When Australia's historic though dormant territorial claim and legal responsibilites under the Antarctic Treaty are included, the total amount of Australian Territory is 28.4 million square kilometres, including 16.1 million square kilometres of ocean territory. It is as big as North America combined, and twice the size of Europe. Though a sparsely inhabited and fragile expanse, it is, by definition, the legal claim of an eco-superpower.

On 15 November 1994, the day before the Law of the Sea convention came into force, the then Minister for Industry, Science and Technology, Senator Peter Cook, told the Senate:

'This imposes on us a huge responsibility ... It is like European civilisation landing on the shores of Australia, but with 21st century knowledge about the environment. We have a chance to get it right from the beginning ... The Convention has given Australia vast new territory to manage and exploit, but it also demands that we manage this exclusive economic zone in a sustainable way to ensure that the living resources in it are not destroyed, depleted or irreparably harmed.'

Four nations emerged under the Law of the Sea with greatly expanded sovereign borders: Australia, the United States, Canada and Russia. Much of the enormous claims by Australia is sea. The magnitude of Australia's claim, both in size and moral obligation, is captured by the author Tim Winton, writing in 1997.

In coming to terms with the sea Australians will have to turn their heads and look hard into the glare and see the reality of our relationship with it. And half of that reality involves our relative ignorance of it. Less than one tenth of one per cent of the deep sea has been explored. Some say we know more about the surface of the moon. If most of life on Earth is indeed aquatic, then humans could do with a little modesty, a sense of perspective. We are a part of life; we are not life itself. We depend upon the

sea, more so because we are islanders. Our coasts and
waterways are among our most significant treasures.
Half our marine species are found nowhere else.

Gone is the casual sense of infinity and the unblemished
openness that shaped the nation. Australia has gathered unto
itself greater power, knowledge and, like all mature entities,
responsibilities. Perhaps the greatest single challenge to Australia is preserving the thin and fragile layer of soil that has
been wasting since long before the European settlers arrived
in 1788. It is the most immediate threat to Australia, more
urgent than the depletion of the ozone layer or global warming. 'The loss of rivers, lakes, soils and forest will have far
more damaging impact on people than climate change or
ozone depletion,' says Dr Graham Harris, head of the CSIRO
Land and Water division. 'Many ecologists has lost the plot.
A very worrying picture is emerging and we can't go on
ignoring it. Yet you could read professional ecological jour-
nals for years and never realise there's a global crisis in
landscape sustainability. Yet many ecologists are still studying the biology of the lesser-spotted-so-and-so when what is
needed is a new kind of science based on large-scale and
regional issues and solutions.' A nation cannot be an eco-
superpower if it is destroying its environment, and two of the
world's largest powers, China and Russia, have showed rapa-
cious indifference to the long-term costs of environmental
degradation. Both China and Russia are involved in environmental piracy. Large-scale smuggling of ozone-damaging
CFC chemicals is taking place out of factories in China and

Russia, which use false paperwork, dummy companies and illegal brokers to smuggle more than 10 000 tonnes of illegal CFCs to Europe each year. Thanks to such practices, the green world will continue to go brown for decades to come. The United Nations estimates that by 2025 two-thirds of the world's estimated eight billion people will be suffering 'water stress' caused by a shortage of unpolluted water.

Into this shrinking world goes Australia, with one enormous advantage: the environment defines the nation and its national character. On Australia Day 1997, when a national poll asked people what defined an Australian, the category that topped the list, by a wide margin, was 'Concern for the Environment'. When historian Lyn Spillman compared national identity-building in the United States and Australia, she found Americans spoke most about their freedom, while Australians spoke most about their land. The environment is Australia's great engine of national and international purpose. Even the national anthem is packed with geography.

Size is not the only determinant of a nation's ability to project power and ideas. If Australia is to act like, and be treated like, a superpower in any form, it has to learn to pick its battles, concentrate on its strengths and not waste precious resources on matters over which it has little control. Contrast the Sydney 2000 Olympics triumph, a contest where Australia was playing to its strengths, with Australia's crushing defeat at the United Nations during the same period, when it sought to win a seat on the United Nations Security Council.

France was one nation quietly delighted by Australia's defeat at the UN. The previous year, France became the first nation to test Australia's role as an emerging ecological power and had been bruised by the encounter. Australia fought a diplomatic war where it was strong. France's program of nuclear testing in the South Pacific, the last significant vestige of European imperialism in the region, became the catalyst which moved Australia toward assuming a more global environmental role. The clash between the two countries was an almost pristine representation of old vanities confronting new realities. The foreign affairs columnist for the *New York Times*, Thomas Friedman, reacting to the story 'Australia superpower' in the *Sydney Morning Herald*, saw the broad sweep of change that lay behind this diplomatic struggle.

> *Beneath the surface, this is a war. It is a war between two very different concepts of sovereignty, and one we are going to witness more of in years ahead. It is a clash between a traditional, inward-looking nationalistic form of sovereignty ... and a very broad, expansive, outward-looking new notion of sovereignty embodied in environmentalism ...*
>
> *This clash between France and Australia, observed the Australian writer Paul Sheehan, will be the first real confrontation between a traditional superpower and an ecological superpower.*

France's decision to test nuclear weapons in the South Pacific was entirely about the past, the obsession with its collaborative humiliation during World War II. Australia's zeal in this dispute was all about the future. In a world of ocean dumping, oil spills and drift-net fishing, the emergence of several eco-superpowers with broad maritime jurisdictions and strong conservation agendas would be an essential barrier to the despoliation of the oceans. In a letter to the Paris newspaper *Le Monde* during the diplomatic tussle with France, the then Prime Minister, Paul Keating, raised the spiritual aspect of Australia's concerns.

We speak on behalf of all the countries in the region, many of them small and ecologically vulnerable, all of them in a profound material and spiritual relationship with the Pacific Ocean.

The Exclusive Economic Zones under the Law of the Sea are not mere diplomatic window-dressing. It did not take long for disputes to break out after these zones became part of international law. Even polite Canada was roused to the point of military violence over fishing rights on the edge of its EEZ, seizing a Spanish fishing trawler and cutting the lines of another during a confrontation with Spain, which then sent its own naval vessels to protect Spanish fishing boats off Newfoundland. Fisheries have also been pirated by Spanish trawlers, operating under Argentinean flags, and the British have been arresting fishing boats. When Japan declared a 200-nautical-mile EEZ around its coast in 1996, it provoked public bitterness and diplomatic protests from China and South Korea. The bitterness was reciprocated by Japan.

Australia and the United States have quietly sniped at each other over Law of the Sea, as befitting the two nations with the most far-reaching maritime claims. 'The Australians claim they're not claiming Antarctica under the new rules,' the State Department's chief ocean policy geographer, Robert Smith, told me with scepticism in 1995. The Americans do not even recognise the Australian Antarctic Territory or parts of its huge continental shelf claims under the Law of the Sea convention. The Australian government rejects US policy.

Once again, the debate over Antarctica is not merely symbolic. Australia's Antarctic claim and Antarctic EEZ (as large as the Australian continent) is aimed at protecting the last pristine continent, a place which Australia has played an integral role in exploring and conserving. It is also aimed at Antarctica's potentially enormous farming future. The CSIRO predicts that the farming and harvesting of Australia's EEZ waters could overtake beef as an export industry early next century, especially given the voracious Asian appetite for seafood. 'By every global measure the sea has twice as much biological richness as the land,' said Dr Peter Bridgewater, Director of the Australian Nature Conservation Authority. 'Our attitude to the sea has to change. Provided we develop our marine science, the opportunities are almost limitless.' Australia's rights under Law of the Sea extend to harvesting the sea, the seabed and the subsoil beneath. The CSIRO calls the coming era of aquaculture 'the blue revolution'.

The sheer extent of Australia's new economic sovereignty should now begin to exert itself in numerous ways, both subtle and unsubtle. It comes at a time when large amounts of arable land, especially in the fertile river valleys of China, have been withdrawn from use, causing global grain reserves to fall. By the year 2020, the world population is expected to be 7.8 billion, two billion more than predicted for the turn of the century. In Australia there are 100 000 fewer farms at the end of the century than there were in the middle of the century. The total area of agricultural land in 1995–96 was less than in 1960–61. A major 1996 survey by the Australian Bureau of Statistics warned:

> *In the 200 years since Europeans first settled in Australia, vast changes have been made to the natural vegetation ... The transformed landscape is more susceptible than natural ecosystems to land degradation including: erosion by water and wind, soil salinisation, soil acidification, and soil structure decline.*

Yet during the time of agricultural land shrinkage, the volume of agricultural production increased by 150 percent through higher productivity. Farmers' margins were squeezed hard, though. Even if the optimists (the technologists) are more right than the pessimists (the environmentalists), Australia's physical resources will grow more valuable as space becomes more finite on a crowded planet. Gains from Australia's new Exclusive Economic Zone have already begun to flow. During the process of mapping Australia's claim to the continental shelf, the Australian Geological Survey Organisation found three major oil fields that could potentially double Australia's oil reserves. They are deep subocean fields, and mining such claims is not yet technologically viable, but their estimated worth is more than 100 billion dollars.

Australia's ocean territory is like its soil: lots of it but mostly poor. Despite having one of the world's most extensive fishing zones, Australia ranks only fiftieth in fisheries production because most of the waters around the Australian continent do not have the major upwellings of nutrient-rich deep water from the ocean floor. Like arid land, these seas are fragile. Serious overfishing of southern bluefin tuna, gemfish and rock lobsters has already shrunk the sustainable levels of these valued species in Australian waters. Australia's only three major commercial fishing grounds have all been reduced by overfishing.

As a child, Tim Winton used to snorkel in abundantly rich waters on the reefs near Trigg Point, off Perth. He saw 'tumbling masses of tailor, lines of crayfish marching out to sea in single file. Plankton passed like dizzy spots before my eyes.' When he left and then returned years later, he found the everyday abuse of a crowded coast had changed everything

> *I returned to my old haunt, the reef I had snorkeled over*
> *obsessively since age eight. But the abalone seemed*
> *small and scarce. There were hardly any fish. No tar-*
> *whine, no sweep. Every scalyfin and red-lipped morwong*
> *had a spearhole high on its back.*

Australia now has obligations to protect not only its coasts and coastal waters but also to preserve the marine environment stretching out into the Exclusive Economic Zone. The challenge is to heal the damage on sea and on land, to concentrate on managing the huge area of the earth's surface where Australia actually has territorial rights. This challenge is intellectual and financial. Australia already has the wealth, the talent and the size. What it lacks is confidence and ambition.

Governments come and go, and in time the intrinsic nature of Australia's ecological strengths and obligations should prevail over political short-sightedness. If Australia takes full responsibility for the 28.4 million square kilometres under its Law of the Sea and Antarctic Treaty claims, a huge and varied system of the earth's surface will be in relatively safe hands. New laws, new communal standards and new ways of thinking can have an enormous impact on the land and sea we have inherited. On Tim Winton's plundered reef off Perth, the local authorities banned spear guns and embargoed the taking of abalone. This is what Winton found when he finally went back:

> *Nowadays, I see as many abalone on the reef as I used to and many more fish than I saw even as a boy. In the midst of a sprawling city, children can swim and snorkel and experience a living reef.*

Asia may still be degrading at an alarming rate, but Australia is renewing. At a time when many advanced cultures are growing in wealth though not in peace of mind, the great step Australians can take is to recognise the extent of their strengths and see the enormous, fragile expanse of their territory as an empire of the soul.

BIG
World's 10 largest
countries (land only)

1 Russia
2 Canada
3 USA
4 China
5 Brazil
6 Australia
7 India
8 Argentina

BIGGER
World's 10 largest
countries (land and sea)

1 Russia
2 Canada
3 USA
4 Australia
5 China
6 Brazil
7 India
8 Argentina

HUGE
World's ten largest claims
under Law of the Sea and Antarctica

1 Russia
2 USA
3 Australia
4 Canada
5 China
6 Brazil
7 France
8 Indonesia

PART TWO

Over time there has been a disturbing historical pattern—the crack and fall of civilizations owing to a morbid intensification of their own first principles.

George Soros

THE MAN WHO WASN'T THERE

WILSON TUCKEY: All you have done is finance growth with debt.

PAUL KEATING: You boxhead, you would not know. You are flat out counting past ten.

TUCKEY: You are an idiot. You are just a hopeless nong ...

KEATING: Shut up! Sit down and shut up, you pig.

TUCKEY: You could not even deliver Christmas presents to Warren Anderson.

KEATING: Why do you not shut up, you clown? ... This man has a criminal intellect ... this clown continues to interject in perpetuity.

On Friday 26 April 1996, five days before the new Parliament was about to be convened, a Parliament in which Paul Keating would be reduced from Prime Minister to back-bencher, Keating tendered his resignation. He thus became the first federal Labor leader in history to decline to take his seat after his government had lost power. All previous Labor prime ministers defeated in battle—Watson, Fisher, Scullin, Chifley and Whitlam—returned to sit in the Opposition benches. Not Keating. For thirteen years he had used the government frontbench to taunt and harangue and patronise his opponents, John Howard in particular.

'From this day onward Mr Howard will wear his leadership like a crown of thorns and in the Parliament I will do everything I can to crucify him.'

'I will do Howard and do him slowly.'

'He is the classic non-deliverer of Australian politics. He is the one person who cannot cut the mustard. The game is too hard for him. Lurking in this chest is not a heart for the political fight, but a split pea.'

'I am not like the Leader of the Opposition [John Howard]. I did not slither out of the Cabinet room like a mangy maggot.'

When John Howard, Prime Minister, led his new ministers into the House of Representatives, Keating, the hard man, was nowhere to be found. The people of Blaxland had voted overwhelmingly to give him the honour of representing them, but he declined to turn up. Ten days before the new Parliament was to begin, he submitted his resignation to the Governor-General when, by convention and as a courtesy to the House he had served so long, it should have been submitted to the Speaker of the House.

'I leave the House of Representatives with my faith not just intact but very much stronger,' his resignation letter said. 'I leave very proud of what the Labor government did, of what the labour movement did, and of what Australians did in the past decade to build a competitive Australian economy and marry it to a good Australian society.'

Keating was right to be proud. He had a glorious career in politics. He was, and always will be, a character who stood out in the mostly stunted ranks of Australian party politics. His structural legacies on superannuation, financial deregulation, native title, the republic debate, plus many other reforms over more than a decade, mark him as a man of vision. As for the manner of his leaving the parliamentary stage, he spent the day of the opening of Parliament at his Canberra home in Red Hill. The contrast was extreme between his absence and the full power and pungency of his parliamentary leadership, where he had refined the art of extemporaneous head-kicking.

... all through Question Time those two pansies over there want retractions of the things we have said about them. They are a bunch of nobodies going nowhere.

Hansard records only the sanitised Keating. The private Keating built his career on backroom tantrums, corridor eyeballings, and the long, crude telephone soliloquies when he told opponents, especially journalists, what he thought of them.

'In and out of the cat's arse.'

'Like a dog returning to its own vomit.'

Keating's departure from politics was no more tainted than his arrival. Twenty-six years earlier, on St Patrick's Day, 1970, Paul Keating, aged twenty-five, rose before the House of Representatives at 10.26 a.m. and uttered his first words in Parliament. It is a bizarre speech when read a generation later in the context of a very different Paul Keating and a very different Australia. It shows how much a man, and a country, can change in twenty-five years.

> *As this is my first speech in the House of Representatives and the beginning of my first term in this place I desire sincerely to thank the 55 000 electors of the Blaxland electorate for the honour of allowing me to represent them here. I wish also to thank the members of the Australian Labor Party for the assistance and unselfish help that they gave me throughout the course of the election campaign.*

Unselfish help? Keating got his red-ribbon seat in 1969 through the time-honoured tactic of branch stacking. Keating lost the 1969 preselection vote on the first and second ballots and won only after the right-wing New South Wales executive intervened and allowed his stacking to stand, thus defeating a left-wing candidate. (The frantic events leading up to this outcome included a late-night motorcycle dash by Laurie Brereton, who would parley his role as a Keating gofer into a long parliamentary career.)

Keating couldn't wait to put Blaxland behind him. During

his maiden speech in 1970, after he had thanked the electors of Blaxland, 'for the honour of allowing me to represent them here', he continued: 'I would like to be able to describe my electorate as a scenic district, as something of beauty, but unfortunately I can't.'

Blaxland never became scenic for Keating. His electoral office was on the second floor of a neat courtyard lined with palm trees. There was a tiny waiting room with four chairs, and copies of a pamphlet called 'Sole Parent' on a table. The office sat between a McDonald's and the Bankstown Adult Migrant Centre. The migrant centre is important. Bankstown, the heart of Keating's electorate, now has one of Australia's largest concentrations of non-English speaking background (NESB) immigrants. Bankstown Plaza is filled with East Asians, Muslims and Pacific Islanders. The chadore, head-cover for Muslim women, is common at Bankstown Square.

This is what the young Keating had to say about immigration in his maiden speech:

The government hopes to be able to offset the present
[small] population situation by immigration. It is time we
considered the enormous cost of bringing migrants to
this country. We must bear in mind this cost when we
consider the cost of subsidising Australian families ...
These figures may sound high but they are not when we
compare them with the cost of bringing migrants to
this country. After all, the best migrant is the infant
Australian.

Paul Keating left Blaxland as fast as he could. He moved to Canberra full-time, where instead of placing his children in the local government or Catholic schools, he put his son into Canberra Grammar and his daughters into Canberra Church of England Girls Grammar. Long before he left politics to pursue a career in business, he had moved as far as spiritually possible from his constituents in Bankstown. After the Lodge, he moved back to Sydney and paid 2.5 million dollars for a mansion on Queen Street, Woollahra, the antiques capital of Australia. Good luck to him.

A man must be judged by his own rhetoric, and this is where Keating has a few problems. Keating spoke often about reconciliation and left some courageous legislative legacies which sought to tackle the intractable problems of indigenous Australians. But the years of Labor government also coincided with an increase in neo-paternalism, welfare dependency, double standards, reverse racism, mismanagement and financial rorting within the Aboriginal aid apparatus. At high social and economic cost, the Labor governments subsidised a multicultural industry with a vested interest in ethnic divides. For twenty-five years, since the days of Gough Whitlam's immigration minister, Al Grassby, Labor and its surrogates pursued an ethnic strategy. Senators Robert Ray and Nick Bolkus, the Ministers for Immigration and Multicultural Affairs in the Hawke and Keating governments, embodied this strategy. 'Our polling,' Senator Bolkus said prior to the 1996 election, 'showed that in the last New South Wales election there was a swing of five to eight percent to [Labor] in the

seats where there was highest non-English-speaking composition. I reckon we can match that in the next federal
election.'

The strategy worked up to a point. The only electorates
that withstood the anti-Labor landslide in 1996 were the
heavily NESB electorates in Sydney and Melbourne that
Labor has so assiduously, and expensively, cultivated. Labor
spent more than a billion dollars building a system of patronage, dependence and influence among ethnic groups. After
the Keating government lost office, the new government
imposed stricter reviews to uncover fraud and abuse and
immediately saw results. The following exchange in the
Senate on 29 October 1997 contains more than enough clues
about the relative laxness of the social security system under
the Labor government.

SENATOR NEWMAN *[Minister for Social Security]: I
am now tabling the Department of Social Security fourth
quarter report on compliance activity ... The Labor
Party said the system was as tight as a drum when they
were in government—as tight as a drum. Former Minister Peter Baldwin claimed that it was of world leading
standard. It is also interesting that the Labor Party's own
review, after they lost the election last year, found that
almost everyone in Australia thought they knew a welfare
cheat.*

SENATOR BOLKUS: *Play to the prejudices. Go on,
keep playing to the prejudices.*

SENATOR NEWMAN: *You just listen ... The taxpayers want this, and so do those who are genuine social security recipients.*

—Opposition senators interjecting—

SENATOR NEWMAN: *During 1996–97 there were over 55,000 tip-offs from the public; that measure alone led to over 12,000 cancellations and reductions. Over three million reviews were conducted during 1996–97; that is up almost 28 per cent over the previous year. Also, 333,120 payment cancellations or reductions were put in place; that is an increase of over 40 per cent over your time in government. Debts recovered were $369 million, which is up 47 per cent over the previous year. And just remember this: almost $28 million every week— $28 million every week—was saved as a result of compliance activity during 1996–97.*

The figures have their own eloquence. The twenty-eight million dollars saved every week, if extrapolated annually, represented payments of more than 1.4 billion dollars a year. The forty-seven percent increase in debt recoveries was a stratospheric increase in just one year. So, too, was the 40 per cent increase in cancellations of pensions. We will never know how many billions were drained away during the previous decade on social security payments to people who should not have been receiving them.

A porous social security system was not even the biggest problem. The Labor government also used millions of 'soft' dollars under the grant-in-aid system which funnelled money, jobs and influence into Labor electorates. Abuse of the grants-in-aid system brought down the Minister for Sport, Ros Kelly, who resigned in the wake of the 'white board scandal'. Other ministers were spending more. Labor sent more than one billion dollars in grants-in-aid to ethnic organisations during its thirteen years in office. A survey of the grants made in New South Wales during its last full year in office shows that ninety-seven percent of the money went to organisations in Labor electorates. The second-largest recipient was the Prime Minister's seat, Blaxland, with its heavy and growing NESB population. In 1994–95 Blaxland received grants totalling $484 304.

The justification for this generosity in Keating's seat and in other Labor seats was that the majority of NESB immigrants moved into Labor electorates. This same cycle of political convenience (which would be repeated, on a much lesser scale, by the Howard government's schemes for assisting 'regional' electorates, i.e. mainly Coalition seats) enabled the Labor government to spend billions in Labor electorates on welfare and job training schemes among immigrant communities which had comparable rates of unemployment to those registered during the Depression.

'By the time it left office Labor was blatantly targeting opinions and votes in a wide range of interest groups through an array of taxpayer-funded grants,' Dr Des Moore, a former Deputy Secretary of the Treasury, wrote in 'How Labor Targeted Votes and Opinion,' a study published soon after the 1996 election. Moore estimated that at least $143 million in identifiable community grants were spent in Labor's last full year in office and the true value was probably greater than $200 million. Moore's study revealed that among the places where this money went were the following:

Twenty-three million dollars to ethnic community organisations, almost all based in Labor electorates, and ranging through the alphabet from the Afghan Community Support Association ($93 200), to the Amal Charitable Association ($89 617), the Assyrian Australian Association ($126 047), to the Immigrant Women's Speakout Association of NSW ($99 684) which, by the way, never returned my phone calls (so much for speaking out).

The biggest recipient among ethnic groups was the Vietnamese community of New South Wales, which received twenty-one grants totalling $844 209, plus another $510 064 for the Migrant Resources Centre. At the same time, Labor was building a political alliance with elements in the Vietnamese community through the Communication Electrical Plumbing Union (CEPU), which had a heavy Vietnamese work force in the mail centres. The CEPU itself received grants totalling $621 303 that year.

Advocacy groups which appeared to be financially independent in fact received subsidies under the community grants system. The Ethnic Community Councils of the various States were completely dependent on government funding. In New South Wales, the Council appears to have received $510,000 in various grants from the Federal government in Labor's last full year in office.

Community organisations which began as privately-funded organisations became almost fully funded by the federal government. A classic example is the Association of Non-English Speaking Background Women in Australia (ANESBWIA), which began as a grass-roots organisation helping immigrant women and now depends on federal government funding.

The use of federal funds became so pervasive under Labor that charities were receiving more than half their funds from the federal government. The cost and breadth of State support for the multicultural industry has become enormous, and the annual reports of the various federal and State agencies committed to diversity reveal a neurotic compulsion towards diversity for the sake of diversity:

- Somali Community of NSW Inc. $2500. To teach the youth the traditional dances of Somalia like zeila, berey and other.
- Serbian National Defence Council in Australia. $2000. To promote the development of folkloric drama from the numerous provinces and states from the former Yugoslavia.
- Pukapuka Women's Culture Group. $1000. To maintain and promote Pukapuka culture and traditions in Illawarra.
- Fleanh Na Locha. $2000. Traditional Celtic Folk Festival. To maintain and promote exchanges of cultures, [sic] involvement youth.
- Echoes of the Cook Island. $3000. Costumes and traditional instruments.
- Woolgoolga Organising Committee. $5000. Purpose: 8th annual national Sikh Games.

These lists, which go on for hundreds of pages, eventually add up to a very big number. Most of it goes on salaries. The link that all these programs have is that the government sector now regards ethnic groups as mendicants that must be helped. The great mystery is how Australia managed to sustain a prodigious and successful postwar immigration program for thirty years without all this new-found bureaucratic and political sensitivity.

An even more blatant political use of the federal grant-in-aid system under Labor was the payments to unions, which received grants totalling 16.5 million dollars. The money went to hundreds of specific projects such as 'developing modules for delivery of language and literacy support for the building industry'.

The close links between Labor's ethnic strategy and its trade union power base was exemplified by endemic branch stacking using ethnic groups reaching historic proportions. Bitter factional fights in western Sydney saw infusions of thousands of Lebanese, Macedonian, Greek and Vietnamese in branch-stacking campaigns. The former Labor minister, Rod Cavalier, described these campaigns as unprecedented in their scope, even including the historic ALP–DLP split in the 1950s.

The Liberals, too, have played ethnic politics. One report by the New South Wales Auditor-General found that during the early 1990s, the Liberal government had increased discretionary payments to ethnic community groups from one million dollars a year to four million a year. The Auditor-General noted: 'Anecdotal evidence suggests that grants could have been made where there was no application and perhaps no immediate need for taxpayer support for the beneficiary.' Peter Collins tried to use the race card, making an attack on New South Wales Labor Premier, Bob Carr, a committed environmentalist.

> *Scrape away this thin veneer of contrived environmental*
> *concern and you have Bob Carr blaming immigrants for*
> *urban sprawl and environmental degradation. At a time*
> *when the community cries out for healing, Bob Carr*
> *opens the wound.*

It was a disgraceful remark, especially as Carr has an Asian-Australian wife who has been a gracious First Lady.

In Victoria, Liberal premier Jeff Kennett played ethnic politics, but playing the race card is primarily Labor's game. So ingrained is the strategy that Labor continued as if nothing changed after the 1996 election. Labor's spokes-man on Aboriginal affairs, Daryl Melham, repeatedly accused the government of 'racism', just as his predecessor, Robert Tickner, did before he lost his seat in Parliament. Then there was Senator Nick Bolkus, an inveterate ethnic player. He once told reporters: 'Part of the portfolio was to attend religious functions and on average I attended about ten every weekend because you knew if you weren't there the Opposition would be.' In Opposition, Senator Bolkus, during one speech by the new Minister for Aboriginal and Torres Strait Islander Affairs, kept repeating: 'Why do you hate blackfellas?'

A full year after the most disastrous rejection in the history of Labor governments, the party's leaders had still not been able to metabolise the real cause of its defeat, which it attributed to fatigue in the electorate after thirteen years of Labor, combined with Paul Keating's pungent personality. The truth was much worse. The depth of community anger at being ignored, patronised and divided showed in the depth of Labor's descent: a mere 38.8 percent of the primary vote. At the 1996 elections Labor was seeking to run a country it had come to patronise.

Everything had been explained in Parliament with perfect clarity. Seven months after the election, during question time in the House of Representatives on 8 October 1996, speaking without notes and with an occasional tremor of anger in his voice, John Howard described the deafening silence, the great unspoken issue of the 1996 campaign. He was responding to a question by the Leader of the Opposition, Kim Beazley, who asked:

> Will the Prime Minister now agree that it is time for him to exercise leadership on the issue and state clearly and unequivocally that the views of the member for Oxley [Pauline Hanson] on racial issues are hurtful to a great many Australians, are damaging to our interests in the region and do not reflect the kind of society that Australia is or wants to be?

Hansard records the Prime Minister's response.

MR HOWARD: *It is a serious question from the Leader of the Opposition, and I hope the House will enable me*

*to give it a serious response ... Have I generally
followed the debate? Yes. Do I have a few things to say
about it? Yes ...*

   *In my view there should be robust debate in this
country about the size of our immigration policy. People
are entitled to attack the present immigration levels without being branded as bigots or racists ... If someone
disagrees with the prevailing orthodoxy of the day, that
person should not be denigrated as a narrow-minded
bigot. That is basically what has been happening in this
country over a very long period of time. It has been happening—*

MR [DUNCAN] KERR: *What about Hanson?*

MR HOWARD: *The Honourable Member for Denison
interjects. When you had people who dared to disagree
with your version of how to handle Aboriginal affairs,
when you had those people being branded as racists
and bigots, then you have a perfect demonstration
of the sort of McCarthyism that was creeping into
Australian politics under the leadership of the former
Prime Minister. McCarthyism was creeping into
Australian politics.*

   *I can remember early in 1992 when unemployment
went to a very high level and the ... former Opposition
leader, John Hewson, and I both called for a reduction in
the overall level of immigration because of its link with
the level of unemployment. For our pains, we were bucketed by the former Prime Minister as racist. He actually*

used that expression. He actually used that expression.
That is the kind of behaviour that I regard as absolutely
unacceptable.

I will always denounce racial intolerance. I will
always defend the non-discriminatory character of
Australia's immigration policy. I believe the contribution
that Australians of Asian descent have made to this
country has been immense ...

Paul Keating's response would have been interesting, but he
was long gone. Also long gone was the Australia that existed
when Keating had first spoken in Parliament twenty-five
years earlier.

It is true that we are experiencing full employment but
this does not mean that our families are enjoying a
standard of living which the wealth of this country
should allow. The real challenge which the
government must face is how to control inflation.
There is only one effective answer—control over prices
and services ...

I believe that the Commonwealth can control prices by
setting up a statutory prices authority to fix prices for all
goods and services used by Australian people. The
authority could include representatives of producers and
consumers and would be responsible to Parliament. The
authority should determine the requirements of an aver-
age family. It should inquire into an average family's
needs in respect of clothing, food, recreation, entertain-
ment, housing and health. From all this information it

*should recommend a wage adequate to provide a stan-
dard of living determined by the authority. This wage
would be set by an Act of Parliament and varied from
time to time ...*

*Family life is the very basis of our nationhood. In the
last couple of years the Government has boasted about
the increasing number of women in the work force.
Rather than something to be proud of I feel that this is
something of which we should be ashamed. The short-
sightedness of the Government's policy was borne out by
the headlines in this morning's newspapers. The number
of unfilled jobs has increased 6 percent while the unemployment figure has fallen by 10 percent. How can we
have national growth without people? How can we survive without a population? Is this Government doing
anything about child endowment? Is it doing anything to
put the working wife back in her home? It is not.*

So much changed, but some things remained the same. The
upstart young member spoke for twenty-five minutes in a
wide-ranging, magisterial, cheeky address filled with references to social justice and jibes against the Liberals, with a
bucketing for the Country [now National] Party as 'a political reactionary Siamese twin of the Liberal Party'. Some
things about Keating's New South Wales Labor Right faction
never change either. The struggle to replace him in the seat
of Blaxland was marked by a formal complaint of 'gross
irregularities' in the preselection contest by a national official
of the Australian Workers Union.

Keating's last speech to Parliament could not have been more different from his first. It was made on 30 November 1995, a speech which no-one at the time (except perhaps Keating himself) realised would be his valedictory address. By tradition, the speech by the Prime Minister before the Christmas adjournment is the time when he thanks all the people, great and small, who make the Parliament run. Paul Keating spoke for thirty minutes and thanked them all, including the parliamentary switchboard staff, Marlene, Margaret, Pam and Gaylene.

It was a long, good-natured, nonpartisan speech and a touchingly prescient farewell to the Parliament that had sustained him for twenty-five years.

> *Public life is a passing parade. Anyone who thinks otherwise is deluding themselves. We can only be on the stage for a while, hopefully usefully to be able to do some things. The good thing about the parliamentary system is that we are all first among equals. If you rise to Cabinet or prime ministerial rank or if you do not, the caucus is where the weight and the responsibility is—the sense, the touch with the community and picking up the plasma of Australian democracy.*

These would have been the perfect words to end his brilliant parliamentary career. But Keating, typically, delivered his last comments for Hansard a few minutes later, as an interjection, during a speech by his old sparring partner, John

Howard. Thus, the final words of Keating's parliamentary career were:

'I'd like to be a fly on your wall, mate.'

To which Howard replied,

'I bet you would, mate.'

7
THE BILLION DOLLAR BLUFF

BARRY JONES IS AN HONOURABLE man. He let the truth escape on 30 August 1997. Speaking at a national environmental conference, the former federal minister and current President of the Australian Labor Party said the unsayable.

The handling of it [immigration] by the previous [Labor] government was, I'd have to say, less than distinguished. Partly because, I think, it was seen as very important, a tremendously important element, in building up a long-term political constituency ... There was that sense that you might get the Greek vote locked up, or, from other party-political points of view, you might get the Chinese vote locked up.

As a result, the idea of bringing groups of people to fulfil family reunion requirements and so on was seen as being a real advantage to the party in power at the time.

It was much worse than that. Any criticism of Labor's immigration policies or multicultural program was described as 'racism'. We will be visiting the issues of ethnic crime, welfare abuse and immigration abuse later in this book. Suffice to say at this point that the problems have been covered up as part of Labor's prodigious political bluff, a bluff that has cost Australian society uncountable billions of dollars and ruined lives. The bluff succeeded.

In the federal election landslide of 1996, the only section of the electorate which held firm for Labor were the urban electorates with the heaviest NESB immigrant populations. Under Labor, these electorates had received a steady flow of federal largesse. We also know, thanks to neutral grassroots activists like Sheila Christofedes, who worked extensively in Sydney for the No Aircraft Noise Party, that Labor successfully targeted the NESB news media, which operate below the radar screen of mainstream media scrutiny. 'When I was door-knocking,' Mrs Christofedes said, 'I could tell that Labor propaganda was really working with migrants who had little English skills. A lot of them told me, "We only vote Labor." They believed that if John Howard was elected that Medicare would be in jeopardy, that immigration would be in jeopardy, that Howard's policies would actively discriminate against ethnic minorities. This is what Labor's foreign-language election material said.'

After Labor's defeat the multicultural industry scrambled to contain the damage and keep control of the debate. When the election was followed, six months later, by the first rush of Pauline Hanson into the national headlines, there was apoplexy in the multicultural industry. At its darkest hour of political defeat, it had been given a lifeline.

At the height of the news media's Hanson mania in late 1996, I attended the monthly meeting of the Ethnic Community Council of New South Wales. The meeting began with the chairperson, Angela Chan, holding up a copy of the *Bul-*

letin with a photo of Pauline Hanson on the cover and the headline: POLL SHOCK: AT LEAST FIVE SEATS. The latest opinion poll had found that if Hanson formed her own party it would win five seats at the next Senate election.

'She is a danger to Australia,' said Chan, who had campaigned vigorously during the 1996 federal election, warning that a Coalition victory could mean 'the death of multiculturalism'. When she handed the meeting over to her vice-chair, Josie Lacey, Lacey continued the rhetoric.

'If the Human Rights Act is weakened, this country is lost.'

Attendance at the meeting was larger than usual, about forty people, because lawyers from the Human Rights and Equal Opportunity Commission had come to talk about proposed changes to the Racial Hatred Act.

'How long does it take before she [Pauline Hanson] goes to jail?' Josie Lacey asked the lawyers.

When told that Hanson could not go to jail under existing laws, she said the Act needed amendment. This led to a discussion about the Act's effectiveness. It soon became obvious that everyone in the room (other than me) wanted to get rid of the section which stated that 'a fair and accurate report' in the news media was exempt from prosecution as an act of racial hatred.

'The British invented the concept of race and used it to rule the world,' said Dr Anthony Pun, a vice-chair of the Council, who would replace Angela Chan as chairperson the following year.

It was not exactly a gathering of civil libertarians.

Although the Federation of Ethnic Community Councils of Australia is nominally a federation of hundreds of community-based organisations around the nation, its real power lies with government, which provides all the funding, and with the news media, which relish accusations of racism. Peter Walsh, another former minister in the Hawke government enjoying the luxury of freedom and writing robust columns for the *Australian Financial Review*, now attacks the multicultural lobby he once helped feed.

The inability to speak English is another leading indicator of migrant unemployability. The suggestion during the election campaign that migrant points should be skewed more towards English speakers induced a threat from Angela Chan to send its proponents off to the Human Rights and Equal Opportunity Commission's thought and speech police for re-education or punishment.

Chan appears not to have noticed that the High Court pulled the HREOC's teeth a couple of years ago. But, if her point is to be taken seriously, she has unwittingly demonstrated how stupid we have been in enacting highly subjective, open-ended clauses in the Race Discrimination Act. If that Act really can be used to block sensible changes, then it is high time it was amended or repealed.

Chan is, of course, a paid-up member of the multicultural industry ... Such people have bluffed governments out of doing sensible things before. Governments have

*swallowed claims that they represent their ethnic commu-
nity; if the government upsets them, then the community
will vote en bloc against it. This always doubtful proposition has been demolished by two [studies] ...*

   *If the government is smart, then it will recognise the
multicultural industry as another paper tiger.*

What has kept this paper tiger growling are the twenty million dollars given each year to the Human Rights and Equal
Opportunity Commission, the federal bureaucracy most committed to the cause of group rights and ethnic divisions in
Australia, even to the point of declaring war on other
government departments.

Long before the costly thought-policing by the multicultural industry, Australia was radically broadening its
immigration base, enfranchising the Aboriginal population
and expanding links to Asia.

Labor greatly expanded the multicultural industry over
twenty-four years because it had to expand the reach of the
public sector, it had to create new categories of grievances,
so that the lawyers, bureaucrats and political activists who are
the party's lifeblood could be sustained. Whereas the Coalition parties have the private sector as their cash cow and
regenerative source of money, talent and ideas, Labor, confronted with shrinking trade unions, had to rely on an
expanded public sector as its other cash cow. Columnist Max
Walsh put it bluntly: 'Thirteen years of Labor has seen political patronage spread to every nook and cranny of the public
sector.'

After Labor lost office, its surrogates inside the bureaucracy conducted a guerilla war against the new Howard government, and strategic leaks claimed at least four ministerial casualties and embarrassments. From the day it lost office, Labor and its surrogates inside and outside the bureaucracy, notably multicultural and indigenous activists on the public sector payroll, kept up an incessant din about 'division' that became self-fulfilling. The most disturbing aspect of this industry is that its most zealous adherents in the bureaucracy and the Aboriginal community give their ultimate allegiance to the sovereignty of international bureaucracies, not Australia. Consider these comments from the 1994–95 annual report of the Human Rights and Equal Opportunity Commission, which includes among its aims:

> *to bring particular concerns or alleged human rights breaches to the attention of the international community (and specifically the United Nations) so as to bring pressure to bear on the Australian government to ensure compliance with appropriate standards ...*

What would this 'international community' know of Australian conditions? Presumably what the diversity industry tells them. What is 'appropriate'? What does 'compliance' entail? The same annual report also refers to 'the need for legal remedies for group libel'. Group libel is another chilling bureaucratic invention from HREOC, part of the general assault on individualism and individual responsibility cloaked in the euphemisms of diversity.

The same annual report also listed some of the juicy measures taken to work toward complying with these human rights goals:

> *Providing Commission representation at the second United Nations Assembly of the Indigenous Initiative for Peace in Paris in 1995;*

and:

> *Attending the Australia Week festivities in Washington in October, 1995, and presenting a paper at the Australian Embassy on the human rights of Aboriginal and Torres Strait Islander peoples ...*

Who were the crusaders who made these arduous tax-funded missions to Paris and Washington?

The Commission's 1995–96 annual report was even more shrill in the wake of Labor's defeat. Zita Antonios, the Race Discrimination Commissioner, wrote in her 1996 report:

> *This new wave of racism has been bubbling under the surface for some time but has erupted in the past year quite publicly. It manifests itself in the view that policies, legislation and even funding for Indigenous Australians and people of non-English speaking background have 'gone too far'.*

Note: criticism equals racism. The same tactic is used again and again. Ms Antonios was mild compared with Mick Dodson, the Aboriginal and Torres Strait Islander Social Justice Commissioner, whose analysis of the 1996 election in the same report showed apoplectic outrage that a conservative government had been elected.

> *A wave of resentment and racism began to take form during the lead up to the March 1996 election, and has washed across this country and the national media ever since. The defining political climate is a disturbing culture of disrespect, disregard, resentment and vilification.*

Not surprisingly, the Howard government tapped Mick on the shoulder and told him his services would not be needed when his term as commissioner expired in January 1998. The government also slashed the Commission's budget. No more junkets to Paris. It also introduced the Human Rights Legislation Amendment Bill 1996 aimed at curbing the Commission's ideological excesses.

Much of the bureaucracy's human rights jargon and ideology has been imported from abroad, particularly the United States, and most of it, wrote the American historian, Benjamin Schwarz, doesn't work.

> *The diversity mythology which we Americans hold up as a light to nations is a sanctimonious tissue of myth and self-infatuation ...*
>
> *We should not forget that our liberal, confident, tolerant, and good-natured bourgeoisie, when for once confronted with a determined and powerful internal foe, forgot its commitment to reason and reached for its revolver ... General Sherman, not the indomitable ideology of liberalism, marched through Georgia ... Our*

history gives us no right to preach. Instead, it should
prepare us to understand the brutal realities of nation-
building.

Peter Walsh admitted in his memoirs, *Confessions of a Failed*
Finance Minister, that the Labor government had suppressed
or ignored the costs of its immigration policies.

In short, migration adds more to demand than it does to
supply, ipso facto it blows out the current account deficit.
(Apologists for immigration, such as the BIMPR [Bureau
of Immigration and Multicultural Population Research]
either deny this fact or claim it applies only in the short
term. This could be true for a once only immigrant
intake, but not for an ongoing program.) ... an immigra-
tion program of 140,000 a year had an adverse current
account effect between four and six billion dollars.

Those billions of dollars helped underwrite Labor's electoral
strategy. This was not the sort of information the Labor government wanted to disseminate. Instead, it set up and
expanded a government agency, the Bureau of Immigration
and Multicultural Population Research, which came to be
regarded as so politicised that the Howard government shut
it down within its first year in office. The BIMPR did not
give Australians the sort of new immigration analysis that
began emerging in the United States in the 1990s.

Immigration has been, and remains, essential to Australia's survival as a nation, but national problems have been
caused by shoddy management and by the racial politics

played by the Labor Party and its surrogates in the multicultural industry. The negative effects of large-scale immigration revealed by substantial new research have been largely kept out of the national debate. For example, the Australian public has not learned about the research of Harvard economists Larry Katz, Richard Freeman and George Borjas, who concluded that immigrants, for their first twenty to twenty-five years in a new country, are a net fiscal drain on society. After studying the impact of immigration at the local level, they found native-born workers responded to immigration by moving out of high-immigration areas or by not moving into them. The same trend is occurring in Australia.

The Harvard economists also found that immigration had a major impact on twenty million native-born high-school dropouts who were competing with unskilled immigrants. Between 1979 and 1995, the average hourly wage of American males who hadn't finished high school fell from $12.22 to $8.92 (in constant 1995 dollars), a drop of thirty percent.

Nor did many Australians learn of the work on immigration at the University of Michigan, where economist George Johnson estimated that the influx of ten million unskilled immigrants to America between 1980 and 1995 raised the annual output of the economy by about US$110.5 billion, of which US$108.8 billion went to the immigrants themselves in wages, education and welfare benefits. This left what Johnson calls 'a trivial net gain to domestic residents' from large-scale immigration. Even this gain was offset by the effect of immigration on internal social cohesion and on the environment.

Another Michigan economist, William Frey, found an America divided by immigration, with a historic level of out-migration by unskilled Americans from the areas of high unskilled immigration—California, New York, Texas, Florida and Illinois. He found immigration patterns which undermined the melting-pot theory and were creating a social geography in which America was increasingly divided into areas either dominated by younger, multicultural populations, or by an older, white and alienated population.

Australian immigration scholar John Atchison wrote a 1997 essay, 'The Sad State of the Immigration Debate,' bemoaning the absence of academic rigour from the public immigration debate. The biggest oversight is that about one-third of those entering Australia as immigrants do not stay for the long-term. 'At a time when some 37 000 persons leave Australia annually on a permanent basis, this is a healthy corrective to easy judgements about the immigration phenomenon.' But he also points out that no country in the Asia-Pacific region, and certainly no country in the wealthy OECD group, matches the scope of Australia's immigration program. Australia has the fastest-growing population in the OECD.

Atchison has also written about what he calls 'the latent fascism' in the constant accusations of 'racism' in the Australian immigration debate. The rhetoric of 'racism' is certainly the weapon used to protect vested political interests. Within a year of Labor losing office, the new government began to clamp down on welfare abuse, immigration abuse and lax spending, and quickly extracted savings of more than one billion dollars a year. It wasn't long before the accusations of 'racism' began to flow from the opposition.

Anthony Albanese, a federal Labor MP from Sydney and notorious factional activist, charged that there were 'strong racist overtones' in the government's attempts to crackdown on false marriages. And why was this racist? Because arranged marriages, where the parties did not know much about each other, were still common among immigrants from Asia and the Middle East.

Senator Nick Bolkus, always reliable, simply described the government as 'racist'. His usual baiting was moderate compared with the speech in the House of Representatives on 16 June 1997, when Laurie Brereton stood up and for twenty minutes bucketed the historian Professor Geoffrey Blainey.

It was Blainey who started it all off. He was the person who lit the fuse in that fateful speech in 1984 when he proclaimed his arguments for a racially discriminatory immigration policy.

In words which have an eerie contemporary resonance, he declared the pace of Asian immigration to Australia to be well ahead of public opinion and warned of conflict and turmoil in the suburbs of our nation. The reaction to those remarks was explosive. By speaking as he did, Blainey fuelled the community fears on which he put so much weight.

More than that, he gave credibility and legitimacy to some of the more ignorant and sinister of the Australian community who quickly found new inspiration and voice

... It was Blainey who unquestionably mapped out the intellectual terrain, prepared the ground for the Member for Oxley and her racist One Nation Party.

Thus spoke Laurie Brereton, the man who introduced to the federal public service the Equal Opportunity mandated categories of 'PWD' (People With Disabilities), 'NESB1' (Non-English Speaking Background, first generation), 'NESB2' (Non-English Speaking Background, second generation) and 'ATSI' (Aboriginal and Torres Strait Islanders).

Why couldn't Professor Blainey just shut up and let the Labor Right, that paragon of virtue and ethics and electoral probity, set the national agenda?

We must not notice that sponsorship of the Commonwealth Bank Cup high school rugby league competition in New South Wales was dropped by the bank after a series of violent cross-racial brawls, and that the Commonwealth Cup high school soccer competition was also marred by violent interethnic brawls, resulting in assault charges. Let's pretend that Cabramatta is not the largest drug bazaar in Australian history. And don't mention that when the large numbers of young Aborigines in juvenile detention centres mixed with Vietnamese gang members in these centres, the spread of heroin into the urban Aboriginal population quickly followed, with disastrous repercussions.

So effective were the tactics of smear and denial over so long a period, and so ingrained is the imposed orthodoxy, that even the incoming Liberal Minister for Immigration and Multicultural Affairs, Philip Ruddock, continued the process of disinformation. In the aftermath of Pauline Hanson's maiden speech to Parliament in September 1996, and the ensuing media frenzy, Ruddock wrote a newspaper article headlined TRUTH AND IMMIGRATION published on 25 October 1996.

Presumably the article was prepared by senior officials within the Department of Immigration, which has a vested interest in making Australia's immigration policy look like a model of virtue and efficiency. Ruddock had an arduous assignment of cleaning up the system keeping open the flow of genuine immigrants, while reducing the flow of people who go straight on welfare. He had moved to tackle fraud, streamlined the Immigration Review Tribunal, which Senator Bolkus had stacked with political appointees, and had been careful not to antagonise any ethnic sensibilities. However, the complexity of this task did not explain why a federal minister would put his name to an article such as 'Truth and immigration'.

Statistics show that people from the many countries that make up the Asian continent comprise only 4.5 percent of Australia's total population. Based on recent immigration patterns, the projection is that by 2031, the Asian-born might be about 7.5 percent. This hardly constitutes an invasion.

Misleading. More than forty percent of all immigrants from Asia (the Asian continent includes the Middle East) settle in just one place—Sydney. Not only do the majority of Asian immigrants concentrate in just two cities, Sydney and Melbourne, they concentrate in clusters *within* these two cities.

The statement that the 'Asian-born' population might be only about 7.5 percent is disingenuous. It ignores the large and rapidly growing numbers of Asian-Australians born *in Australia*. Various demographic projections have placed the Asian-Australian population at around twenty percent of the total population within a generation. This twenty percent figure is borne out by a major study of immigration trends, *Immigration and Ethnicity*, by demographer Charles Price, published in 1996. Professor Price used Australia's long post-war immigration history and the ethnic composition of immigrants from 1983 to 1995 to project the population in twenty-five years. 'The work of Charles Price remains absolutely essential for anyone wanting to appreciate the social and demographic processes of integration, especially on marriage patterns,' wrote John Atchison in 'The Sad State of the Immigration Debate'.

Price's study projected the Asian-Australian population (which includes Middle-Eastern) at 19.5 percent in the year 2025, plus one percent ethnic Pacific Islanders. This level has already been reached in large areas of Sydney. According to the New South Wales Health Department, one in four births in central Sydney and one in five births in the south-west are to Asian-born mothers.

There is nothing wrong with this trend. But there is a great deal wrong with pretending that such a major demographic shift is not underway. This shift is the product of social engineering, and the highest population growth among advanced nations.

Ruddock went on:

Research has consistently indicated that a properly balanced immigration program has a neutral effect on a number of the key aspects of economic life ...

Wrong. Broad, bipartisan community support does exist for a properly balanced immigration policy, but as we don't have such an immigration program, there is no broad community support, a fact confirmed by poll after poll. Ruddock does not even acknowledge the growing environmental dimension of immigration, a dimension now of concern to a majority of Australians.

A long-term survey being undertaken by my department shows an unemployment rate of 20 percent 18 months after arrival for migrants in the Preferential Category, covering spouses and children.

Wrong. This twenty percent figure is bad enough, but it carefully understates the problem. The journal *People and Place* has repeatedly found astronomic unemployment numbers among some immigrant groups, including an overall long-term unemployment rate of 24.3 percent among settler arrivals entering the work force in 1988–89. Among immigrants from Vietnam who entered the work force in 1988–89, the majority, 55.3 percent, were receiving Jobsearch or Newstart payments five years after their arrival. The figures were even worse for settlers from Lebanon, 71.1 percent, and Turkey, 79.1. In contrast, the extremely low rates of long-term unemployment among settlers from Hong Kong, 2.4 percent, and Malaysia, 5.5 percent, who arrived in 1988–89 illustrate the huge disparities within the diverse 'Asian' immigration stream to Australia.

> *Are we really importing criminals as some would have us believe?*

Yes. Check the prison statistics.

> *The truth is that all migrants undergo character checks before they get a visa.*

Fantasy. According to figures in the 1996 *NSW Inmate Census*, twenty-eight percent of the non-Aboriginal prison population of New South Wales is foreign-born, not exactly a bargain for taxpayers. Somehow the Department of Immigration also did not notice that career criminals were arriving among the refugee intakes in large numbers.

> *Last year, in a speech to the National Press Club, Tom Sherman, the outgoing chair of the National Crime Authority, noted that 'empirical information consistently shows that people from non-Anglo communities commit fewer offences than those from the Anglo population.*

Disingenuous. The categories 'Anglo' and 'non-Anglo' are not only uselessly broad but also deliberately misleading. Once again the prison inmate figures put the lie to such happytalk. Apart from Aborigines, who are exponentially overrepresented in the prison populations, four immigrant groups stand out, per capita, in the prison population: those from Vietnam, Lebanon, New Zealand and the former Yugoslavia. These same groups tend to be negatively over-represented across the spectrum of official statistics. Yet Ruddock has claimed it is 'unfair' to use small statistical groups like prison figures. Far from being unfair, these statistics are signposts to wider illegality.

> A report on South-East Asian organised crime also noted that there is no basis for the argument that South-East Asian Australians are more likely to be involved in criminal activity than any other community within the Australian population. An Institute of Criminology study prepared in co-operation with my department refuted the 'portrayal of rampant youth violence in the Vietnamese community'.

Wrong. There is no such country as 'South-East Asia'. The category is meaningless, given the wide disparity in the crime/unemployment rates of immigrants from the various nations of South-East Asia. This broad category is used to mask problem areas. The Department of Immigration, despite its best intentions, helped to create Australia's largest ever drug market in Cabramatta. In the face of a multitude of quality control problems with Australia's immigration stream is a Department of Immigration so cautious it cannot even bring itself to charge those illegal overstayers who are actually caught. A 1997–98 report by the Australian National Audit Office expressed dismay at the department's habits.

> *People detained or removed from Australia are legally*
> *liable to pay for the cost of this action. However, in*
> *1993–94 the ANAO observed there was very little recov-*
> *ery of costs by DIMA.*
>
> *Three years after the previous audit, 0.1 percent of*
> *nearly $10 million in compliance costs of people who*
> *were removed was recorded as paid before departure on*
> *the computer compliance system ...*
>
> *ANAO was advised of instances where people who*
> *had breached their visas and were being removed from*
> *Australia had substantial liquid assets with them and yet*
> *did not pay for their detention and passage.*

After noting this pathetic 0.1 percent recovery rate, the ANAO also recommended that the immigration department 'eliminate the futile effort involved in sending a debit note after the person has departed Australia'. The ANAO also expressed disapproval of the department's poor record in clamping down on passport rackets.

> *In 1993–94, the ANAO noted limited progress in DIMA's*
> *investigation of a significant rate of 'lost' passports in*
> *Australia amongst a particular class of entrant. The*
> *ANAO saw a need for vigilance on misuse of passports*
> *more generally.*

The problems of passport rackets and immigration scams are examined later in this book. The Australian people need real information, not sleight-of-hand numbers and misleading generalities like those packed into Ruddock's 'Truth and immigration'. The electorate continues strongly to support economic expansion and cultural tolerance, but the majority are tired of being patronised on the issue of immigration. Barry Jones admitted as much on 30 August 1997, when he not only said that Labor had politicised immigration but added: 'What we were fearful of ... has proved to be correct.'

What they feared has come to pass—a nation increasingly divided along racial lines, cultural enclaves, high unemployment and high crime. In 1997 the suburb of Auburn was a place where police and firefighters were attacked by youths hurling rocks, a place where ambulances received police escorts after one ambulance had a window shot out. The problems were generated by groups of young people who were 'known to police'. Many of them came from a section called Little Lebanon, a concentration of families from the same region, even the same village, who had come to Australia as refugees and immigrants. They had created an Islamic Lebanese enclave in many ways disconnected from the Australian mainstream. A few months after this incident, firemen were attacked by a large group of youths after being called to a fire at the Villawood housing estate, not far from Auburn, and another troubled immigrant enclave. In December 1995 two firefighters were bashed by about thirty teenagers at the same Villawood estate, which has become so crime-ridden and derelict that it is being demolished.

Belatedly aware that such problems had cost Labor dearly, Labor under Kim Beazley began quietly supporting immigration reform. It allowed the Howard government to impose a ban on welfare payments to immigrants in their first two years in Australia, supported measures which allowed the government effectively to almost abolish the immigration of parents, a category that was slashed by ninety percent. Labor also allowed the imposition of English tests for the family program. Bob Birrell of Monash University, wrote an article asking: 'How did such radical changes get through Parliament? What happened to the previously influential lobby groups who had helped prompt governments to put out the welcome mat?' It was a rhetorical question. He knows the multicultural industry is, with a few exceptions, a surrogate for Labor.

It will take at least a decade to dismantle the problems caused by years of politicised and poorly executed immigration programs, and even longer to deal with the potent cocktail of economic rationalism coupled with large-scale, low-skill immigration. Structural reform is already underway. Quietly.

The seed of the race divide in Australian politics was sown on 25 August 1988 when a young Liberal MP, Philip Ruddock, was one of four Liberals who crossed the floor of Parliament and voted against their leader, John Howard, on a motion that, 'no Australian government would use race or ethnic origin as a criterion to determine the composition of the immigration intake'. Clearly, almost all Australian politicians agree with this sentiment. The motion was a stunt. It was designed as an attack on John Howard's handling of Asian immigration to Australia, an issue he has since admitted he handled maladroitly.

Ruddock voted as a matter of conscience. His motives were unimpeachable. But his gesture came at a high price. Philip Ruddock unwittingly helped the Labor government continue to mask its ethnic strategy. He unwittingly helped legitimise a cynical race ploy by then Prime Minister Bob Hawke. He thus helped execute a political move that contributed to a chilling of honest debate from which the country has yet to recover.

8
A KICK IN THE TEETH

AMONG THE MANY LETTERS flushed out by my article, 'The multicultural myth' in May 1996, was one from emeritus professor Jerzy Zubrzycki, who sent a paper he had presented at the Global Diversity Conference in 1995. The paper explained that the term 'multiculturalism' had been 'transported to Australia from Canada in 1973 by the then Minister for Immigration, Al Grassby'. He said the term had been 'subject to misunderstanding and confusion ever since'. The first person in Australia to misunderstand multiculturalism, Professor Zubrzycki wrote, was Al Grassby.

Ah yes, Al Grassby. Given Grassby's fondness for historical allusions, and given his key role in the introduction of 'multiculturalism' to Australia, it is worth revisiting the final chapter in his public career. In 1986 the Nagle Special Commission of Inquiry, conducted by John Nagle QC, examined the aftermath of the 1977 assassination of anti-drug crusader Donald Mackay in Griffith, New South Wales, a country town in Al Grassby's former federal electorate. In the course of his inquiry, Nagle examined certain actions by Albert Jaime Grassby. Nagle gave a damning summation of Grassby's behaviour in his final report. He found that Grassby had distributed an anonymous document, obtained from highly dubious sources, containing 'scurrilous lies' that grossly defamed the family of Donald Mackay. The document suggested that Mackay had been murdered by his wife and son after a family argument. It also suggested that the family solicitor was an accessory after the fact.

Nagle said the writing style in the document was characterised by a 'sneering nastiness'.

He said the document 'appears to be written as a parliamentary speech'.

He said none of the accusations withstood factual examination.

He rejected Grassby's defence of his actions—that he was trying to prevent the 'racial defamation' of the Calabrian Italian community in Griffith over the disappearance of Donald Mackay.

> *The commission makes only one comment—that no decent man could have regarded the attacks on the Calabrians as justifying him in propagating the scurrilous lies contained in the anonymous document.*

He described Grassby's behaviour as a witness during the hearings:

> *He was long-winded, dissembling, and unconvincing, and was constantly driven to uneasy claims of defective memory ... [Grassby] was, at the best, less than frank about, and at worst concealed, what he knew about the origin of the documents ...*

He claimed to have no memory at all of the parlia-
mentary speech which he handed to Maher.

The now infamous document had first surfaced in July 1980
when Grassby, by then long voted out of office, gave it to a
New South Wales State Labor MP, Michael Maher. At their
meeting in Grassby's office, Maher found two men and a
woman with Grassby, who, on behalf of this group, gave him
twelve pages containing the allegations about the Mackay
family. Grassby also gave documents to the *Sun-Herald*
newspaper, whose editor at the time, Chris Anderson, knew
Grassby. In August 1980 a front-page story in the *Sun-Herald*
claimed Michael Maher was about to make allegations in
Parliament on the Mackay case. The story ran under the
front-page banner: NOT THE MAFIA ...?

Wrong. During the Nagle inquiry, Grassby's barrister suggested to Maher that Grassby had merely suggested he 'raise'
the matter in Parliament. Maher strongly disagreed:

> *My recollection is that he said 'read' because he became*
> *quite heated—more emotional than I had ever seen him*
> *before.*
>
> *He [Grassby] said: 'If they stop you, keep going, if*
> *they take a point of order, keep going.'*

Maher also said Grassby had told him he had given the document to the then shadow Attorney-General in South
Australia, who would read it in State Parliament. Maher, far
from reading the document in the New South Wales Parliament, gave it to the New South Wales police. Nagle would

describe Maher's evidence to the inquiry as 'cogent and convincing'.

Grassby, and others, were later charged with conspiring to pervert the course of justice. He was cleared of the charge after a five-week court hearing. After the Nagle Inquiry report was released, the Labor Premier of New South Wales, Barry Unsworth, accepted Grassby's resignation from his $48 000-a-year job as Special Adviser to the Premier on Community Relations. The job, worth more than $100 000 a year in today's dollars, had been created for Grassby by the previous Labor premier, Neville Wran. In the New South Wales Supreme Court on 12 March 1987, Grassby apologised to the Mackays and to their solicitor, Ian Salmon. He was ordered to pay them $5000 damages. In making his apology, he accepted that the document he wanted read in Parliament 'makes the most serious allegations imaginable'.

The Mackays sued Grassby for criminal defamation. In 1991 a jury found Grassby guilty on three charges. Supreme Court Justice Allen, in fining Grassby $7000, said he had considered jailing Grassby but had decided not to because, 'There must be hurt in having a lifetime of public service crowned not with honour but with disgrace and humiliation.' The following year the jury's verdict was overturned by the New South Wales Supreme Court.

The greatest mystery in this episode is why Grassby would choose Michael Maher, a famously honest man, as the target for an attempt to defame the Mackays and abuse parliamentary privilege. When I asked Maher in 1997 why Grassby had chosen him, he replied: 'Because I had the biggest number of

Italians in my electorate. I had big concentrations of Italians in Haberfield, Five Dock, Concord, Drummoyne and Chiswick.' He thought he could play the Italian vote.

> At the start of the meeting he suggested that I could represent him on some overseas trip. I think it was to the Middle East. I just dismissed that. He then produced the document. I was appalled. I thought, 'That poor woman [Mrs Mackay]'.
>
> I clearly remember how agitated he became. I refused to even read it. This document could not be read. He was certainly acting for forces in Griffith who wanted to damage Mackay. I sent it to the police.

That was effectively the end of Al Grassby's political career, but the episode set a precedent for the tactic of personal abuse and the claim of 'racial defamation' of entire ethnic groups. The political self-interest behind the rhetoric of tolerance, all these qualities remained at the heart of the multicultural industry's methods as it grew large in the decades 1973 to 1996.

The central fantasy of the multicultural industry is that Australia should be a cultural federation. But Australia has a distinct, dominant, cohesive, assimilative, blended culture that has been painstakingly built through trial and error. There is an enormous difference between the self-evident diversity of Australia's multiracial society and the big protective tent under which this diversity is thriving. Take away that big tent—Australian culture—and this diversity curdles into state-sponsored tribal animosities.

These animosities are helped by the well-oiled machinery of complaint and victimisation. The New South Wales Anti-Discrimination Board, for example, actually celebrates the growing litigiousness it is fostering, as if this were a measure of community health. The Board's 1994–95 Annual Report gushes:

- *1994–95 was a fantastic year for the Aboriginal and Torres Strait Islander Outreach Program. The number of complaints that we received rose dramatically ...*
- *The Labor government is ... committed to extending the grounds of unlawful discrimination in NSW to include more types of discrimination.*

One of the jewels in the bureaucratic crown of the multicultural industry is the national broadcaster SBS, which started with laudable goals and bipartisan support but, having to please a babel of constituencies, has been plagued by endemic in-fighting and racism. The following leaked memo from an SBS manager was the quote which opened the 1996 story, 'The multicultural myth', the seed which planted this book.

... the following remarks were [allegedly] made in the context of an application for the job of [a management position]:

- *'There is no way I'll accept having that woman in the job. We don't need someone from that sort of background, an Anglo.'*

- *'An Anglo shouldn't be given that job; it should go to an ethnic. We don't need people like that.'*
- *'How can she know what the ethnic community needs? She's an Australian.'*

If you transpose the words Anglo and ethnic, I believe it is immediately clear that these comments were racist.

When the job of general manager of SBS became vacant in 1997, the successful applicant was Nigel Milan, who had a long history of successful senior media management and had also come to Australia as an immigrant. He was the wrong choice according to members of the multicultural industry for reasons that had little to do with media management. A New South Wales Liberal politician, Jim Samios, even complained publicly that two of the failed candidates—Angela Chan, who runs her own immigration consultancy, and the chairman of the New South Wales Ethnic Affairs Commission, Stepan Kerkyasharian—'would have excelled' if they had been chosen. Why? Neither Chan nor Kerkyasharian had any experience as senior managers or entrepreneurs in the media business. The big problem with the successful applicant appeared to be that he had migrated from the wrong country—Britain.

In his 1997 book, *Liberal Racism*, the American author Jim Sleeper argues that modern liberal orthodoxy has placed racial identity as the 'central organising principle of our public life', a process that divides the infinitely complex community into rigid racial groups and reflects a 'primordial' desire to classify people according to their skin colour. In

1996 Australian multicultural ideologues produced a book entitled, *The Teeth are Smiling,* subtitled, *The Persistence of Racism in Multicultural Australia.* One of the book's coeditors was Stephen Castles, Director of the Centre for Multicultural Studies at the University of Wollongong, who appeared earlier in this book's chapter 'It Wasn't Luck' with his description of Australia's past as racist, sexist, elitist and genocidal. His co-editor, Ellie Vasta, a sociologist at the university, wrote a chapter entitled 'Dialectics of Domination: Racism and Multiculturalism,' which describes the 'loss of identity' felt by many Anglo-Australians 'because they feel they have lost their hegemony over the cultural and geographical spaces they once controlled.'

As an example of this sense of loss, she quotes an attack made by the poet, Les Murray, against the Australia Council:

> *They are creating an Australia that is exclusive.*
> *Multicultural, they call it. But they are discrimina-*
> *tory, they exclude. 'They' are not just the Australia*
> *Council; they are the ruling elite of today's Aus-*
> *tralia: the cultural bureaucrats, the academics, the*
> *intellectuals ... They are excluding people like me*
> *from their Australia—the country people, the red-*
> *necks, the Anglo-Celts, the farming people—they*
> *have turned their backs on us. They act as though*
> *they despise us ... We Old Australians, not always*
> *Anglo but having no other country but this one, are*
> *now mostly caught and silenced between the indige-*
> *nous and the multicultural.*

*This is a fairly articulate lament from someone who
feels he has lost his sense of hegemonic identity within
the cultural scene. It is instructive to know that Murray
has formed the Australia Council Reform Association
with Mark O'Connor who is a leading member of Australians for an Ecologically Sustainable Population, a
well-known organization whose anti-immigration dis-
course is part of a broader racist rhetoric.*

Note what is going on here. This Wollongong academic presumes to find Les Murray 'fairly articulate'. She also
presumes to call him, by association, a racist. The logic is
that anyone who wants lower immigration is pursuing a racist
agenda. This allegedly includes groups such as Australians
for an Ecologically Sustainable Population, an organisation
which is part of 'a broader racist rhetoric'.

I attended the 1997 national conference of Australians for
an Ecologically Sustainable Population (as a reporter not a
participant). It was opened by the Premier of New South
Wales, Bob Carr, and a key speaker was Labor Party President, Barry Jones, who would tell the truth about immigration
and politics under the Labor governments. There were six
other speakers, all scholars, and one of them, Associate Professor Frank Stilwell of Sydney University, touched on the
big issues latent but largely unspoken beneath the stresses in
Australian politics:

*The delicate balance between diversity and social
cohesion is at the heart of the matter ...
    Size itself is not a crucial variable on economic matters*

*... In any case, there is no possibility of competing with
our regional neighbours in terms of absolute scale ...*

Speaker after speaker said Australia would no longer become
stronger and better by simply bulking up its population. Jim
Downey, executive director of the Australian Conservation
Foundation: 'It is no longer necessary to have high net migra-
tion to boost per capita economic growth ... ' Then came
Barry Jones, MP.

*Population policy cannot be a long-term side-effect of ad
hoc immigration practice ... One factor contributing to
the unanimous [bipartisan] adoption of the 1994 Report
by the Standing Committee ['Australia's Population Carrying Capacity'], was that the members were
increasingly concerned that an exaggerated emphasis on
immigration, in isolation, was potentially very divisive,
with migrants then becoming scapegoats, being blamed
for a cultural threat ... We were very well aware that in
France, for example, with the rise of Jean Marie Le Pen,
that migration was blamed for every social problem,
especially crime, unemployment, pressure on health,
social services and even the environment ... I [also]
spent some time in Bulgaria last year. Bulgaria was very
striking, a country with a very sharp population
decrease. You become conscious that Bulgaria is, to a
very large extent, a culture of death ... the lack of new
life contributes to the sense of decay, ruined buildings
and a sense of fatalism and the sense that nobody's
going anywhere.*

The conference room was packed. The audience listened carefully to Barry Jones's warnings that immigrants are easily scapegoated for society's problems. Few if any of the predominantly middle-class people in the conference hall believed that such scapegoating was fair or useful.

The defining picture of Australia at the end of the twentieth century was being told at this conference. On any given day so many different stories were flowing into each other like the tributaries of a single large river. Take, for example, the reports from a single newspaper on 5 June 1996.

AUSTRALIA PLACES JOBS BEFORE OZONE
The Federal Government has vowed it will not sacrifice tens of thousands of jobs by agreeing to inequitable greenhouse gas reduction strategies.

GUN REBELS FORCE GOVERNMENT TO RETALIATE
Alarmed by the growing backlash against the proposed gun law reforms, the federal government is planning a nationwide campaign to try to stem revolts from conservative voters.

WE'RE WRONG: SYDNEY SHOULD BE CALLED WEERONG
If Dr Tim Flannery's dream is fulfilled, Sydney will be given back its Aboriginal name, Weerong, Sydneysiders will be called Cadigals, the Harbour will be called Cadi and Botany Bay Cameera.

TOUGH JOB AHEAD TO REIN IN THE DAMAGE
The first attempt to fully document the economic and

*social importance of Australia's environment and its
health has revealed that the nation is facing vast ecological challenges from pollution, land degradation,
irrigation and deforestation.*

OUR 'BREADBASKET' IS IN BIG TROUBLE
*The economic importance of the Murray-Darling Basin
and its precarious health makes the waterway, which
drains four states, one of Australia's most important
environmental issues, according to a report released
yesterday.*

PERMIT SYSTEM URGED TO SAVE TOURIST ICONS
*Some of the most fragile and beautiful parts of Aus-
tralia—including the Great Barrier Reef and Tasmania's
World Heritage areas—are being loved to death, a
national study has found.*

ANGER AS TWO FACE CAB MURDER CHARGE
*Family and friends of a murdered taxi driver and the
supporters of one of the accused clashed outside
Bankstown Local Court yesterday. Davina Leaituaalesi,
19, and Julius Graff, 19, were refused bail by the magistrate when they appeared on a charge of having
murdered Mr Youssef Chmeis on May 25 at Riverwood.*

VET POO-POOS TINNED PET FOODS
*There are 6.8 million pets in Australia, and they produce
1.7 million kilograms of excrement a day, three times the
volume of the excrement which would be produced if they
were eating natural foods, such as meaty bones, and it is*

sticky, putrid and contaminated with bacteria. 'It gets into waterways and causes environmental havoc,' said vet Dr Tom Lonsdale.

UN WARNS OF BIG DRY TO COME
Most cities in the developing world will face extreme water shortages by 2010, according to the opening paper at the United Nations human settlement conference.

CHINA: POLLUTION CRISIS
AS ECONOMY GOES INTO OVERDRIVE
Beijing—China's pollution woes continued to mount last year despite strenuous efforts to tackle its environmental problems, according to a government report.

JAKARTA SHIPPING PLAN SPARKS ANGER
Australia and Japan are deeply concerned about Jakarta's plan to limit the passage of military and commercial shipping to three sea lanes running north-south through the archipelago state. The curbs could add millions of dollars to the cost of shipping between Australia and Japan.

39 FACE TRIAL IN IRIAN JAYA
Thirty-nine people are to be tried in Irian Jaya for taking part in riots in March in which four people were killed.

SYDNEY'S ALIEN NATION
Few of the early Chinese settlers saw Australia as home but those families who stayed endured hardship and discrimination that have spanned five generations.

A KICK IN THE TEETH

QANTAS STEADY
*Qantas Airways is adding a second flight to Ho Chi
Minh City beginning in July.*

I clipped all these stories and put them in a folder which I
marked 'Zeitgeist'. That day, the fifth of June 1996 was the
day I decided to write this book.

Connect the scattered pieces and a single portrait emerges.
The mosaic of news depicts a tolerant, advanced, prosperous
and democratic country enduring social and environmental
stress, the side-effects of economic growth, high and undis-
ciplined immigration, racial politics, a growing divide
between city and the bush, a growing awareness of the magnitude of the Aboriginal issue, and a nation increasingly
interdependent with an Asia whose economic growth carried
costs as well as benefits.

The people of the bush, those closest to the ethos on which
Australian culture and mythology was built, feel so margin-
alised by the new dominance of urban politics that many
believe they are being thrown on the historical scrap heap.
Rural Australia, while still having thousands of successful
farms and a significant export industry, also has dying country towns, large areas of shrinking job prospects and growing
crime. In some rural towns up to eighty-five percent of
people are living on some form of assistance. The level of
crime in many country towns is endemic. This sense of siege
in the bush provided the white heat in the historic Wik debate
on native title.

On 11 December 1997 the *Sydney Morning Herald* ran a

front-page banner headline 500,000 CHILDREN ON BREADLINE based on new figures from the Centre for Population and Urban Research at Monash University which showed that Australia's working poor are concentrated in the bush. On the same day the newspaper also carried a front-page headline THE GREAT SYDNEY GRIDLOCK, a story about increasing 'traffic paralysis' in Australia's largest city. It was a perfect juxtaposition of two separate yet linked trends: country drain and city strain. The stress of increasingly crowded big city streets showed up in a 1997 survey by the insurance company AAMI, which found that fully two-thirds of drivers said they frequently encountered what we now call 'road rage'. The survey found that young women had become as susceptible to road rage as men.

The collective unease, caused by these underlying stresses erupted on 2 March 1996 when a powerful government was thrown out of office. The Keating government was humiliated despite twenty consecutive quarters of economic growth, low inflation, high business confidence and sound economic management. Despite all this, the ruling Labor Party was suddenly reduced to a rump thirty-nine percent of the primary vote. No election since Federation has combined such a benign economic environment with such a savage electoral rebuke. The deafening silence imposed on debate cloaked the real issues of concern during the election campaign—the politics of intolerance masquerading as tolerance.

Speaking of which, within months of the publication of *The Teeth are Smiling*, which sank without trace in the public debate, Les Murray's new collection of poems, *Subhuman*

Redneck Poems, became a bestseller with more than 20 000 copies sold, extremely rare for a book of poems in Australia.

Where will Australia be held?
Ethnics who praise their home ground
while on it are called jingo chauvinists.
All's permitted, though, when they migrate;
the least adaptable are the purest then,
the narrowest the most multicultural.

From 'The Suspension of Knock', *Subhuman Redneck Poems*

Murray is a provocateur, a bush eccentric, a man of feuds, ideologically uncompromising. His poems about multicultural orthodoxy are not written to make people feel comfortable. His work is included here because he has been smeared and because, like all original artists, he does not fit the prevailing artistic orthodoxy. One of his primary targets is this new orthodoxy which, having largely swept away the old Eurocentric, male-dominated value system, has settled into some of its own intolerant rigidities.

Our one culture paints Dreamings, each a beautiful
   claim.
Far more numerous are the unspeakable Whites,
the only cause of all earthly plights,
immigrant natives without immigrant rights.
Unmixed with these are Ethnics, absolved of all blame.

From 'A Brief History', *Subhuman Redneck Poems*

AMONG THE BARBARIANS

Les Murray is a writer with an international literary reputation whose fans include the 1996 Nobel Laureate for Literature, poet Seamus Heaney. *Subhuman Redneck Poems* won the 1997 Victorian Premier's Literary Award for poetry. It was one of the three finalists for the 1997 New South Wales Premier's Literary Award for poetry. Several months after being smeared by multicultural zealots in *The Teeth are Smiling*, Les Murray won the TS Eliot Award, one of the most important poetry prizes in the world.

9
LOVE AT FIRST SIGHT

HANSARD, HOUSE OF REPRESENTATIVES, Tuesday, 10 September 1996:

> *Mr ACTING SPEAKER: Before I call the honourable member for Oxley, I remind the House that this is the honourable member's first speech. I ask the House to extend to her the usual courtesies.*

> *Ms HANSON (Oxley) (5.15 p.m.): Mr Acting Speaker, in making my first speech in this place, I congratulate you on your election and wish to say how proud I am to be here as the Independent member for Oxley. I come here not as a polished politician but as a woman who has had her fair share of life's hard knocks.*

Pauline Hanson spoke for twenty minutes, concluding her speech at 5:35 p.m. Within minutes, the switchboard at Parliament House began to light up. People were calling asking for copies of Hanson's speech. The density of the phone traffic was highly unusual and unprecedented for a political novice.

The news media's immediate reaction to the speech was to fixate on the sentence: *'I believe we are being swamped by*

Asians.' Although clearly the best bite to take from the speech, Hanson's statement immediately beforehand, rarely quoted, was even more important to understanding her rise to prominence:

> *Immigration and multiculturalism are issues that this government is trying to address, but for far too long ordinary Australians have been kept out of any debate by the major parties. I and most Australians want our immigration policy radically reviewed and that of multiculturalism abolished. I believe we are in danger of being swamped by Asians. Between 1984 and 1995, 40 per cent of all migrants coming into this country were of Asian origin.*

It does not matter whether people loathe her or love her or use her, the key to Pauline Hanson's rise in Australian politics are these words—'for far too long ordinary Australians have been kept out of any debate by the major parties'. Prior to the arrival of this unpolished politician in 1996, an anger had built up in the electorate over the furtive, bipartisan dissembling by politicians and the press over the issue of social cohesion. So strong and so ruthlessly imposed were the protocols constraining discussion of racism, discrimination, affirmative action and immigration, it would be a foolish move to smash through and express, with undisguised resentment, the unpleasant fears felt in much of the electorate. Pauline Hanson made that move. That's why the phones lit up at Parliament House.

'It all soon became like a fan club, a personality thing,' said the man who helped draft that maiden speech, John Pasquarelli, Hanson's chief political adviser, who was later sacked amid spectacular discord. 'Barbara Hazelton [Hanson's office manager] started telling her all the time she could become Prime Minister. She thinks she's doing an Eva Peron.'

* * *

One of the ANZACS who landed at Gallipoli in 1915 was Frederick Charles Webster. He was wounded in action. Shot in the chest, he lay on the battlefield surrounded by dead soldiers. In her 1997 biography, *Pauline—The Hanson Phenomenon*, Helen Dodd (an Ipswich pharmacist with a PhD in biotechnology) writes that the young soldier was found by a Turkish doctor who saved his life. After he returned to Australia he married Alice McKee and they had a daughter, Nora, who in turn had a daughter, Pauline.

Pauline Lee Seccombe was born on 27 May 1954 near Brisbane. Three of her grandparents had migrated to Australia from England prior to World War I. The fourth, her maternal grandmother, Alice McKee, was Queensland-born and the one who gave Pauline her red hair and her red temper. Pauline left school at fifteen, got a job as a clerk, worked most nights at her parents' hamburger shop, married at age seventeen to Walter Zagorski, a Polish immigrant, had two children, divorced in 1977 after six years. She married Mark Hanson at age twenty-five, had two more children, and divorced again after six years. By then she was Pauline Hanson, living in Ipswich.

Her bridge to politics was Rick Gluyas, a friend whose influence led her to run for Ipswich City Council as an independent in 1994. She won a seat in an anti-Labor swing against the council, but her friendship with Gluyas did not survive this development.

Hanson's fourth confidant was Maurie Marsden, an ex-boyfriend who was her campaign manager in the council election and when she ran for the federal seat of Oxley in 1996. Hanson's success in gaining Liberal pre-selection was not seen as a great prize. Oxley was a safe Labor seat, needing a mammoth 14.7 per cent swing to change hands. Any Liberal candidate would likely be cannon-fodder. Hanson did not even last until the election before her pre-selection was stripped away. The catalyst for disendorsement was a letter she wrote to *The Queensland Times*, published on 6 January 1996 in which she wrote of indigenous Australians:

How can we expect this race to help themselves when governments shower them with money, facilities and opportunities that only these people can obtain no matter how minute the indigenous blood that flows through their veins, and this is what is causing racism. Until governments wake up to themselves and start looking at equality not colour then we might start to work together as one.

The letter became her unintended campaign manifesto, especially after the sitting Labor member, Les Scott, refused to appear on the same podium with her at a pre-election debate. Local Aboriginal elders Elsie Geebung and Gladys Graham described Hanson as 'ignorant as a pig in mud'. This, like Les Scott's boycott, merely served to enhance her cause. On election day, 2 March 1996 Hanson won a 19.3 percent swing, the biggest in the nation. *The Queensland Times*, in noting her resounding success in ending 'the unspectacular career of Les Scott', and also noted what the national news media chose to ignore:

> *While some supported her comments, others simply supported her right to speak out on the issue and still others admired her for the bravery of her convictions in the face of the party machine.*

On 3 March, the day after her victory, a complaint of racial discrimination was lodged with the federal Human Rights and Equal Opportunity Commission. Thus began the surreal political phenomenon of Pauline Lee Hanson. Right from the start, it was propelled by a ferocious level of attention from the media, which accorded her the news status of a redneck Princess Diana. 'There's no doubt the media attacks were magnificent for her,' John Pasquarelli told me. Denis McCormack, a leader of Australians Against Further Immigration and Australia First Party, also shared the belief that the international attention on Hanson was in large part a media phenomenon.

> *She is on centre stage completely because of the*
> *news media. Pauline is straight out of the movie* Being
> There. *She is the Chauncey Gardener of Australian*
> *politics.*

Privately, her career was marked by incessant feuds and a stream of personal casualties. The first to go was her campaign manager, Maurie Marsden. 'Ten years of friendship just went out the window,' he told me in 1997. 'I felt I wasn't wanted after 2 March. I never got paid a salary. I never took a cent. It does offend me that I was treated as an outcast by a stranger who came in after Pauline won office. There was a paranoia about who got credit. They were paranoid about a lot of things.'

The stranger who ousted Marsden was Barbara Hazelton, who had previously worked as a secretary for National Party MPs. After Hanson's federal election victory, Hazelton came for an interview and got a job as office manager the same day. 'Pauline and I just clicked from day one,' she said. 'She gave me the job on the spot.' Maurie Marsden did not last long after that, and he remains bitter.

> *It was playground stuff. I was told not to come back to*
> *the office. She said she felt I was disrupting her office*
> *... They didn't like being told problems. They only*
> *wanted to be told they were wonderful ... The situation*
> *became ridiculous. Pauline can't take criticism. She was*
> *taking notice of strangers. People came in from nowhere*
> *wanting to run the show ... I see a lot of our work on*
> *important issues going down the chute. She hasn't got*

*policies. The whole thing is turning nasty. She's fighting
with everybody. All the original grass-roots campaign
organisations are going down. I've seen a turn against her
in Ipswich.*

John Pasquarelli didn't last long either. He had come to her
office on the recommendation of the anti-immigration
crusader, federal MP Graeme Campbell. Pasquarelli tried
to play Svengali with the inexperienced, inarticulate
Hanson and it blew up. He was fired within a year. He
told me.

*Nobody ever goes away a friend. They all go away
enemies. I used to have to tell her to ring people
to thank them. It never occurred to her ... There
was a big element of curiosity value about her, but it's
basically a sideshow. She can't carry the big arguments
... The one thing that may save Hanson as a political
force, at least in Queensland is black racism. Australians
will resent reconciliation if it's rammed down their
throats. If this happens, people may be prepared to over-
look Pauline's inadequacies.*

Pasquarelli was sacked on 9 December 1996. Sacked on the
same day was Jeff Babb who had barely arrived. Both Babb
and Pasquarelli sued for unfair dismissal in the Industrial
Relations Court. Babb's claim went to Federal court and was
unresolved as this book went to press. Pasquarelli's claim
was settled out of court.

Several early grassroots organisers also angrily broke with
Hanson, notably Bruce Whiteside, founder of the Pauline

Hanson Support Movement, and Vic Piccone, who headed the movement in north Queensland. Piccone was threatened with a lawsuit by One Nation. Within a year of One Nation's operation, the party splintered. In December 1997, a dozen branches in Queensland, New South Wales and South Australia endorsed the formation of the Australian One Nation Party. 'If you don't agree with them you are labelled a "white ant",' said David Archer, one of the leaders of the splinter faction in New South Wales. The director of One Nation, David Ettridge, dismissed the split: 'In every rapidly growing organisation a few branches are going to turn out to be duds.'

In 1997, the main adviser in Hanson's life became a Sydney Liberal Party activist, David Oldfield, a bachelor in his early thirties who met Hanson after defending her from a shouting abuser in a Canberra restaurant. This story, often told, is actually true. Hanson's new adviser did little to hide his long-term desire to win a seat in federal Parliament. He also brought in a friend and professional fund-raiser, David Ettridge, to run the new Pauline Hanson's One Nation party.

For a new political party dealing with the highly loaded subjects of racial discrimination and immigration, Hanson's new principal political adviser brought plenty of emotional baggage. Oldfield came from a home indelibly printed with scars left by Japanese atrocities in World War II. 'My father is a decorated gunnery officer,' Oldfield told me.

*He served all through Indonesia. He was shot down
by the Japanese in October, 1944, and was a POW for
seven months. He came close to being murdered many
times. His bomber crew was held for interrogation,
moved six or seven times, and never put in a camp
with other POWs. They were beaten, tortured. My father
was fourteen stone when he was captured, and six and
a half stone when he was released. He was bashed so
violently he had to hold his eyes open. They would line
them up and say, "We are going to decapitate you".
He had two friends lopped during the war. They would
also line them up and put them in front of firing squads,
and simulate an execution. The Japanese killed all
the bomber crews and they were planning to kill my
father's crew when the war ended. My father would
not say anything about the war until the 1980s, but we
weren't allowed to have anything in the house that was
made in Japan.*

David Oldfield did not arrive at Hanson's office in time to
save his new boss from her greatest debacle, the book *Pauline
Hanson—The Truth*, which destroyed any credibility she
might have been building through electoral success. Nearly
everything about the book was amateurish, paranoid, mean-
spirited, and fifth-rate. No serious politician could have put
their name to it. 'People say she received bad advice about
the book,' said Maurie Marsden, who was still around when
it was being compiled, 'but she was the one making the decisions. The copyright is in her name. Her name is on the cover.

So she is responsible for what's in the book. She can't just walk away.'

The book, with its comments about cannibalism among Aborigines, and its parody of a future Asianised Australia run by a lesbian Asian who was partly genetically engineered, was nominally by Hanson but its true authorship soon became highly secretive after controversy erupted immediately after publication. One of the authors was Bruce Whiteside, a Gold Coast pensioner who had formed the Pauline Hanson Support Movement as a spontaneous grass-roots eruption.

'The media created her,' said Whiteside. 'She was a small target while she was the member for Oxley. She could be nicely naive, inarticulate. That even worked in her favour. But when she became leader of a party she became a big target. She needed a lot of help, but she won't accept help. She's ego-driven.' By the time Hanson made her rise from battler to national figure she had left in her wake a formidable list of estrangements—Walter Zagorski, Mark Hanson, Rick Gluyas, Maurie Marsden, John Pasquarelli, Jeff Babb, Bruce Whiteside, George Merrit, Vic Piccone, and even, for a few years, her eldest son, Tony. 'She will never run a happy ship,' predicted Maurie Marsden.

Whiteside admitted he was one of the authors of *The Truth*. 'I wrote the foreword and the conclusion, but after we broke Pauline wanted them out and she wanted my name out of it completely. The book that is called *The*

Truth is the book that nobody would put their name on. That disturbed me.'

'The book is bigger than Pauline Hanson,' Denis McCormack told me. A retired Adelaide engineer, George Merritt admitted he had pulled it together from work by several collaborators. Merritt, too, fell out with Hanson. One Nation's leaders quickly stopped further publication after the book blew up, but the damage was done.

* * *

The performance of Pauline Hanson after the 1998 Australian of the Year awards marked her as a woman who was determined to strip her following of its large contingent of the sympathetic, the curious, and the disenchanted, until only a rump of zealots remained.

On Australia Day 1998, the world champion sprinter and one of Australia's most beloved public figures, Cathy Freeman, was named Australian of the Year. The award recognised the moments of national communion she had given Australians at the 1996 Atlanta Olympics and the 1997 World Championships when, after brilliant performances, she had carried the flags of Australia and Aboriginal Australia with pride and dignity on an international stage. Several days prior to Freeman's being honoured, a Vietnamese-born, twenty-year-old Melbourne law student, Tan Le, was honoured as Young Australian of the Year for her work with immigrants and refugees. Tan Le herself had come to

Australia as a refugee, but in accepting the award she described herself as 'an ordinary Australian'.

Pauline Hanson told a radio station that while she had 'no problem' with either woman, the awards smacked of tokenism and the honouring of Cathy Freeman was meant to make Australians, 'forget about the Wik, forget about the stolen generation and I think appointing the young Asian lady, the government's been pushing us to become Asianised and I'm totally against becoming Asianised ... I think it's all very political. I'm not very impressed by it whatsoever. I think the majority of Australians will know what I'm talking about.'

When this was passed on to the Prime Minister, John Howard, he responded later that same day: 'Her remarks were not only inaccurate, they were stupid, they were petty, and they're very divisive remarks to be made on Australia Day.' Nothing more needed to be said.

Pauline Hanson's crusade, however, asked some questions that the political heavyweights had been ducking for years, and she attracted some heavyweight critics. Henry Reynolds, a distinguished and remarkably influential historian, expressed outrage about the racist references to Aborigines in *The Truth*.

Henry Reynolds is the same historian who has argued, with great impact and moral authority, that Australians had tried to sweep the dark side of their history out of the collective memory. Yet, he also, in effect, says it is acceptable to pump up the moral volume with claims of white 'genocide' but not acceptable to play the tough rhetorical game of references to infanticide, routine violence toward women, and endemic clan hostilities even though scholarly literature is filled with dispassionate references to brutal practices among the indigenous peoples. One of many examples is A.W. Howitt's landmark 1904 study, *The Native Tribes of South-East Australia*, republished in 1996 by the Aboriginal Studies Press, whose comments include some harrowing references to the fate of newborn children in some clans during droughts. Kenneth Maddock, a visiting professor of anthropology at Macquarie University, was prompted to write a rebuttal to Reynolds in April, 1997. In raising the issue of double standards and selective history, Professor Maddock brought into focus perhaps the most important issue that spun out of the entire Hanson debate:

> *What we are seeing is a struggle for the high moral ground using the method anthropologists call the politics of embarrassment. The aim is to soften up your opponents by making them feel bad about themselves or their ancestors. This puts them in a mood to make concessions. Indigenous groups have become adept in these tactics. The trouble is the method is not particularly useful for identifying problems, let alone solving them. But it is being resorted to so often that it would be hypocritical to raise an eyebrow just because a popular but unfashionable politician uses it.*

Exactly. Within a year of Hanson's arrival in federal Parliament, she had unwittingly rewritten the language of political debate in Australia. Her name became the standard weapon with which to bludgeon opposition. Labor's defeat in 1996, and the vulnerability of the enormous grievance industry it had left behind, saw an escalation of shrill rhetoric and an assault on the middle ground from those who had lost power. As for the news media, Helen Dodd wrote of their relationship with Hanson:

> *Styled as the 'race debate', it was never a debate among average Australians. It was written, orchestrated and performed by the media. The media have peddled the idea that Australia is a racist country so widely that our Asian neighbours are beginning to accept this twisted reporting as fact [and] the media have now placed Australia in a precarious position.*

This comment, by an educated non-journalist, reflects a dismay widely felt in the community at the media's combination of shedding crocodile tears over the divisions Hanson was creating while at the same time fermenting these divisions. For the media, the story was simple. It was black and white, good versus evil, middle-class enlightenment against redneck prejudice. There was more than a touch of class war—focaccia and cappuccino versus fish and chips. Even Zita Antonios, the federal Race Discrimination Commissioner, a leader of the politicised bureaucracy of the Human Rights Commission, expressed disgust at the class condescension that lay behind many of the attacks on Hanson. 'I get so angry about some of the criticisms of Pauline Hanson,' she told the *Australian* in 1998.

Whatever one thinks about her position on any of the issues that she speaks about, it is supremely offensive to me that she is ridiculed because she lacks a formal education, or because her grammar is poor, or because she struggles over reading speeches, or indeed that she is a fish and chip shop owner. I grew up with fish and chip shop owners. It's symptomatic of the very things we are arguing against ...

Trevor Watson, a former head of ABC Radio, crystallised the problem at a conference on the Australian news media in 1996. 'Today the emphasis seems to be on conflict and sensation. The objective doesn't seem to be to inform the public any more, it seems to be to entertain the public through some sort of conflict.' He described Australia as a tolerant, non-racist country but a very different impression was given to Australia's Asian neighbours by the media's coverage of the Hanson debate. The Hanson public relations disaster for Australia in Asia was largely media-made.

Above all, the media declined to investigate the fire that lay beneath the smoke of Pauline Hanson. Thrashing Hanson as a racist and a fool is no substitute for actually doing some work. Moral outrage does not explain what caused the widespread unease that found expression in the 1996 federal election and the huge swing Hanson received in that election. The collective attitude of the press pack was that this complex issue was actually simple: white racism was still common in Australia.

The possibility of community anger at political duplicity never seemed to enter the equation.

This softness is not merely an Australian phenomenon. The Harvard economist and immigration scholar, George Borjas, expressed dismay at the bias of the American media, led by *The New York Times*, when they covered a major report on immigration in 1997.

> *The big news, which was not in the headline in* The
> Times, *is that there is a growing consensus among econ-*
> *omists that the gains from immigration are small.*
> *Overall, the National Academy of Sciences report is not*
> *as favourable as the press made it out to be, and I'm sort*
> *of stunned by the way it was spun by the press.*

He should not have been stunned. The news media, whether in the United States, Britain, Canada, Australia or Western Europe, is extremely leery of reporting negatively on immigration or ethnic crime or non-white racism. The only racism it feels unconstrained in reporting is white racism. Anything else produces a professional rash. John Cassidy, economics correspondent for *The New Yorker*, a journal as liberal as it is prestigious, confronted this problem in an article on immigration published in July 1997.

> *According to opinion polls, about two-thirds of Ameri-*
> *cans now believe that immigration should be restricted,*
> *yet support for an open-door policy is virtually a badge*
> *of respectability among the political and media elite*
> *[even though] immigration may also be affecting internal*

*migration patterns in ways that undermine the notion of
the melting pot.*

Cassidy then cited the distinguished demographer, William
Frey, the scholar who first identified 'white flight', who is
now writing about what he calls the 'Balkanisation' of
America.

Similar concerns are expressed in Australia by Pauline
Hanson's One Nation party. Hanson herself says she is
opposed to racial discrimination in all its forms. When she
was running her seafood shop, she employed a young Laot-
ian immigrant, Lilly Vichitthavong, who says she enjoyed
working for Hanson. 'Everyone in the shop was spoken to at
the same level,' she said. 'I never heard any racist comments
at all.' Hanson's maiden speech contained numerous references to racial equality, few of which were ever quoted by the
media:

*Paul Hasluck's vision was of a single society in which
racial emphases were rejected and social issues
addressed. I totally agree with him, and so would the
majority of Australians ... Reconciliation is everyone
recognising and treating each other as equals, and everyone must be responsible for their own actions ... I do
not consider people from ethnic backgrounds currently
living in Australia anything but first-class citizens, provided, of course, that they give this country their full,
undivided loyalty.*

Hanson's general ineptitude meant that these comments were dismissed as disingenuous. The video address she recorded in November 1997 to be released in the event she was assassinated—'Fellow Australians, if you are seeing me now it means I have been murdered'—further enhanced her reputation for paranoia.

But another reality of Australian politics is that Pauline Hanson has been spat on, subject to numerous threats, her younger son has been stalked and she has received a torrent of racist abuse from Aborigines. One Nation's opponents covered themselves in disgrace in 1997. Hundreds of people were subject to a gauntlet of insults and projectiles as they attended One Nation meetings. Many were threatened, some were beaten. A docile news media and Labor Party both watched as a systematic assault on freedom of speech and freedom of assembly took place—in the name of tolerance. The violence culminated, inevitably, with a serious assault when fifty-nine-year-old Keith Warburton was bashed by three goons calling him a 'Nazi' as he came out of a One Nation meeting in Dandenong, Victoria. He had attended the meeting out of curiosity. 'I'm just an individual without political leanings,' Warburton said later. Political curiosity carried a high price in Australia in 1997.

For much of that same year, the formal complaint of racial discrimination made against Pauline Hanson after her election victory was working its way through the Human Rights and Equal Opportunity Commission. The matter was finally adjudicated in October 1997. The claim was dismissed but not before it had hung around for almost twenty months.

Meanwhile, back in Parliament, Pauline Hanson, though greatly discredited and diminished, was still able to ride the silences that had brought her to power. During question time on 30 October 1997 she asked a question which produced a stunned silence from both sides of the House and muffled applause from sections in the public gallery:

Ms HANSON: My question is to the Prime Minister. Would the Prime Minister please explain how his government can justify making available to Indonesia what may be as much as 1.7 billion dollars when we already give approximately 90 million dollars in foreign aid, 8 million dollars of which is for their defence forces? Has the government considered that perhaps it is more appropriate for President Suharto to help bail out his own people with some of the billions he and his family have profited from during his time in office? Is it the policy of this government to prop up questionable and militaristic regimes with appalling human rights records?

The most discomforting thing about this question is that it was a good question. Leaving aside that the government's decision to help Indonesia was the right thing to do, everyone in Parliament knew that the Indonesian ruling elite was a deeply corrupt military plutocracy which had funnelled away billions of dollars for its own enrichment, especially the enrichment of the extended Suharto family. Everyone knew that the Indonesian economic system was collapsing under the weight of unchecked cronyism.

The Prime Minister responded:

*Mr HOWARD: I think the question raised by the
member for Oxley deserves a serious and considered
response.*

*The measure that I announced was designed not to
prop up a regime but to help the Indonesian people ... a
demonstration of regional neighbourliness; I describe it
as regional mateship.*

*... it is a situation where it is in Australia's national
self-interest to have a strong Indonesia capable of buying
goods and services from Australia ... It would be a very
short-sighted and narrow-minded Australian government
that passed up the opportunity to extend a strong hand of
economic support in a time of difficulty to a friend and
neighbour.*

Despite East Timor, despite all the corruption, despite the
destruction of the rain forests, despite the burning of hundreds of Christian churches, despite the growing threats
toward the Chinese minority in Indonesia, Howard's answer
was the only possible answer. Australia and Indonesia must
be allies, not enemies. There was, however, a time when the
left wing of the Labor Party would have been willing to ask
such morally pointed questions, but that time has passed. The
historian Geoffrey Blainey had warned, accurately, that the
silences being imposed on Australian political debate had
become dangerous:

*Democracy in Australia is not quite as healthy as it
should be. There is a strong view, reinforced by a section
of the media based in Canberra, that certain topics are
too dangerous to be handed to the people for decision at
election time. Immigration is one topic ... We hear,
again and again, that the Australian people themselves
cannot be trusted to vote on immigration ... Aboriginal
affairs is another topic not to be trusted to the people.
The press joined with Mr Keating in wiping it from the
agenda at the 1993 Federal election. And of course the
Native Title Bill was deliberately introduced to Parliament without any chance of members of the public seeing
that Bill, and a strong attempt was made to push it
through as quickly as possible ... It will remain a smol-
dering topic in Australia for many years to come.*

The coalition that imposed this silence was formed by Labor,
the multicultural industry and the selective news media, three
heavily overlapping constituencies, especially at the Government-controlled ABC and SBS. This coalition created a
vacuum in Canberra. The vacuum was filled.

PART THREE

'*People need to see how their tax dollars are being pilfered on an enormous scale—every conceivable rort and deception is used to beat the system. Medicare rorts, dealing in prescription drugs, obtaining multiple identity papers, milking the social security system, even stealing electricity.*'

NSW Police Commander

10
STRIP MINING

DR RICHARD BASHAM seems normal. He is not. He deals with murder, blackmail, organised crime, gangs, prostitution, human smuggling, immigration fraud, tax evasion, welfare abuse and racism. Strange, because Dr Basham is a teacher, with an office on the lovely main quadrangle at Sydney University. He gives classes, marks students' papers, attends committee meetings. He is the head of the Department of Anthropology at Sydney University. But Richard Basham leads a double life. He spends a lot of time talking to cops. He is one of Australia's leading authorities on the links between crime and culture. He advises the New South Wales Police Commissioner.

He is also worried.

Organised crime, drugs, gangs, extortion, tax evasion, fraud, these have now reached a level where they are damaging the national economy. What has happened at Cabramatta is just the tip of the iceberg, but it often seems that anyone who dares to talk about Asian crime in this country is shouted down as a racist.

Richard Basham lives at an interesting cultural intersection. He speaks Thai and teaches courses on South-East Asian societies. He is an immigrant to Australia and an advocate of Asian immigration, yet he investigates abuses of the system by immigrants. He is an academic anthropologist, yet has deep knowledge of crime and corruption. He is American but has spent the bulk of his career in Asia and Australia. He has a Thai wife and a Eurasian daughter, both now Australian citizens, and both have experienced racial prejudice. Even so, he is passionately opposed to using race as a tool for political censorship.

> *Racial prejudice against Asians in Australia is real. It hurts. My own wife has experienced it. But to use charges of racism as a moral skewer to silence discussion of ethnic-based crime is arrogant and, ultimately, dangerous. Censorship has divided this country. All crime has its cultural base and it is foolish to pretend, for example, that Asians don't dominate the hard drug trade in Australia.*

The police agree with him. 'Australia has never had anything like Cabramatta before,' one NSW police commander told me, requesting anonymity. 'The gangs have got guns, and the violence within the Indo-Chinese community is noticeably higher than in other communities. They are very confronting. European-style cops do not represent much of a threat ... Cabramatta has the highest homicide rate in Australia. It has the highest number of foot soldiers in the drug trade. It has the largest number of people who die in the streets from heroin overdoses. It has the highest concentration of cases of Hepatitis C. It has the highest incidence of drug-related arrests. Fifty-seven percent of drug- related arrests in New South Wales are Indo-Chinese ... Cabramatta is the largest retail outlet for heroin in Australia. Nothing competes with it ... People go to Cabramatta because it is the purest dope. It can be cut [diluted and on-sold]. Roughly two-thirds of the drug abusers also deal. They come to Cabramatta in taxis to pick up stocks ... We arrest them, and they are soon back on the streets ... When security cameras went into Cabramatta, we discovered street-level violence—bag-snatching, drug-dealing, assaults, and multiple heroin deals —were far worse than we had realised. A real eye-opener.'

Cabramatta is the extreme, but many of the same characteristics are evident on a smaller scale in pockets of the west and south-west of Sydney. In Melbourne, the heavy concentration of Vietnamese in Springvale was followed, as in Sydney, with this enclave also becoming a drug centre. Vietnamese gang activity has now spread from Springvale, Footscray and Richmond to parts of at least eight other Melbourne suburbs, and continues to spread.

Cabramatta and Springvale became the focus of the urban drug trade not because many of the Vietnamese who congregated there were criminals—exactly the opposite is true—but because poor bureaucratic oversight had allowed many hardened criminals into the country among the inflow of Vietnamese refugees after the Vietnam war. Hundreds of criminals arrived. They formed the original Cabramatta gangs, and the 5T gang was the prototype. The five Ts stand for *tinh* (love/sex), *tien* (money), *tu* (prison), *tu* (death) and *toi* (criminal convictions). Over time, the 5T gang was gradually worn down, but Vietnamese have emulated the gang style. 'Once the Vietnamese learned the networking originally used by the Chinese they just replicated it,' the commander told me. 'The Vietnamese have now supplanted the Chinese in retailing. They took over by offering the highest quality at the best price.' Increasingly, Vietnamese drug importers are also cutting out the Chinese wholesalers, importing heroin through Vietnam in vertically-integrated operations.

Each year, between 2000 and 3000 kilograms of heroin are sold and consumed in Australia, and most of it goes undetected. 'We're only getting about 10 percent or a little less,' said Peter Lamb of the National Crime Authority, adding that police seize about 220 kilograms of heroin a year. While Vietnam has emerged as a major transhipment route for heroin to Australia, Vietnamese authorities have offered little cooperation because of a mixture of incompetence, corruption, and lack of resources. The ethnic Chinese remain the big money players. 'The major heroin dealers are in Chinatown,' said Federal Agent Ray Tinker of the Asian Organised Crime Group. 'Cabramatta is the end of the chain. The major heroin dealers are in Chinatown because that's where all the orders and brokers are. The amounts that are dealt with down there leave Cabramatta for dead.'

'Organised crime in Australia is different to the traditional Mafia-style where you're in a permanent family arrangement,' said Assistant New South Wales Police Commissioner Clive Small. 'Groups do their own thing but come together when it's mutually of benefit to them.' The new Asian crime operations follow the lead established by traditional Australian criminals, a loose group of mainly Australian-born criminals which the National Crime Authority calls the 'East Coast Milieu'. The backdrop to all this is a disturbing upward curve in crime in Australia, particularly violent crime. In her 1997 study *Rising Crime in Australia*, Lucy Sullivan gives the problem its historical perspective:

> *Violent crime more than doubled between 1981–82 and 1993, and increased by a factor of seven, or 700 percent, between 1964 and 1993, attesting to the accuracy of public perceptions of the growth in, and people's growing fear of, personal violence ...*
>
> *Our penal system, also overtaken by the escalation in crime, has allowed the 'economic' rewards of crime to rise markedly.*

Gang crime is Australia's biggest criminal growth area. The arrest of Chinese and Vietnamese for heroin importation has become routine. Typical—it was a minor news item— were the arrests made on 19 December 1997 after raids by police on several Sydney homes yielded twenty-one kilograms of heroin with a street value of around thirty-two million dollars. All those arrested in possession of the heroin were Chinese. One of those arrested came to Australia from China as a political refugee. He was unemployed and had been receiving government welfare benefits.

Tongan dealers have moved aggressively into cocaine, importing from Colombia through Tongan contacts in Hawaii. Tongans and other Pacific Islanders are also active in the Kings Cross drug trade and in drug trading in Western Sydney. Lebanese criminals have been building a network since the early 1970s, according to the National Crime Authority: 'A number of family-based Lebanese criminal networks in Australia [are] involved in the importation and sale of heroin and hashish in the Bekaa Valley [in Lebanon] which is under Syrian control.'

'Romanians are disproportionately represented in criminal activity,' said an NCA report. The Romanians sell heroin—they were selling heroin in Cabramatta before the Vietnamese—and rort the social security system. Their exploits have even made the front pages of the Romanian, if not the Australian, press.

The police are desperate for more resources and more political will in the areas of ethnic crime and foreign-language community liaison, particularly to meet the challenge of rapidly-growing Asian crime. 'Let's not deceive ourselves,' the NSW police commander told me. 'It does not help or serve the victims of Asian crime when we are not frank with our problems. The overwhelming majority of victims of Asian crime are Asians. Yet a lot of the decision-makers in this state are intimidated by the issue.'

It is not difficult to see why. The NSW Police Commissioner, Peter Ryan, was set upon by the Thought Police when he dared to wander into the no-go area of ethnicity and crime. Commissioner Ryan's sin was to make the following remark in an interview with a British police magazine:

Here [in Australia], the crime is partly Lebanese-based,

partly from the old Soviet Union, Hong Kong, Vietnam and China.

The political pain was immediate and it was personal.

'I am disgusted, I am not happy at all,' responded Helen Sham-Ho, a Liberal member of the NSW Upper House. *'For the past eight years I've been trying to persuade police not to identify even suspects by race. Now the top man in the force comes and reverts back to the old ways. I couldn't believe it when I read it ... You have to back up claims with evidence.'*

Franca Arena, a Labor member of the same Upper House, called the Commissioner's remarks 'pathetic'.

Angela Chan, a spokeswoman for the Federation of Ethnic Community Councils of Australia, said the Police Commissioner's comment 'stereotypes people as criminals on the ground of race and in today's climate, with all this anti-Asian sentiment and racism debate going on, it just adds fuel to the fire.'

Joe Wakim, the secretary of the Australian Arabic Council, said there was no statistical basis on which to connect cultures with criminal activity. He said the Commissioner was using 'a few bad apples' to tarnish an entire community.

In the wake of these and other public rebukes, Commissioner Ryan and the police went quiet on the issue of ethnic crime. Dr Basham regards this climate of censorship as dangerous:

The charge of racism is being used to suppress information.

The comfort level of Asian criminals in Australia is now very high. It is almost as if they have political protection. This imposed silence is one of the reasons why Australia now has Pauline Hanson. Australians have to realise that attempting to cope with crime among people living in different cultural worlds without trying to understand those worlds is not foolish but a waste of resources. What is unacceptable practice in Australia can be regarded as acceptable in much of Asia. Common viola-tions of Australian law, such as tax evasion, immigration abuse and money laundering, are often not really viewed as criminal at all. This extends to bonded servitude, which is found in China, Thailand, Cambodia and Burma.

In a 1997 graduation speech at Bond University, delivered before a large audience including many Asian students and their families, Basham praised the self-evident vitality that Asian immigration has brought to Australia but also chal-lenged those in the Australian and Asian news media who were exploiting Pauline Hanson while expressing outrage about her:

In contrast to Australia, no Asian society genuinely pro-hibits racial discrimination in immigration or before the law. Indeed, racial discrimination is so deeply imbedded in the moral premises of Asian societies that it often goes unnoticed. While someone of Asian ancestry who is born in Australia can expect citizenship, the same cannot be

*said for someone of Caucasian ancestry born in
Malaysia or Japan.*

This is not the sort of stuff that usually comes out of Australian universities. Richard Basham's personal world has seen too much struggle between life and death in recent years for him to care about political convenience. For a decade he watched his wife slowly dying.

*We had ten years living under a death sentence; it
changes the way you live your life. My wife, Charoen,
was diagnosed with leukaemia in 1981. It was chronic
myeloid leukaemia, for which there was no cure. The
average survival rate was three and a half years. All the
other people who were diagnosed at the same time have
died.*

Today, Charoen is alive and well.

*We don't know how she lived so long until the technology
existed to cure her. But she took a Buddhist response.
She wasn't afraid of death. She hung on until new drugs
were invented which permitted her to undergo a bone-
marrow transplant using marrow from her sister, who did
not even have the same blood type. At that time, no operation involving such a mismatch had been successful in
Australia. The odds were bad. But the doctors gave their
all for her.*

By the time Charoen Basham was out of danger, Richard Basham had stripped his own life down to the fundamentals.

He knew there were big problems with Australia's immigration program and he wasn't going to be intimidated by politicians and political activists with racial agendas. Because his web of contacts and experience allowed him to see not merely the vitality and talent that Asian immigration is bringing but also the problems seeping into Australia from countries where corruption is endemic, Basham became much more active in his work with the police. One of the highlights of this work was his contribution to the investigation of the Ivan Milat serial murders, which one police document describes as 'extraordinarily accurate intellectual input'.

His unusual preparation for police work included work with psychotic patients for the National Institute of Mental Health in Washington, DC, and a doctorate in psychological anthropology from the University of California, Berkeley. He arrived at Sydney University as a lecturer in the 1970s, by way of lecturing in Malaysia, and has built expertise in cultural psychology, interethnic relations, Asian business practices, and the cultural elements of organised crime.

From this vantage point Basham believes one of the greatest threats to Australia's long-term stability is complacency about the rise of international crime syndicates, the dark side of capitalism's rise in Asia and the former Soviet Union. He sees the rise of these syndicates as afflicting the entire region.

In **Burma**, where most of the world's heroin is produced and processed in the rugged jungle region known as the Golden Triangle, the drug trade has become so important it is by far the nation's largest export industry, and drug profits have helped the closed and dictatorial military junta through its foreign currency crises. The junta, known as the State Law and Order Restoration Council (SLORC), has financed its military spending with drug profits. The military has then been used to suppress the democracy movement led by the Nobel Peace Prize laureate, Ms Aung San Suu Kyi. United States intelligence reports state that economic growth in Burma is now largely underpinned by the heroin trade.

In **Vietnam** the heroin trade has flourished in an atmosphere of police duplicity, causing alarm for the government. In a spectacular show trial in 1997, which saw eight men sentenced to death before a firing squad, the lead defendant was a police captain. He had led a trafficking ring which flooded Vietnam with heroin from the nearby Golden Triangle. Half of the twenty-two convicted were members of the security establishment.

In **China** the top police official, Tao Siju, describes the growth of organised crime in China and South-East Asia as 'extremely grim'. He says that even though China deploys army units along its border with the Golden Triangle, the drug trade had surged in Yunan province, which adjoins the Golden Triangle. Hard drug use, ruthlessly stamped out by the old communist regime, was spreading along with the new economic liberalism. A major new industry is human smuggling—trafficking in illegal immigrants to Australia, North America and Europe.

In **Taiwan** violent triad crime is so pervasive that more than 50 000 people demonstrated outside parliament in 1997 after the body of yet another kidnap victim was found dumped in a canal. Triads have been woven into the politics of the long-dominant Kuomintang party, skimming multi-billions off national infrastructure programs, engaging in wholesale vote-buying exercises and dominating the gambling industry. The biggest triad, United Bamboo, with more than 10 000-members, has its own political arm.

In **Japan** the influence of organised crime on the corporate sector, after decades of systematic and routinised extortion by gangsters known as *sokaiya*, has been so great for so long that it has siphoned off enormous resources, impeded reform, destroyed confidence and led to a succession of public disgraces for senior corporate leaders. The serious anti-*sokaiya* reform process has only just began. *Sokaiya* money has been laundered into Australia.

In **Canada** murder, extortion, loan-sharking, counterfeiting, robbery, drug importation, and home invasions have followed the arrival of the triads in Vancouver as heavy immigration from Hong Kong and China brought the largest Chinese population in Canada. 'I would say very few Asian restaurants in Vancouver are not paying extortion and protection money—they use Chinese restaurants like ATMs,' says Andy Nemmo, head of the anti-triad police task force in Vancouver. 'These guys specialise in going after "satellite kids" whose parents live in Hong Kong.'

In the **United States** the Federal Bureau of Investigation has warned that expanding foreign criminal enterprises in the United States, based in Asia and the former Soviet Union, pose the greatest crime threat since the emergence of the Mafia in the 1950s. The FBI states that the largest triad in the world, the Sun Yee On, based in Hong Kong, has at least 47 000 members and is expanding its reach overseas, including into Australia.

In **New Zealand** the Commissioner of Police, Richard Macdonald, has warned that an 'alarming trend has emerged' with the penetration of Asian triads in New Zealand, including the first known contract placed on the life of a police officer. Triads followed an influx of Chinese immigrants, and the usual crime pattern—extortion against restaurants and Chinese citizens—has flowered. The New Zealand Asian Crime Squad says the Hong Kong-based 14K Triad has recruited more than 500 teenagers from Auckland's Chinese community.

In **South Korea**, when a major new tourism market for Australia began to blossom, the plane-loads of Korean visitors also contained Korean gangsters following the money trail to Sydney and new business in extortion, loan-sharking and prostitution. Difficulties with detecting Korean criminals entering Australia were revealed, embarrassingly, in 1997 when four Korean 'businessmen' went on a house-breaking crime spree soon after arriving in Sydney. The four men all had convictions in South Korea for major theft; and one of them also had convictions for rape, assault, blackmail and trafficking in women. The system failed yet again when, after police discovered the men's criminal records in Korea, the information was not passed on to the magistrate. The men were only given eighteen-month sentences.

In **Australia** police intelligence believes the Hong Kong triads, notably the Sun Yee On, are diversifying beyond heroin, gambling and protection rackets into food importation and property portfolios. Sun Yee On hopes to use the food business to insinuate itself into Australian casinos, regarded by Asian syndicates as a potential honeypot for money laundering and loan sharking. A criminal pattern similar to that in Vancouver has emerged in Sydney and Melbourne. Home invasions, almost unknown in Sydney prior to the arrival of triads and criminals hidden among the legitimate refugees from Vietnam, are occurring in Sydney at a rate of three a week, according to the Bureau of Crime Statistics and Research. An unknown number of home invasions go unreported. An attempt by New South Wales police to break the code of silence in the Asian community met with only limited success.

> *Home invasions and extortion are real barometers of Asian crime in Sydney and if they are going up we are in for trouble,'* said Dr Basham. *'If they are left unchecked, then kidnappings become more common. If police cannot provide protection against home invasions and kidnappings, then people will seek out those who can.*

Gang crime, modelled on the Triads, has penetrated the schools.

> *There have been numerous instances of extortion attempts involving Asian school children,'* said Detective-Inspector Tom Sharp, who ran the Oak Investigation Unit into Asian organised crime. *'It's happening at a lot of schools. We have had some prosecutions ... Some people*

have paid up, and some people have withdrawn their
children from school in Australia … We always have a
lot of trouble finding people to come forward in all
crimes.

Many of those targeted have been from Hong Kong, where
the most wealth is generated and where most expatriate children are from. Triad-style influence is evident in the
recurrence of the number 36, a traditional triad number, in
school extortions.

'If they say 36, they mean $360, if they say 360, they
mean $3600,' said Inspector Sharp. 'The triad traditions
have mostly gone, but the numbers have carried on. The
leader is the 489, the 'dragonhead'. His deputy is 438.
The fighters are 426. The messengers are 432. The chief
of staff is 415. The number four means death.'

Asian organised crime is so widespread it has even replicated elements of the coastal piracy practised in South-East
Asia. Vietnamese gangs are operating a large-scale black
market trade in abalone, a shellfish delicacy highly prized in
Asia and now being poached from Australian waters. Black
market abalone fetch about 100 dollars a kilo. Black market
abalone fishing became so significant that a special police
task force was set up in New South Wales in 1996, and the
problem extends to fisheries in Victoria and South Australia.
'These are well-organised, highly professional thieves,' said
Warren Spooner, general manager of NSW Abalone Pty
Ltd. 'They damage juvenile fish stocks and threaten our

reputation for quality on the export market.' An active black market has sprung up between Asian gangs. They exchange abalone for heroin.

Richard Basham sees all this as part of the evolution of what he calls 'parallel moral universes' in Australia.

I have spoken to so many Australian businessmen who are just stunned when their supposed Asian partners have robbed them blind. In my business consultancy I tell companies they should forget about signing contracts at first, they are better off with a memorandum of agreement, because in much of Asia a contract will bind the Westerner while leaving the local partner free to behave as he likes.

Exactly the same warning is given by Reg Little and Warren Reed in their 1997 book, *The Tyranny of Fortune*. They buttress Richard Basham's argument that 'parallel moral universes' are developing in Australia.

We don't just have a crime problem, said Basham. *The reality is that there are all kinds of immigration, taxation and welfare rorts in the Asian communities and a lot of them are simply seen by Asians as using the system that exists. On arrival in Australia, many immigrants, often so-called 'students' from countries such as China, will be forced to work at a number of jobs to repay debts upwards of $15 000. Failure to repay will invoke serious sanctions.*

Many Australians have come to believe, wrongly, that the growing prevalence of violent and drug crime among some immigrant groups in Australia is the product of a criminal mentality. This is not true, and it is dangerously misleading. There are a number of logical antecedents for crime problems among immigrant groups:

(1) Geography. The Golden Triangle lies between southern China and Indo-China. If the remote mountainous opium fields lay in Australia, native-born Aussies would no doubt be lining up for a piece of the enormous profits this export crop brings.

(2) History. Triads and triad-style groups have an ancient history in Chinese communities and in some ways evolved to fill the role filled by the police in Western society. Although this role mutated into crime, many protection rackets do operate as a (warped) form of police, keeping restaurants and businesses safe from other criminals.

(3) Culture. Some immigrant groups simply have a different value system to the one prevailing in Australia. This division breaks down with the second generation.

(4) Familiarity. The people who suffer most from immigrant crime are other immigrants from the same ethnic group, especially business operators. They are the ones robbed and extorted.

(5) Politics. The Immigration Department, under political pressure from the multicultural industry, has allowed criminals and parasites into the country by the thousands. Abuse of the immigration system has been integral to the penetration of Australia by criminal groups. 'The Family

Reunion Program has been widely abused, and the Migrant Business program has been widely abused,' says a Chinese adviser to the Asian Organised Crime Unit set up in 1997. 'To get a business visa, many people took loans and paid them back after they came to Australia. Gangsters came into Australia this way. Of course, they had access to plenty of money.' Asia scholars Dr Stephen Fitzgerald and Dr Richard Basham have both written about abuse of the business visa system, which, despite these problems has been an overall success.

(6) Inadequate police resources. 'The thing about the Vietnamese criminals who came as refugees is that they quickly understood that Australian law can't really touch them,' said Dr Richard Basham. 'So the payment of protection money in Cabramatta has become so routine that it's almost ritualised.'

As long ago as 1988, Carmel Chow, senior investigator with the National Crime Authority said that Chinese 'triads' had a near monopoly on heroin importation into Australia. He also said Hong Kong police expected many triad members to migrate to Australia in the decade prior to the Chinese takeover in 1997. He was proved right.

In the real world, it is a fact that one of the engines of growth in crime in Australia is the high levels of crime among some immigrant groups. In New South Wales, the state with by far the most immigrants, as well as a raging crime problem among young Aboriginals, assaults surged twenty-six percent in 1996, accounting for most of the national increase. Break-ins were up twelve percent, three times the national average. The problem is particularly acute among young Indo-Chinese, mostly Vietnamese, whose numbers in the prison and juvenile detention systems rose dramatically in the 1990s.

When I compared statistics from two very different New South Wales government documents—the 1996 green paper, *Building on our Cultural Diversity*, and the 1996 NSW *Inmate Census*—I found that the Vietnamese-born prison population was between three and four times overrepresented compared with the per capita Vietnamese population in the state. The strong anecdotal evidence from police of heavy Lebanese and Turkish involvement in the illegal drug trade was also borne out by these statistics. The proportion of Lebanese-born prisoners was double the per capita Lebanese-born population. Turkish-born prisoners were also doubly represented, per capita, although their number was small. Drug arrests accounted for most of the Lebanese, Turkish and Vietnamese in the system. Other sharp disparities showed up in the per capita representation of various immigrant groups. New Zealanders, for example, were overrepresented on a per capita basis.

The prison census data actually understates the problem. The figures are based on country of birth and so do not include those born in Australia in homes where English is a second language, a segment of the population from which a large proportion of Australian gang members are recruited.

One disastrous by-product of the heroin abundance was the rapid spread through already vulnerable Aboriginal communities after young Aborigines in juvenile detention centres mixed with young Vietnamese gang members. Aborigines were once rarely seen in the Cabramatta hard drug market, but that changed. Detective-Sergeant Debbie Wallace of the Cabramatta police watched it happen. 'We are seeing a lot of Aborigines in Cabra now, and we never used to see them here.'

An anthropologist who spent years studying the heroin sub-culture, Dr Lisa Maher, foresees enormous costs to the health care system. Dr Maher found that patterns of teenage addiction began with smoking heroin in cigarettes or cannabis but progressed to addiction and injecting within three months. She found about forty percent of young addicts were females. She also found most heroin dealers were heroin users. Another disastrous by-product has been the flowering of gang culture based in immigrant communities with extremely high unemployment and low English-language skills.

It takes courage to raise, as Richard Basham does, the issue of widespread abuse of the immigration and welfare systems in Australia because anyone who does so in the past has routinely been vilified as a racist. Dr Basham, clearly, is not a racist. 'It is interesting to see how many people fail to make a distinction between criticism and racism,' he says. A growing number of people are voicing informed concern about what amounts to the strip mining of Australia.

'The problems have been exacerbated by silence,' says Basham. Intercepting criminals at Australian airports has been made more difficult since the rules were changed preventing immigration officers from selecting incoming passengers at random. An exasperated secretary of the Australian Federal Police Association, George Nichols, says the practice of random searches was stopped, 'because certain groups started claiming they were being victimised.'

'We have our heads in the sand,' says Mark Craig, a former intelligence analyst with the Queensland Police who at the time of publication was being eased out of the force for his outspoken views.

> *The Immigration Department suppresses certain issues.*
> *The human smuggling trade is very big, much bigger*
> *than people realise. Immigration also doesn't like to talk*
> *about which provinces in China do the overstayers come*
> *from. In most cases, it is Fujian.*

Craig said a boatload of 139 illegal Chinese entrants was picked up in Queensland and nobody from the Immigration Department called the police. 'They were all from Fujian. They all had Queensland driver's licences. We didn't get a call. It was an immigration matter. They sent 135 of them home, and kept four. They spent $360 000 flying them to Port Hedland. And they didn't get any information out of the entire group.'

'Australia really needs to wake up to what is going on,' says Richard Basham. 'I'm very much in favour of Asian immigration, which I think has enhanced the texture of Australian life, but we need to select carefully the people we are taking in.' He regards curbing abuses as important to preserving an open immigration system and preserving Australia's proven cultural commitment to equality, which he believes has been dragged through the mud by the Australian media. Like all courageous people, he refuses to wallow. He concluded his 1997 graduation speech at Bond University with these words:

> *Far from being pessimistic about Australia's racial future, I hold out great hope for it. I cannot but be reminded of my family's return to Australia from a trip to Thailand late one night in January. Exhausted, the three of us, my Thai-born wife, my Eurasian, Australian-born teenage daughter, and I, with my distinctive American accent, approached the immigration officer and handed him our passports. After stamping them, he handed them back to us with a warm and genuine smile and said, 'Welcome home.'*

RICO

The resource gulf between police and drug traffickers is growing, not narrowing. The drug trade generates so much cash that dealers can buy sophisticated electronic equipment and discard cellular phones like wrapping paper. Police surveillance is becoming increasingly difficult.

But there is a powerful American weapon that could be adapted: the Racketeer Influenced and Corrupt Organization Act, known as RICO. The groups that would most fear RICO's arrival are crime gangs and corrupt unions. The law was devised in the United States when it became obvious that existing laws had failed to stop the virulent spread of the Mafia. RICO proved a formidable tool against the Mafia, and Mafia control of the Teamsters union. It has now become the primary weapon against Asian crime syndicates.

'RICO has made a huge difference in the United States,' says Dr Richard Basham. 'The beauty of RICO is that it introduces the notion of collective responsibility for crimes to an entire criminal organisation. Since an entire gang can be charged with crimes its members commit, previously untouchable bosses go down with everybody else. So it's more difficult for gangs to intimidate informers.'

The first hint of RICO's power against the code of silence came in 1985, when twenty-seven members of the Ghost Shadows were sent to jail on charges including murder, robbery, kidnapping, extortion and running a racketeering enterprise. The Ghost Shadows had previously been the largest and most feared gang in New York's Chinatown.

Since that victory, more than a dozen major RICO prosecutions have succeeded against Asian gangs. In 1991, a single murder investigation by the Federal Bureau of Investigation led to the unravelling of the Green Dragon gang, ten of whose members were charged on thirty-six counts, including seven murders, extortion, robbery, bribery and running a racketeering organisation. Nine of the ten went to jail. The tenth, the leader of the Green Dragons, fled to China. In 1996 the former head of Tsung Tsin Association in New York, one of the largest and oldest civic associations in the Chinese diaspora, was sent to jail on RICO charges.

'Australia is going to have to do something,' says Dr Basham. 'The level of police resources to tackle organised crime is pathetic. The existing laws aren't enough.'

11
THE BIG NOWHERE

EACH JANUARY, IN THE annual initiation rite when young people around Australia receive the final results of their high school careers, newspapers carry photographs of happy students who have received the ultimate result—perfect scores. One joyous front-page picture in 1997 showed some of the best new faces of Australia: Denise Lee, Johnny Wong, Sanushka Mudaliar, Philippa Webb, all Asian or Eurasian, part of a regenerative immigrant surge from Asia that the country needed and continues to need.

The impact of Asian intellectual muscle was affirmed the next day when the top 5000 Higher School Certificate results were published. The list confirmed, yet again, the role that Asian students, mostly ethnic Chinese, are playing in boosting the standards of excellence in Australian education. More than 1800 Asian names were on that list, far out of proportion with the per capita numbers of Asian-Australian students in New South Wales, by a magnitude of around 500 percent.

The list of Asian-Australian and Asian students who topped or shared the top place in the State was a long one: Johnny Wong in Mathematics 4 Unit; Anna Lam in English 3 Unit; Louisa Chan in Mathematics 3 Unit; Vidian Choi in Music (Board) 3 Unit; Kenny Chan in Physics 2 Unit; John

Lee in Chemistry 2 Unit; Colin Tan in Geography 2 Unit; Sarah Cheung in Accounting 2 Unit; Raymond Lam and Saurabh Kumar in Business Studies 2 Unit; Anita Chandrasekaran in Economics 2 Unit; Ju-Lee Ooi in Agriculture 2 Unit; Po-Tsang Chui in Electronics Technology; Amar Maini in Contemporary English; Gia Din Vuong in French Z, and Deepa Jamnadas in Industry Studies (Hospital). Asian students—again, mostly ethnic Chinese—dominated several disciplines:

> Eight of the top ten in Chemistry 2 Unit
> Seven of the top ten students in Mathematics 4 Unit
> Seven of the top ten in Music (Board) 3 Unit
> Six of the top ten in Mathematics 3 Unit
> Four of the top nine in Physics 2 Unit
> Four of the top ten in Economics 3 Unit
> Four of the top ten in Economics 2 Unit
> Three of the top ten in Electronics Technology

It was much the same again in 1998: Ruiyi Wang topped the State in Mathematics 4 Unit; Gladys Wing Man Lam in Mathematics 3; Wendy Wing Man Yung in Biology; Cindy Fang in Chemistry; Lok Man Ho (jointly) in Physics; Melissa Yee Seeto in Business Studies 3; Timothy Cheung in Business Studies 2; Anson Cheuk Hin Mak in Economics 3; Rami Banna in Computing Studies 3.

When the list of the forty-two top students in New South Wales was released, seventeen of them—forty percent—were Asian-Australian. The two students who scored a perfect 100 on their tertiary entrance rank were Ju-Lee Ooi and Kavita Enjeti. This is a social revolution.

Asian academic success in Australia has become part of the social fabric. The large number of talented Asian school students has flowed through to disproportionate success in the university honours lists, especially in medicine, science and mathematics. Although many of these students return to their home countries, the majority of them are Australians whose high productivity will flow through the system. Typically, when a major new cancer treatment was announced soon after these HSC results, an Asian-Australian, Associate Professor David Ma, was the coordinator of the Australian contribution. When a breakthrough was made in solar energy efficiency, smashing the world record for solar cell energy production, an industry in which Australia has a vital stake, it was by Dr Aihua Wang and her husband, Dr Jianhua Zhao, at the University of New South Wales. The Australian of the Year in 1996 was Dr John Yu, the driving force behind the New Children's Hospital in Sydney.

Australia has benefitted from the economic surge in Asia in the past thirty years, a period when East Asia's share of the world's GNP jumped from four percent to almost thirty percent and East Asia accounted for the bulk of the growth of Australia's exports. The growing blends of Asian influences in Australian culture and cuisine, and the growing number of young interracial couples, are happy by-products of this evolution. A pro-Asian immigration policy is not merely the best policy for Australia, it is the only viable immigration policy.

It is important to the country's economic, cultural and moral future.

But while newspapers were showing the happy, and heavily Asian, face of perfect graduation success, the front page of the *Daily Telegraph* did exactly the opposite in 1997 with a headline THE CLASS WE FAILED, and the Year 12 class picture of Mount Druitt High School, representing the bottom of the graduation success scale. Mount Druitt is a suburb named often when demographers talk about the formation of ethnic enclaves with high socio-economic problems. The *Daily Telegraph* was sued for its troubles. A group called the National Children's and Youth Law Centre, using lawyers donating their services, coordinated a series of defamation actions on behalf of nineteen students at Mount Druitt. The lawsuits argued that the front-page photo and accompanying story caused the students to be embarrassed and ashamed, and the newspaper had breached the privacy of the students. The New South Wales Teachers Federation described the story as 'appalling.'

But if someone comes first, someone also has to come last. The school system, always the front line of cultural cohesion, has shown clear signs of social stress as Australia's booming trade and cultural links with Asia, the Middle East and the South Pacific have percolated through society. A national survey of high-school teachers in 1996 found that half the teachers said immigration levels should be reduced because of high unemployment. The inflow most identified by the teachers as causing social stress came from Asia and the Middle East. Replicating the experiences of France, the

United Kingdom, and the United States, Australia's immigrant flow in the 1980s and 1990s has brought extremes of social behaviour. At the high end, the great majority of immigrants are contributing to their new country, especially the thousands putting in the long, slogging hours of small businesses. At the low end, groups within this diverse immigrant stream are overrepresented in welfare abuse, extortion, drug importation, gang crime, marriage rackets, visa abuse, insurance fraud and tax avoidance.

'There are immigration and welfare rackets of all kinds, and some of them are organised by government officials in Asia,' says Dr Richard Basham. 'Since the moral authority of the larger society is often rejected by Asian immigrants, and since people may have lied to its agents—in immigration, social services, and the taxation department—there is always the fear of being turned in if they cooperate with authorities. So there is a silence, an opaqueness, between the mainstream society and the Asian societies within it.' In the context of their own cultures, he says, they are merely continuing the ancient habits of self-interest, thrift, family commitments, group ties and fear of the oppressive central authorities. 'I'm very much in favour of Asian immigration, but I think our naivety is dangerous.'

David Reid resigned from the Department of Social Security because he believed the system, for political reasons, was winking at a lot of rorting by immigrants.

'The abuse is extensive, it is upsetting, I resigned on principle,' said Reid, a former determining officer handling sole parent claims in a Sydney social security office serving a largely Vietnamese population.

The system is biased in favour of people who lie. Most of the people I saw were hard-working people, survivors, opportunists. But they regard the social security system as a source of income, not a safety net. When the Vietnamese claim a sole-parent benefit, the first thing they usually do is give a separate address for the wife and the husband. I have run those addresses through the computer and found up to six so-called separated husbands listed at the same address ... When they are denied benefits, they appeal. They sign statutory declarations. They back each other up. When I challenged people, they retreated behind the language barrier. This was a standard practice.

The most extreme example he encountered was a Vietnamese family who lived in a North Vietnamese enclave in inner Sydney.

They were a family of seven: mother, father and five daughters. Three of the daughters had children, and two were receiving sole-parent benefits. The third daughter was on unemployment benefits. Her boyfriend was also on unemployment benefits. A fourth daughter was working in a cake shop but got paid in cash and was claiming unemployment benefits. The mother was on unemployment. The father was on unemployment. Six of the seven

family members were receiving benefits. The seventh was
at school. There was an industrial sewing machine in the
home. It was going all the time. They all worked. The
piecework was never declared as income for tax purposes.

The widespread combination of unemployment benefits and
illegal garment industry work is well known as an integral
part of the Vietnamese black economy. The combined income
from welfare payments, based on sole-parent benefits and the
range of unemployment benefits extant at that time was
$1745 a fortnight. Plus the income from illegal garment
industry piecework. All tax free. Black money.

'They were all keen to get their Australian passports and
get the whole scheme rolling again for their relatives,' David
Reid told me.

The worst individual case I saw was a Vietnamese girl
who was already married, in a Buddhist ceremony. She
went to Vietnam and married a second man, for a fee.
She brought him to Australia, and moved back with her
husband. She went on unemployment benefits ... Her
second husband went on the dole. After they officially
split up, she applied for the single-parent benefit. On the
same day she claimed the sole-parent benefit, her real
husband came into the social security office with her to
claim unemployment benefits.

Another classic was a Lebanese woman who told us
her husband had left her two weeks before. She got the
benefit. Then she left for Lebanon. She would come back
each year to maintain her single-parent benefit. She

wasn't a single parent at all. Her husband was in Lebanon. She was able to keep this up for two and half years until she stayed away for more than a year, then came back to Australia with a return ticket to Lebanon.

David Reid's stories are supported by other sources including, most importantly, official statistics. A Monash University researcher, Earnest Healy, pointed out in 1995 in the journal *People and Place*: 'An exploitative informal labour market based on the clothing industry, and related to social security fraud, has assumed major proportions.' The New South Wales Minister for Fair Trading, Faye Lo Po, confirms that tens of thousands of Asian immigrants are working in illegal sweatshops in the garment industry in Australia. Another former social security officer, an Asian woman then working as a review officer specialising in Asian clients, told me David Reid's comments were consistent with her own experiences. 'Most of the clients I see treat the system as a piggybank. They test the system for what they can get.'

If these various claims were wrong, the social security statistics would show no significant per capita variations among ethnic groups. But the official statistics do show extreme disparities. Checking David Reid's comments on Vietnamese single-parent claims, I found the latest figures available—for 1996—showed that Vietnamese-born comprised 1.8 percent of sole-parent beneficiaries, but were only 0.8 of the Australian population. The per capita discrepancy is thus more than 100 percent. In contrast, immigrants from Malaysia and Hong Kong put very little strain on the social security system, much less so than among people born in Australia. At the other extreme, welfare usage is endemic among immigrants from Lebanon and Turkey.

Other stand-outs: forty-two percent of Turkish-born adults in Australia were receiving welfare benefits in 1996. They receive disability payments at a rate 330 percent higher than Australian-born. Thirty-seven percent of Lebanese were receiving benefits, and disability payments at a rate 300 percent higher than Australian-born.

> *I never had a decision overturned by a review officer,'* says David Reid. *'Because I was an ASO-4 [Administrative Services Officer, grade 4], I didn't have authority to look at addresses in the computer. I had to get an ASO-5 to do it. But when we ran addresses through the computer we found the same addresses coming up repeatedly ... I referred blatant cases to review officers, but I found the regional office often did not check them. Social Security cannot enter a person's home. If they make a home visit, which is rare, and the person is not there, they must leave a card requesting an interview.*

Checking for fraud is especially hard among the Vietnamese community because there is so little variety in the names. And the multicultural industry is particularly vigilant on the matter of rorting among immigrant groups. Both social security officers said the department's culture was completely intimidated by accusations of discrimination. 'If we push too hard in Cabramatta, they go to the welfare rights people,' said the Asian Social Security Officer.

'Our officers used to live in terror of the Welfare Rights Centre,' said Reid.

'The Welfare Rights Centre automatically assumes the recipient is always right and we are discriminating against them ... Local staff are not supposed to imply that any particular ethnic group are disproportionately accessing the system. The department discourages the compilation of such statistics, saying it breaches the nondiscriminatory ethic of the department.

The Department of Social Security confirms this. 'We select people for examination on the basis of risk factors, not ethnicity,' said a spokesperson. The department does, however, practise active discrimination in other ways. Its staff is carefully divided, in accordance with the equal opportunity mandated categories, into 'PWD' (People With Disabilities), 'NESB1' (Non-English Speaking Background, first generation), 'NESB2' (Non-English Speaking Background, second generation), 'ATSI' (Aboriginal and Torres Strait Islanders) and 'Women'.

The Department of Social Security had explanations when asked about the extreme variation among ethnic groups. Turkish migrants are high welfare users and receive disability pensions at a rate three times higher than Australian-born because they are primarily engaged in manual labour and heavy industry. The Turkish category also contained Kurdish war refugees and refugees are often severely disadvantaged. Similar reasons were given for Lebanese being similarly overrepresented. As for the high number of Vietnamese-born sole-parent beneficiaries, Social Security provided a written response.

> *SPBs born in Vietnam represent around 1.8 percent of the SPB population but Vietnamese-born people represent only 0.8 percent of the total Australian population ... The Vietnamese-born community may contain a higher proportion of women of child-bearing age ... The Vietnamese-born community may have been particularly affected by negative experiences often associated with refugee immigration: for example, the death of a partner ... The experience of immigration and re-establishment may have been particularly difficult for Vietnamese couples ... [and] led to separation while in Australia.*

Translation: Vietnamese immigrants are expensive and will continue to be so for some time. In fact, Australia's entire refugee program is proving extremely costly. 'It is basically a refugee problem, not an immigration problem,' said David Reid. 'The refugees are the people who are most exploiting the system because refugees bypass the normal checks in the immigration system.'

Even the Minister for Immigration, Philip Ruddock, acknowledged in 1998 that thousands of people were trying to turn the refugee system into a racket. Although 85 percent of refugee applications are found to be unsustainable, an applicant with good legal advice can string the system out for years, staying and working in Australia while appealing through the Refugee Review Tribunal and then the court system. The full extent of the problems in the welfare system only became evident after Labor lost office and the Howard government, without even tightening the rules, discovered 333 120 people receiving social security payments to which they were not entitled. The government did not break up the figures on the basis of Australian-born and immigrants, but the whole nexus between immigration and welfare was tightened when the budget-cutting Coalition came to office.

While presumably the majority of these payments were going to people born in Australia, Richard Basham regards the hypersensitivity about rorting by immigrants as a failure of Australia's moral system.

> *The reality is that there are all kinds of immigration rorts and welfare rorts and crime in the Asian communities. Everyone knows it. On arrival in Australia, many immigrants, often so-called 'students' from countries such as the PRC [People's Republic of China], will be forced to work at a number of jobs to repay debts upwards of $15 000, debts which while unpaid attract usurious rates of interest. Failure to repay such debts will invoke serious sanctions. I saw a case of a Sino-Thai who had actually been kicked out of Australia. He bought a new identity from a 'Tiananmen refugee' who had gone back to China, and he came back to live in Australia with a new identity.*

The Australian embassy in Beijing backs up these claims. In 1997 the embassy complained to Canberra about chronic visa abuse by Chinese. 'The current overstay rate by Chinese nationals is unacceptably high,' said Todd Frew, the top immigration official in Beijing. He said a large number of applicants for tourist, student or business visas end up working in restaurants or sweatshops. The Australian diplomatic missions in Beijing, Shanghai and Guangzhou granted visas to 54 000 Chinese visitors in 1996, a fifty percent surge on the previous year. The diplomatic missions cannot cope with the increase in demand, a fact exploited by immigration consultants in Australia and China, who often create bogus job offers in Australia. The Beijing embassy also conceded that obtaining false Australian passports by switching identities was a common practice.

Once in Australia, the evolving culture of abuse and opportunism among some immigrants feeds a variety of illegal schemes, such as the underground trade in stolen Medicare cards, which are sold to new immigrants who are not entitled to benefits under stricter new government rules. When New South Wales police arrested one New Zealand immigrant for tax fraud in 1998, they found twenty-one driving licences, multiple birth certificates and numerous false bank accounts.

A former principal of Randwick Primary School, which has a large Asian enrolment, says she interviewed many newly arrived Asian families who immediately asked for letters that could be given to welfare agencies to establish residency requirements. She remembers instances where 'the child was enrolled, the letters written, and within a day the child removed from the school'.

The owner of a Vietnamese restaurant in Sydney was even more damning about tax avoidance than the Social Security officers. 'It's very hard to keep staff because they want to work the social security system or the tax system or the immigration system. We are always losing staff because they only want black money. It's lucky my wife is such a great cook.'

The luckiest place in New South Wales is Cabramatta-Fairfield, according to the New South Wales Racing and Gaming Commission. These adjoining suburbs are the biggest source of Lotto winners. In a period of seven years, Cabramatta residents won fourteen first prizes. Cabramatta's winning run has little to do with luck and everything to do with gambling fever, tax avoidance, money laundering and the black money that dominates Cabramatta's economic life. Direct buses operate between Cabramatta and the Sydney casino. The Cabravale Ex-Servicemen's Club, in the heart of the Vietnamese enclave, has so much money flowing through its poker machines that it borrowed nineteen million dollars to expand and paid the money back within ten months. The 'casino rooms' at the Cabramatta Inn, the Stardust Hotel and the Kookaburra Hotel in nearby Canley Vale are all thriving.

'When we investigated organised crime, we found Asians were using the casinos as money laundering operations,' says retired Justice Athol Moffitt, QC, who headed the Moffitt Royal Commission. 'We found that some of these so-called Asian high rollers were bringing drug money and Asian crime syndicate money into the country,' he told me. 'The [federal Labor] government wasn't interested.' So concerned about the rise of organised crime is Justice Moffitt that he believes sweeping new law enforcement powers are essential. He advocates giving police greater power to seize the assets of drug carriers by the imposition of a much less onerous civil, rather than criminal, burden of proof in asset seizure cases. Drug dealers have benefited enormously from the often impossible burden of proof required in criminal cases.

Millions of dollars in profits from the Vietnamese black economy of cash-skimming restaurants, illegal garment-making outlets, welfare rorts, unregistered businesses, gang activities and the booming drug trade are laundered through gambling. Millions more are simply funnelled into gold bullion and literally carried onto flights back to Vietnam. Last year QANTAS doubled its service to Saigon/Ho Chi Minh City, from one flight a week to two.

A tremendous amount of money is going out of the country through the gold bullion exchange,' said a source in AUSTRAC [Australian Transaction Reports and Analysis Centre], the agency which tracks money transactions into and out of Australia, and which estimated that criminals laundered about $3.5 billion overseas in 1995. 'The Vietnamese buy gold off dealers and pay cash. They buy less than $10 000, so it doesn't have to be reported to AUSTRAC. The increase in the bullion going out of Australia coincided with the upsurge of heroin importation through the Vietnamese community.

The practice of making multiple deposits of less than $10 000 to avoid currency controls is known in America as 'smurfing' and the term has come to Australia. In March 1997 the National Crime Authority arrested a group of

Vietnamese money launderers who used to drive around Sydney in a Tarago filled with packets of cash, making $9000 deposits to numerous bank accounts in numerous branches, then transferring the money overseas. The NCA believes these Vietnamese smurfs sent twelve million dollars overseas in 1200 transactions in the year prior to their arrest.

Cash is king in Cabramatta and the surrounding suburbs where more than half Australia's 160 000 Vietnamese live. 'When I worked in Cabramatta,' said an officer with the Commonwealth Bank, 'I saw an unbelievable amount of cash. Most of it wasn't in accounts. It was in bags put on the table in front of me by people making applications for property loans. I used to wonder where the money came from. They had these pyramid and savings schemes that people contribute to, but I still wondered where a lot of the money came from.'

The theme of tax avoidance also recurs repeatedly among the ethnic Chinese immigrants interviewed by Sang Ye in *The Year the Dragon Came*.

> *I've already reached the $30 000 mark. A few people have couriered most of it back to China for me. You never know when there's going to be a change in government policy. This way the tax department won't catch up with me either.*

The biggest immigration scheme of all is phoney marriages. 'So many Asians are working the marriage racket that the price for a marriage has plummeted in the past year,' says Dr Basham. 'The price has dropped from $35 000 to less than half that, and a lot of people are ticked off. I know a restaurant chain that is involved in massive marriage scams. It has hundreds of illegal workers.'

Bob Birrell of Monash University, writing in *People and Place*, argues that spouse migration was the largest single component of Australia's immigration program, and the most abused.

> *With spouse migration now accounting for 40 percent of the immigration and likely to grow in size, especially with the prospective PRC [China] flow, questions about its economic costs and benefits need to be asked.*
>
> *We know that very high proportions of recent spouse arrivals from countries like Turkey, Lebanon and Vietnam are dependent on unemployment benefits ...*
>
> *For example, there was a total of 1,518 arrivals from Lebanon in 1991–92, of whom 770 were spouses. Many of the others were children and elderly persons. Yet as of May, 1994, according to Department of Social Security files, 553 of them were receiving unemployment benefits. The availability of our welfare benefits (generous by the standards of most Third World countries) is a standing inducement to spouse migration. As a spokesperson for the Arab Community Welfare Centre stated in October 1994 of Lebanese spouses: 'A lot of them don't want to work. They want to be on the dole.*
>
> *... It is not clear that the [tough] new rules have discouraged fraudulent applications ... It may be that those whose prime objective is to utilize marriage for immigration purposes have simply moved offshore to make their*

*applications. By doing so they can avoid any serious
evaluations of the bone-fides of their marriage ... the
number of spouse/fiance visas issued offshore has
increased* [since the tough new rules] *from 17 000 to
over 19 000 a year ...*

*It seems likely that some migrants have taken advan-
tage of the system. The best data source is the pattern of
divorces. In the case of PRC [China], there have been a
large number of successful onshore marriages (937 in
1989–90 and around 500 a year since). The number of
Chinese-born persons involved in divorces has since
increased sharply from 533 in 1990 to 1,390 in 1993.*

'There are 120 000 marriages a year in Australia and an
astonishing proportion of these, about thirty percent, involve
offshore spouses,' Birrell told me. 'China and Vietnam now
provide the two largest flows of offshore spouses ... A substantial number of these people do not have the wherewithal
to cope in Australia. Many go straight to the Social Security
office.'

The high ratio of divorces to marriages among Chinese is
part of the worst kept secret in the immigration business—the
widespread abuse of the system by immigrants from the
PRC. Using Australian laws to advantage has been openly
discussed in numerous Chinese-language articles and books,
such as *My Fortune In Australia* and *I Married A Foreign
Woman*, published in China, and *The Year the Dragon Came*
and *Bitter Peaches and Plums,* in Australia. Many of the

Chinese immigrants interviewed in *The Year the Dragon Came* are blunt about using the system:

> *As soon as I got to Melbourne I arranged a phoney marriage. It cost me over $10 000 but I got PR [permanent residence] out of it ... Now I realise that if I'd stuck it out I would have been able to stay on "humanitarian" grounds.*

Another man in *Dragon*, a librarian, expressed pain at the general attitude of his fellow immigrants from China who, he said, were always trying to take advantage of loopholes and were 'outraged' if they were refused. 'They never stop complaining about Australia, cursing the place and feeling that somehow Australia hasn't done the right thing by them.'

The Department of Social Security does engage in a ceaseless effort to sift the welfare roles of abusers, conducting three million data checks a year. The department compares databanks from the Australian Taxation Office, other departments, and other compensation payers looking for discrepancies, a process known as data-matching. The number of reviews more than doubled in the five years to 1993–94, then really took off when the Howard government and its budget razor gang arrived in 1996. In the first full year of administration by the new government, 1996–97, the number of reviews of social security payments rose twenty-eight percent; the number of payment cancellations or reductions increased forty percent, and the amount of debts recovered soared forty-seven percent, all producing net savings to the system of $1.5 billion without any important change in policy.

The cumulative effect of all the small and large abuses of the social security net, the immigration system and the tax system is a huge black economy which mingles with the black economies from money laundering, drug profits, organised crime, extortion rackets and human trafficking. Richard Basham has warned police they should treat documentation from Asian consulates with caution because of corruption among consular officials in some countries, and proceed with caution in information shared with some Asian police forces, including Vietnam. 'Australians can remain naive for only so long,' he said. 'At a certain point it becomes dangerous. I think we have reached that point.'

12
THE VOTE EATERS

AUSTRALIA'S FIRST assassination of a political figure occurred at 9.30 on the night of 5 September 1994, when a member of the New South Wales Parliament, John Newman, was murdered at his home in western Sydney.

Newman had been warned. The Labor member of the NSW lower house had been campaigning against the burgeoning Cabramatta drug market since his election to State Parliament in 1986. Death threats started in 1991, followed by a bullet through the window of his electoral office. A warning was left on his answering machine: 'You dead, Newman. We kill you.' The voice had a heavy Vietnamese accent. The brazenness of the warnings increased. Newman's car was splashed with white paint, a standard warning. On the night he was killed, he was in the driveway of his home, putting a cover over his car to prevent further paint daubings.

He was shot twice in the chest at close range. The murder was carried out in front of his fiancee, Lucy Wang. After an investigation lasting three years and a coroner's inquiry, on Friday, 13 March 1998, three Vietnamese immigrants were charged with Newman's murder. One of them was the most well-known member of the Vietnamese community in New South Wales, Phuong Ngo, a local councillor and operator of the Mekong Club in Cabramatta. The other two men charged with murder, Tuan Van Tran and Quang Dao, were both associates of Ngo and worked for him at the Mekong Club.

Phuong Ngo had come to Australia as a Vietnamese boat refugee in 1982. Five years later he became the first Vietnamese to win political office in Australia when he was elected to Fairfield City Council. Over time, he developed a fierce political rivalry with John Newman, the state parliamentarian whose electorate included Cabramatta. Ngo wanted to enter Parliament. Newman wanted to destroy his career.

Whether Phuong Ngo, Tuan Van Tran and Quang Dao conspired to murder John Newman we do not know. Their trials had not begun when this book went to press.

The assassination of a political figure is a frontal assault on the democratic system and Australia was miraculously free of such an assault through its democratic evolution. Newman's killing may prove to be a political aberration, but a more insidious assault on the democratic system—electoral fraud—was also carried out that same year by Vietnamese and their Australian allies inside the union movement. The election fraud took place, ominously, inside the major mail centres, which have predominantly immigrant workforces, especially Vietnamese and Filipino.

More than a thousand workers had their votes manipulated or improperly gave their ballot papers to fixers. It was a major fraud. A key element in the rorting of the system was ethnic politics, specifically the manipulation of workers with poor English skills who were culturally susceptible to pressure from ethnic group leaders. Prominent among the people who illegally collected blank ballots and intimidated voters were a group of Asian fixers. The Australian Federal Police obtained the names of a number of those believed to be responsible for illegal vote-gathering, and many of them were Vietnamese. But the police were not brought into the case until long after the events and could not do much without physical evidence, such as handwriting samples, or witnesses willing to testify in court. None of the fixers was ever prosecuted or reprimanded.

The year 1994 was not a good one for grassroots democracy in Australia. Not only was John Newman assassinated, but the election for the postal workers branch of the Communications Electrical Plumbing Union (CEPU) was found to be so tainted that it was declared void after a court challenge before Justice Michael Moore of the Industrial Relations Court of Australia. The electoral irregularities took place within a culture of bureaucratic inertia that worked to the advantage of the then federal Labor government, which was aligned with the same Right faction controlling the CEPU.

Justice Moore expressed dismay at the problems which escaped the notice of Australia Post, the Australian Electoral Commission and the investigating arms of the government. Even amid the ponderous language of the law, his summation and judgement sometimes read like a novel.

Ms Mary Buenaflor said she was approached before the ballot opened by Mr Paul Michel, who asked her to give him her ballot paper ... he wanted the ballot so it could be filled in for the [incumbent union group led by Jamal] Natour. She said she would give it over.

A few days later she was approached by Mr Chamrod Ratnavirawatana who made a similar request. Again, she said she would hand it over ... She later saw a notice on a bulletin board indicating that vote buying was a crime [and] completed the ballot and posted it herself.

Justice Moore found Ms Buenaflor to be a credible witness. He found similar credibility in other witnesses called to give evidence of standover tactics and ballot rorting. His opinion of several of the other witnesses who appeared before him was different: 'I do not accept them as truthful witnesses.' The judge also quoted two union activists speaking prior to the announcement of the ballot results.

I approached [a Vietnamese organiser] and said, 'Well I got 200 [votes] in the East and how much did you get in the North?' He replied, '70 percent [of the votes].'

I then said, 'And in the North West?' He replied, '70 percent.'

I then said, 'And in the South?' He replied, '80 percent.'

I then said, 'And in the South West?' He replied, '70 percent.'

Commenting on this exchange, Justice Moore wrote:

The words ... have the appearance of someone who is gloating ... That they were said is entirely credible ... He had an obvious interest in denying evidence that suggested widespread electoral fraud.

Yet not a single person ever received more than a mild rebuke for their actions in this election, and the federal agencies entrusted with preventing and prosecuting such manipulations remained inert throughout. In fact, of all the hundreds of union elections that took place during all the years of Labor government, I was not able to find evidence of a single prosecution for union election manipulations.

Control of the postal workers union has always been one of the prizes of intra-Labor fighting. Control translates into Labor Party delegates and factional power in cabinet or shadow cabinet. For political zealots, political power in mail centres means some degree of potential influence, however small, in all elections.

Australians believe their basic institutions, like the postal system, are free of political influence. They are not. They are, and always have been, a one-party state. It is revealing to see what befell the two men who, through their court challenge to the 1994 election, successfully revealed the scandal.

One of them was an ordinary postman, Quentin Cook, working in the Blue Mountains west of Sydney. In the midst of what would prove to be a successful court challenge that would eventually lead to reforms of the entire Australian system of industrial elections, Quentin Cook was sacked by Australia Post. Cook was handed his dismissal papers in front of his family, at the front door of his home. The reason given was 'insubordination'. He continued to fight his election court case but, broke, living on debt and his wife's earnings, and no longer employed by Australia Post, he could not afford his union dues for several months. When the new election was held in 1996 to replace the one he helped overturn, he was barred from standing for office by the Australian Electoral Commission because he had been an unfinancial member for several months. So the man who helped expose the tainted election was barred from standing in the new one.

Cook sued Australia Post for unfair dismissal and won a delayed but emphatic victory. Judicial Registrar Joan Locke, in her 1997 judgement, scorched Australia Post management.

'The response was so out of proportion, ill-founded, unjust and illogical that by independent, objective standards it was tantamount to capriciousness and spitefulness.'

She also noted that Cook and his ally had purportedly been called 'Liberal shits' by an Australia Post manager who drafted the allegations against Cook. She found Cook to be, 'a faithful and industrious employee'. He was reinstated, with back pay, by a begrudging Australia Post management.

The other key figure in exposing this fraud was a veteran and colourful union organiser, Noel Battese, also known as 'Cementhead'. He, too, would be abused for his role in the affair, this time in federal Parliament. At 7.20 pm on 12 September 1996, Senator Stephen Conroy, a member of the

Labor Right faction in Victoria, also a former official of the Transport Workers Union and a protege of the factional headkicker Senator Robert Ray, stood in Parliament and began defaming Noel Battese.

> *Justice Moore has exposed that supporters of the Cook-Battese team were involved in electoral fraud. Was there any indication of who might have been involved with this? ... A member of the Cook-Battese team has pointed directly at who is responsible. Yet Battese is the instigator of the challenge to the election on the grounds of electoral fraud. One of his own team has given him up.*

Senator Conroy knew, or should have known, that the judge, while making no finding as to who might be responsible, had noted that the faction which controlled the union, the Labor Right, Conroy's faction, was overwhelmingly the beneficiary of the tampered ballots. Senator Conroy made his speech on the eve of the new union election campaign, the one held to replace the rorted election. Within twenty-four hours of his speech, thousands of copies of the Hansard record were printed and distributed anonymously around the mail centres under the heading 'The Cheat Team'. A second version of the speech was printed in Vietnamese. Senator Conroy ended his speech with bravura, saying: 'I look forward to the inquiry into electoral matters.'

Outside the Parliament, we didn't hear from him again. Noel Battese challenged Senator Conroy to repeat his claims outside the Senate.

Silence.

I faxed the senator a dozen questions several weeks after his speech.

Silence.

On 9 November 1996 the *Sydney Morning Herald* published a highly critical description of his behaviour in this affair.

Silence.

The day before his remarks in the Senate, Stephen Conroy was the subject of a profile in the Parliamentary newsletter, the *House Magazine*. He had recently returned from a trip to Europe and told the newsletter he had been impressed in Germany because, 'There was no narrow, vindictive, small-mindedness of spirit in their politics ...'

While Senator Conroy was remaining aloof from vindictive, small-minded politics, another member of the Right faction, Leo McLeay, swung into action. Mr McLeay's most famous episode in a long parliamentary career is receiving $60 000 in taxpayer-funded compensation for falling off his bicycle. On 31 October 1996 McLeay stood in the House of Representatives and repeated the same attack on Noel Battese that Senator Conroy had made in the Senate the previous month. He noted that the team which had won the rorted 1994 election had also just won the 1996 election. McLeay ended his speech by saying: 'This sends a clear message to the government to let the new team get on with the job of running the CEPU.'

The message this episode sends is that the Australian legal and political system does not have the tools to prosecute cases such as the one exposed by Quentin Cook and Noel

Battese. The 1996 CEPU election, like the voided 1994 election, was marked and tainted by a campaign of anonymous character assassination by supporters of the incumbent Right faction, who distributed thousands of anonymous circulars known as 'shit sheets'. The worst of them depicted one of the reform candidates plus this description of his life:

> *My wife left me. Her and her solicitor squeezed me for every cent I had. I have lost my home and I am now living out of the back of my car. They made up stories about my drinking and gambling. They even told lies about my visiting prostitutes. So then I lost custody of my kids.*

The man in question was not living in his car. In fact, when I spoke to him soon after this 'shit sheet' had been distributed he had just completed putting an extension onto his house. Everything else in the sheet was untrue. At least the matter was given an airing in Parliament by the Minister for Workplace Relations, Peter Reith, on 11 September 1996.

> MR REITH: *The electoral fraud consisted of multiple voting by a limited number of persons. The court found that members of the union had been approached by other members to hand over their uncompleted ballot papers, which had been completed by a limited number of other persons … In all, some 930 ballot papers were tampered with in this fraudulent election.*
>
> MR [JOHN] HOWARD: *Any motorbikes?*

MR REITH: *All in good time, Prime Minister. The court ordered a new election ... The [CEPU] is a big union. It has 187,000 members. The relationship between the former government and this union is on the public record. For example, in 1992–93 the former Labor government granted to this union $100,000 directly and in return the CEPU donated to the ALP $140,000.*

—Opposition members interjecting—

MR REITH: *We have got plenty of time. The last point to be made is that the CEPU has been run by the New South Wales Right, and of course there are close links between some of the leading affiliated unions in the New South Wales Right and current members of this House, including former ministers for communications, including the member for Dobell, and there are others who may similarly be named. We are concerned about these matters, and investigations are under way.*

Investigations into the conduct of the CEPU election, which had petered out during the Labor government, did resume after the Coalition came to government. Peter Reith also gave the scandal another airing during question time on 19 March 1997.

I think any fair Australian would be pleased to see that Quentin Cook has received a favourable outcome in this particular case, requiring his reinstatement to Australia Post. The words used in the decision, I think, are quite damning of Australia Post in the way they handled this matter ...

    It is also timely to note that Quentin Cook has been having a running battle with the factional allies and mates of those on the other side within certain elements of the trade union movement. It was Quentin Cook who was able to expose the rorts in certain trade union elections. Members might remember the spectre of four trade unionists sitting around a kitchen table, filling out the ballot papers to get their mates back—who just happen to be mates of certain people on the other side. Members won't forget that, as Quentin Cook was raising his concerns, there was nothing but silence from the members [opposite] ...

In the end, a joint standing Parliamentary committee investigated the AEC's conduct of this and other elections. The committee noted that the 'notorious' CEPU election had sparked its inquiry, and recommended that the *Workplace Relations Act* be amended to greatly increase the penalties for election rorting; to make it easier to conduct investigations and prosecutions, and to make illegal the manufacture and distribution of smear sheets that engage in character assassination:'It is appropriate that the legislation reflect abhorrence for the practice and enable a penalty to be imposed.'

By the time a vigorous examination of the CEPU election rort was finally conducted, the various arms of the federal bureaucracy had managed to see nothing, hear nothing and say nothing for so long that the trail had gone cold. The union official who police believe helped organise the rort, Jamal Natour, had died of a brain hemorrhage. He was buried with full honours in 1995, and his funeral was attended by a long list of dignitaries from the Labor Right, including a federal minister.

13
IN THE FOOTSTEPS OF ALEXANDER

COMPLAINANT WITNESS: *... It was only after the fifth century that they [Macedonians] gradually became part of the wider Greek world, but there's no doubt that scholars have found that linguistically and religiously they were part, they were Greeks. They shared the same language and religion as the other Greeks.*

COMPLAINANT COUNSEL: *They worship the Gods of Olympus?*

WITNESS: *Yes.*

DEFENCE COUNSEL: *I object at this point Mr Chairman. It's now too far from anything raised in cross-examination. I didn't cross-examine about the Gods of Olympus.*

...

COMPLAINANT WITNESS: *... The opposing argument always refers to the Greek politician Demosthenes who's probably the most famous orator of antiquity, who hated Philip very much. But most sources ... refer to the fact that in Athens when Demosthenes was attacking Philip there were also two others ...*

DEFENCE COUNSEL: *I object Mr Chairman. There has to be a limit drawn to this! It's an expensive exercise.*

Limits? Costs? This is the Equal Opportunity Tribunal. This is the Anti-Discrimination Act. The case of Hellenic Council of NSW v Macedonian Youth Association is too bizarre not to warrant a close look, especially as one of the most dangerous trends in Australian democracy would be to allow foreign animosities to be played out in the Australian legal system under the guises of multiculturalism and anti-discrimination.

The dispute, which took more than five years to resolve, began when, in the wake of the creation of a Macedonian state in the break-up of Yugoslavia, a full-page ad was placed by Greek cultural zealots in the *Sun-Herald* in 1 March 1992 under the headline MACEDONIA IS GREEK. Among the more provocative statements in the ad were:

> Nobody took the notion of a 'Slav' Macedonia seriously because the whole world knew that Macedonia was always Greek and could be nothing else.
>
> We encourage the Skopian community both abroad and here in Australia to search their rich and beautiful Slavic history for the appropriate naming of their new independent nation. However, continued usurping of the name 'Macedonia' will firm the resolve of Greeks and Phil-Hellenes around the world to defend this glorious heritage from further plunder and rape.

It came as no surprise when, two months later, in a full-page ad in the *Sun-Herald*, zealots from the Macedonian community returned the provocation, under the headline *MACEDONIA*—LAND OF LEGENDS! LAND OF GLORY! BUT *NEVER* GREEK, along with a map of a barb-wire-enmeshed greater Macedonia.

> Had the misguided Greek community known the truth of their history, they would never have infected Australia with the elements of a cancerous European epidemic known as nationalism, thereby transforming 'The Lucky Country' into another arena for foreign dispute ...
>
> The Macedonians (tall and fair) were in Europe long before the beginning of time itself, and were referred to by the Achaeans (short and dark) as 'Endopi', which means 'Old Settlers', inferring that etymologically Macedonia was a name borne by the Macedonians before the Achaeans had even arrived in Europe ...
>
> Well, no more! We can only take so much. Fellow Australians, you have read the facts, now it's time we stood up to these hostile fascists. It's these radical community sects which entangle our politicians within the labyrinth of foreign policy, translating foreign issues into domestic ones ...
>
> Always remember: 'Phillip II, Alexander the Great and Aristotle were Macedonians.'

This, in turn, prompted the Hellenic Council of New South Wales, to lodge an action with the Equal Opportunities

Tribunal of New South Wales in May 1992. They also made a claim to the Press Council. The existence of the Anti-Discrimination Tribunal and the Anti-Discrimination Act provided an avenue to sue. Even so, when the case was about to begin after a four-year delay, the plaintiffs had still not lodged a statement of claim, and sought an immediate postponement. This prompted exasperation from the chairman of the Anti-Discrimination Tribunal, Michael Bieddulph: 'I'm talking about a statement of claim in the Supreme Court … It was ordered to be filed. The tribunal relies on the points of claim. It was never filed.'

If this nonsense had taken place before one of the dragons on the bench of the New South Wales Supreme Court, the Hellenic Council case would have been over before it began. Instead it was allowed to lurch ahead, and in its own unintended way it illuminated nearly every dubious trend in the fetish for tax-supported 'cultural diversity'.

For Australians, a disturbing statement appears in a book by an American anthropologist, Loring Danforth, who quotes the then Greek consul in Melbourne as stating: 'Australia is the first line of defence in the battle for Macedonia.'

In 1992 there were mass demonstrations by Greeks in Australia and one of the speakers at these demonstrations was federal Labor MP Andrew Theophanous, a product of the left-wing ethnic 'Greek' Labor branches in Melbourne. According to the *Age* of Melbourne, Theophanous told the crowd that Slavic people were the most recent arrivals in the region of ancient Macedonia and had no right to misrepresent history by monopolising the name. This was exactly the same line propagated at the time by the then government in Athens which, in addition to the stated reasons of cultural defence, used the emergence of a Macedonian state to deflect attention from several domestic scandals.

Greek nationalists exerted pressure elsewhere. Cambridge University Press refused to publish an ethnographic study of the Greek-Macedonian dispute following advice from the Foreign Office and the M16 security service that publication could provoke terrorism against Cambridge University staff in Greece. The warning was acted upon because a British Council official was murdered in Greece in the 1980s and a Greek scholar received death threats two years ago for publishing her work on Slavic speakers in Greek Macedonia. The censored book, *Fields of Wheat, Hills of Blood*, challenges the official Greek government line that there is no Macedonian minority in Greece. So does Loring Danforth's book, *The Macedonian Conflict: Ethnic Nationalism in a Transnational World*, published by Princeton University Press. Danforth first came to Australia in 1988 as a guest of the Melbourne Greek community. He was later disowned when he deviated from the official line.

PLAINTIFF WITNESS: *By adopting the name Macedonia, Macedonians automatically aspire to adopt the history of ancient Macedonia, thereby creating confusion in the man in the street. The man in the street associates Macedonia with Alexander the Great, whereas Alexander the Great and ancient Macedonia are part of the history*

*of Ancient Greece and no serious scholar can dispute
that.*

I, as a man in the street, had always assumed that ancient
Macedonia and Alexander were self-evidently part of modern
Greek tradition. But that was prior to the Hellenic Council
case, which revealed the truth was far more intricate.

PLAINTIFF'S COUNSEL: *You would disagree with the
proposition that the Macedonians are not Slavic?*

DEFENCE WITNESS: *Well, language is one thing and
national and ethnic identity is another. You will find, for
example, a lot of people who came from Asia Minor who
were Greeks but spoke Turkish, so what would you say
about them?*

Loring Danforth points out that neither the household of
Alexander the Great nor his Greek contemporaries regarded
him as Greek. He argues that the melding of the two hostile
and distinct cultures began only centuries later under pressure
from a common enemy, Rome, and even then Macedonia was
regarded as marginal. Macedonian identity, he argues, has
largely been fostered by Greek oppression. He lists in elabo-
rate detail the long and often brutal suppression of minority
rights in Greece, a record which explains why the two groups
in Australia have fought each other in soccer riots, fire-
bombings and insulting newspaper ads.

The Anti-Discrimination Act states that 'a public act, done
reasonably and in good faith … for public purposes including discussion or debate' cannot be rendered unlawful. This

means it was always going to be a difficult case for the Hellenic Council activists to win, or to win more than a token or symbolic victory. They wanted to send a message.

When the case resumed in August, 1996, after another delay of several months, the bizarre elements also resumed:

PLAINTIFF'S COUNSEL: *Mr Chairman, there is somebody swearing behind me. I would ask that he be evicted. Justice cannot be done if members of the audience behind counsel swear at every question.*

CHAIRMAN: *Has it been going on without my knowledge, has it?*

COUNSEL: *... it is disconcerting to me, the questioner, because I have a program of questions in my mind which rolls along and when this kind of disruption occurs it really destroys my train of thought. It's not fair.*

Although the plaintiff's counsel rightly did not like being insulted inside the court, he did not mind making some general remarks that many Australians would find grossly insulting.

COUNSEL: *You were aware, were you not, that there were a large number of Australians who were very touchy when it comes to this aspect of the loyalty of migrants?*

DEFENDANT WITNESS: *Yes, I was, I was one of them.*

> COUNSEL: *And there are a large number of Australians who feel that if somebody comes from overseas they should have cultural lobotomies performed upon them and that thereafter they have no interest at all in the cultural activities of their former homeland?*

It was not clear what exactly the Hellenic Council was trying to achieve with this case. Was the council trying to remind people that there is an independent state called Macedonia? To remind Australians that Greece has practised suppression of minorities? The author and journalist Robert Kaplan, writing in the *Atlantic Monthly* in 1997, was brutally succinct in depicting how the modern Greek state was formed: 'Greece is a stable democracy partly because earlier in the century it carried out a relatively benign form of ethnic cleansing, in the form of refugee transfers, which created a monoethnic society.'

Is that what the Hellenic Council wanted to revisit? Or did it want to reopen the issue of irresponsible meddling in Australian affairs by the Greek government? Or examine the links between the Australian Greek community, the Greek government and the federal Labor government? If so, Hellenic Council of NSW v Macedonian Youth Association succeeded on all fronts.

> PLAINTIFF'S COUNSEL: *Would you agree that following FYROM [Former Yugoslav Republic of Macedonia] seceding from Yugoslavia that the Australian government made a decision ... that your type of*

Macedonia would hereafter be classified as a Slav-Macedonia? And that decision annoyed you?

DEFENCE WITNESS: *I didn't see that as to the interests of multiculturalism in Australia. I saw it as an attack on the principles of multiculturalism ... I saw it as an attempt to deny our right of self identification and self determination. A right that all other Australians enjoy ...*

PLAINTIFF'S COUNSEL: *You realise that by being called Slav-Macedonians the government of this country was entertaining the idea, at any rate, that, that there could be other types of Macedonia like Greek Macedonians and Bulgarian Macedonians?*

DEFENCE WITNESS: *Well, from the conversations that I had with Prime Minister Keating, Foreign Minister Gareth Evans, and Multicultural Minister, Nick Bolkus, the reason for the decision was pressure from within the Greek community.*

It was inevitable that the name of Nick Bolkus would turn up eventually. This case was another window into the career of Senator Bolkus, whose brand of ethnic politics was also placed under a microscope by scholar Ernest Healy in *People and Place*, the journal of the Centre for Population and Urban Research at Monash University.

Recent decisions by the Minister for Immigration and Ethnic Affairs, Senator Bolkus, raise serious questions about the Minister's preparedness to tolerate open

*debate about immigration and multicultural issues, and
about measures he has taken to control the debate ...*

*During 1993 Senator Bolkus appointed Stephen
Castles [of the University of Wollongong, and joint
editor of the book The Teeth are Smiling] as Chairman
of the advisory council and included Mary Kalantzis
as a member—both have written disparagingly of
Australia's past ...*

The role of ethnic blocs as tools in Labor politics found its
most naked expression in the large Greek community of Melbourne, which was allowed to set up fourteen 'community
language' branches. These branches, in turn, formed the
bedrock of power of the Socialist Left of the Labor Party.
This regressive move was justified in terms of Labor's support for multiculturalism. It legitimised the rampant ethnic
branch stacking that had taken place. Greek activists within
the Socialist Left faction argued that these stackings were
countermeasures against the Labour Unity faction recruiting
from the Turkish and Macedonian communities.

In 1994, the year of the most sustained ethnic violence in
Australia as Greek and Macedonian nationalists waged a
campaign of demonstrations, threats and bombings against
each other, Senator Bolkus gave his closest Victorian ally,
Andrew Theophanous, the role of directing the community
access program by the Office of Multicultural Affairs. This
program produced a document, *Our Nation*, which advocated
changing the Australian Constitution to incorporate 'multicultural principles'. These and other measures were among

the reasons for the Labor government's emphatic rejection by the electorate in 1996.

By 1997 the legal battle between the Greeks and the Macedonians in Hellenic Council of NSW v Macedonian Youth Association was still working through the legal system.

> PLAINTIFF'S COUNSEL: *Mr Chairman, there is somebody swearing behind me ... It has happened on three occasions. I decided to ignore it on the first two occasions.*

> CHAIRMAN: *All right, I will ask that gentleman withdraw himself from the court and remain outside. [Pause.]*

> CHAIRMAN: *No, outside, and remain outside the precincts of the court.*

Finally, on 25 September 1997 the Equal Opportunity Tribunal handed down its judgement. The Hellenic Council lost. In dismissing the complaint, the tribunal found that:

> *... the Macedonian Youth Association showed that they had an honest belief in the statements within the article, and believed the article itself to be a reasonable response to what had already been published by the Greek community. The Tribunal accepts this submission and finds that the public act was done reasonably and in good faith, for academic and research purposes and for other purposes in the public interest, including discussion and debate about the Macedonian issue.*

Freedom of speech may have won in this case, but the matter had dragged through the system for five years and four months. It cost the respondents $15 000 and the Australian taxpayers much more than that. It revealed the weaknesses of the antidiscrimination, equal opportunity and racial vilification legislation.

The great majority of Australians do not care about the arguments raised in this case. What they do care about is any meddling in Australian domestic politics by foreign governments. They do care about free speech, and they do care about having to pay thousands of dollars to subsidise ancient, alien disputes such as this case, which managed to portray one of Australia's most successful migrant groups—a smart, educated, diverse, entrepreneurial community—as if it were a foreign enclave whose heart is 10 000 kilometres from home.

PART FOUR

It is lack of confidence, more than anything else, that kills a civilisation. We can destroy ourselves by cynicism and disillusion just as effectively as by bombs.

Sir Kenneth Clark

14
WHITE DREAMING

'I'm not a nice guy. I don't even want to be a nice guy. I have to overcorrect for the mealy-mouthed quality in contemporary Australian life. I try to draw attention to it by behaving in a different way. I just say what I think and it blows up in my face more often than not. But without honesty there can be no literature.'

David Foster may or may not be a nice guy, but he won Australia's highest literary honour, the Miles Franklin Award, in 1997. It gave him a little room to move. He says some things I would not dare to say, or even dare to believe, but his courage, his willingness to defend the maligned bushies, the breadth of his knowledge, and the sheer scope of his family, which stretches across the country, up to the Top End and into an Aboriginal clan, make him a remarkable Australian. In some ways his story is Australia's story.

The eucalyptus are in heat at present, determined to seize the window of opportunity which has opened to them; dry storms over dry forests.

Until he won the Miles Franklin and became a bestselling author he was the country's finest unfamous author. It only took him ten novels to make it. 'David Foster is one of a very small handful of Australian writers writing today who will still be read in fifty or a hundred years from now,' wrote the literary critic Andrew Riemer. When his novel, *The Glade Within the Grove,* won the award, it went to a writer who lives so far from the cappuccino ghettos of Sydney and Melbourne that he has worked on prawning trawlers in the Gulf of Carpenteria and knows how to kick his way out of trouble in a fight.

His strongest literary influence is the first-century Roman writer Juvenal, whom he reads in the original Latin. 'Juvenal showed what could and should be done by an artist working in a decadent, or if you prefer, postmodern age such as ours.' Twenty years ago Patrick White described Foster as the most individual and most interesting writer in Australia. Geoffrey Dutton called him the country's most original and daring novelist. Rodney Hall wrote in 1996: 'I am yet again astounded that Foster is not more celebrated. Too much adulation is squandered on light-weight novels masquerading as literary works.'

David Foster's mother was an orphan and his father abandoned them. He finished high school at Orange High and did well enough to graduate with honours from Sydney University. Even though he went on to earn a doctorate in inorganic chemistry and do postgraduate work, he left university to work as a postman in a country town, Bundanoon, and take a succession of literary grants. 'No PhD likes to put a postman's uniform on. You swallow your ego. But I was trying to write, and I had to earn an income.'

As recently as the month before he won the Miles Franklin he was working as crew on his son-in-law's prawning trawler in the Gulf of Carpentaria. 'Professional fishing is not much fun. Though green deckies are probably Australia's most highly paid teenagers. It's dirty, dangerous and unremitting work, with stonefish and catfish in the prawn. Deckhands lose fingers. The boats wallow in the big swells.' He goes north so he can visit his scattered family, including those in the Top End, the family one of his sons married into, the Aboriginal branch of the family. Aboriginal with a big dash of Chinese.

'The High Court's Wik decision came to mind as I sat in the galley of our trawler, at anchor off the red bauxite beach at Weipa, Gulf of Carpentaria, not far from the Archer River Mission. Wik territory. We were preparing to hunt banana prawn. It's one of Australia's most lucrative fisheries, the northern prawn fishery. A licence for an eighty-footer like ours will cost you $2.4 million. It's the world's best ocean shrimp, too good for the likes of us. It is destined for the Tokyo fishmarket, the Tsukiji.

'This is not fishing the way the Wik fish. I'm not sure the Wik ever fished bananas. But the Croker Islanders want their cut of my percentage. We fishermen understand the Wik. What could be more pathetic than a warrior defeated in war, a hunter deprived of his hunting ground? The prawn farm is the future, but prawn fishermen despise prawn farms. They won't work on prawn farms for the same reason the Wik don't want to work at all: when you have known the real thing, a surrogate becomes unacceptable.'

Until he won $27 000 and bestseller status from the Miles Franklin, the rainshowers of high critical praise for Foster had produced little in the way of widespread recognition. Even now, he remains a niche novelist, a dense stand of old-growth rainforest amid a sea of prevailing eucalypt.

> *Olaf becomes aware he is entering a warm temperate rainforest of amplitude: not the customary, pitiful remnant, which has made a valiant stand in the narrow confines of a moist gully by deploying itself down a watercourse ... but a rainforest broad and capacious, extensive, dominant and relaxed, with nothing to fear, for now, from the eucalyptus, who keep a subdued, and respectful, distance. Not much in the way of understorey, but thick leaf mulch, with a touch of orange thorn, and everywhere rivulets, because of the rain, and a dank, forbidding darkness, tempered by the inviting wistfulness of wood pigeons in flight, and the brilliance of glossy green leaves, up to a foot broad in the case of the giant stinging tree. A monumental stand of coachwood, well south of its recognised range, descends from one bench to the next. Tall blackwood and pinkwood (mainland leatherwood) and cedars pierce the canopy. Milk and passionflower and lawyer vines festoon the blueberry ash, while prickly little white starworts twinkle on the verges of the road.*
>
> *'Don't you log this Valley?' inquires Olaf.*
>
> *'We took the corkwood,' replies Attis, 'and we cleared the Flat, but we thought it would be nice to leave some*

old-growth standing somewhere, just so people would
know what this country was like once. But it turns out
this country wasn't like this at all.'

As this extract from *The Glade Within the Grove* suggests, Foster writes about Australia with a lucid affinity. Among his many skills, he is a gifted naturalist.

I felt humiliated that I knew so little of the bush I grew
up in and liked to spend so much time in. I'd done a
couple of years of botany, and I more or less had to start
a field herbarium. I really liked botany. It's one of the
less egotistical fields.

Foster is a wiry, weathered, piratical figure who once bemused an academic conference by delivering a large part of his address in Latin. He can be a mesmerising performer. When giving a reading he usually wears the bush working uniform of boots, moleskins and blue singlet, and while he recites he rolls a cigarette with one hand. At the 1996 Adelaide Festival he recited from memory an unbroken passage from his *The Ballad of Erinungarah* for forty minutes. He's memorised the entire 200 stanzas.

While red and black cicadas
Add their stridulating song
To the ceaseless play of rapid spray
Could human voices sing so strong?
Can human voices sing as long?
Why should the glade within the grove
Yield to a city paved with gold?

His vantage point on the world is an old stone cottage in Bundanoon with views of the escarpments and gorges of the Blue Mountains. It is the area where Foster was born, where he has lived for more than twenty years, and where he worked as a postie. He writes in a little studio behind his home. Two certificates on his wall say he holds advanced black belts in martial arts. 'Tae kwon do, hard style,' he says. 'Don't worry about that. To a certain extent I don't like to be presented as a martial artist. I did it because it went against the grain.'

Outside his studio window is an enormous eucalypt. 'That's a big ribbon gum. It's one of the reasons we like the place. It's a big fella. We white people have always been uncomfortable with the eucalypt. They are an extraordinary species, and the more you learn about them the more they take your breath away. Especially as they are evolving enormously while most other species are disappearing.'

I prefer to be alone and I believe a white man can be more alone in the Blue Mountains than almost anyplace, because we European settlers don't as yet have eucalypt dreaming. I have oak dreaming. A spell of walking in Ireland left me in no doubt of it.

'Most of us have no idea what we are looking at when we go out into the bush. It's a tremendously varied landscape here. We never had an ice-age to wipe out botanical species as they did in Europe. And there is a tremendous number of species in Australia, even given the rates of extinction. It doesn't reveal itself in a walk-through once a month.'

The dingoes are still out there. Two days back I disturbed
five dingoes as I drove at dawn in my Landrover down
the old Oberon Colong stock route. Big red handsome
dingoes, within a hundred kilometres of Sydney's CBD.

'My first wife's an anthropologist. My son went through
early phases of initiation into an Aboriginal people, one of
the few full-blood whites ever to have done so. It was
because he was very gifted with the language, and a good
dancer, and a good kind of boy. It's a great place for young
boys, an Aboriginal camp. Not so good for grown men.'

Much of Foster's life—his experiences visiting his Aboriginal family in the Top End, his spiritual life as a martial
artist, and his work in the prawning industry—coalesces in
one of his finest novels, *Mates of Mars*, in which Foster, typically, never lapses into sentimentality or cheap second-hand
moral superiority:

Cyril and the boys had a country once, but that country
is dead and all the best wishes of well-intentioned folk
from Glebe to Carlton will not revive it. And let these
folk live and work with Cyril and the boys for a while,
and see how red their necks get.

'A lot of sentimentality obscures the issues. It's an intractable
problem. The issue of colonised peoples. It won't go away.
There's a conviction in our society that every problem has a
solution, but certain problems don't have solutions. Problems
that arise between colonisers and colonised, problems that
arise between men and women. There are certain intractables.

A proper intelligence recognises that and uses those tensions in their art or in their thinking. The notion that all problems can be removed is not even intellectual.'

All eyes are on Cyril that evening when a young lubra collapses, drunk, next to the bowsers at the service station opposite the pub.

Cyril doesn't look as though he cares as much as his white colleagues, and why should he? He has nothing to do with these Arunta. He inhabits the richest part of the continent; they inhabit one of the poorest. He doesn't speak the same language as the men, doesn't sing the same songs, doesn't dance the same dances. Only a white man would put them on the same committee.

'When you actually look, as distinct from fantasise, you realise that the health problems that so concern us among the blacks are really not of overwhelming concern to them. They are very tough hunter people. Injuries and wounds are something they don't take a great deal of notice of. With all the consequences. They die younger, they get sick, they get injuries, they live in a state of chronic ill-ease. But being healthy and living for a long time is not their goal in life. In that they distinguish themselves from whites ... They are very different to us. Plus we're talking about a culture that has been assaulted and brutalised and really hardly exists any more, except in people's memories. We idealise it.'

Opposite, a young woman, kicking and screaming, is being dragged by her hair from one camp to another.

*The young men pulling her are swigging at a 2-litre
moselle bottle, which is hot stuff and banned.*

*'I can only apologise,' says Jade to Cyril, 'for what we
have done to your people. I think it's absolutely scan-
dalous that they have been introduced to alcohol.'*

   *'Ah,' Cyril replies, 'reckon dey gotta make up dere
own minds dere. Same as de rest of us.'*

'I find it difficult to feel an overwhelming sense of guilt or
an overwhelming sense of violation about the Aboriginal
issue. Many of them went into the stations—they weren't
rounded up with stockwhips—because they liked flour and
sugar and wanted to avail themselves of some of the advantages of white civilisation. And that's where the problems
began. It wasn't only a matter of forcing our civilisation upon
them. They changed. There is not one of them who wants to
hand in his semiautomatic, I imagine. Things like guns and
beer are nonnegotiable attributes of modern civilisation
which they are not prepared to now do without.

   'The big problem for me as a scientist is the word "Aboriginal". What does it mean? Most of the people who call
themselves Aboriginal have not been initiated. They don't
speak for the cultural elders. People assume they understand
Aboriginal issues, but once they get among real experiences,
this quickly cures them of their misconceptions ... Genital
mutilation is basically the system of Aboriginal initiation.
They first circumcise the penis. Some tribes also then subin-
cise the penis. They open the penis up to the urethra ...

   'I don't know why they are as they are. Those tribes are

very different to us. But if someone is not circumcised in a traditional ceremony, are they an Aboriginal? Nobody has a definition. Is it culture? Is it blood? Are my black grandsons Aboriginals? What does that make me? What is my son, an initiated man? I've got white grandsons and black grandsons.'

> *If we define an Aboriginal Australian as a person of unmixed Aboriginal descent, no longer living the traditional nomadic lifestyle but residing in a settlement of some sort, retaining traditional language and culture, then such Australians, most to the north of the continent, are held in widespread awe today. There exists towards them, from white country and city both, an unstinting affection ...*
>
> *But towards the mixed blood Aboriginal there is not much goodwill. Their proclivity for white vice, in the boredom of their chronic unemployment, has also worn the patience of their black kinsmen, many of whom disown them utterly as non-initiated yellow trade-offs. Their seemingly intractable behaviour evokes the wringing of distant white hands, while whites obliged to contend with them daily have a battle on their hands, quite literally ...*

In an opinion piece published soon after he won the Miles Franklin Award, Foster suggested that the classification of race in Australia, with people claiming to be Aboriginal with just the barest mix of indigenous blood—hence the explosion of 'Aboriginal' numbers in Australia in recent decades—was exactly the wrong way to go.

> *A first step toward reconciliation would be to show some of that generosity our indigenous peoples have tradition- ally shown towards peoples of mixed blood by accepting such mixed blood people as our own. Let us throw this whole business out of reverse gear. Let us regard any person born in Australia as Australian, pure and simple, excepting only those who are initiated and retain a tribal culture.*
>
> *By this definition my full-blood white elder son, an initiated man, is Aboriginal, and my three coffee- coloured mixed-blood grandsons, who go to school in Darwin, Australians, nothing more. Just Australians, albeit Top Enders with a skin better suited to the climate than most of us. In fairness, I ought to add my son sees himself as white and his boys as Aboriginal. I think he's wrong.*

For his frankness Foster was given a head-kicking by the Thought Police in Sydney. But he had raised a fundamental issue. The number of indigenous Australians is exploding. The 1996 census shows that 352 970 people (1.9 percent of the population) described themselves as indigenous, an increase of 87 599, or thirty-three percent since 1991. The key factor in this surge in numbers, which itself is surely a clear sign of surging indigenous pride and strength, was inter- marriage with whites. In contrast with the United States, where the intermarriage rate between blacks and whites is between ten and twelve percent, the intermarriage rate between indigenous Australians and whites is forty-seven percent. Because one Aboriginal parent is enough for someone to claim Aboriginal identity, this accelerates the growth in numbers. The reality of race in Australia, and it is a healthy reality, is that a majority of the 352 970 indigenous population are actually mixed-race Australians. The overwhelming majority of indigenous Australians receive government benefits. Thirty-nine percent of the adult population are long-term unemployed; another thirty-eight percent are recipients of indigenous employment schemes or Community Development Employment Projects. Almost all receive free tertiary education at all levels if they want it, but only seven percent finish Year 12.

Forty percent of indigenous Australians now live in the big cities, and the growing stream of mixed-race Australians claiming indigenous status—and indigenous rights—is causing problems described bluntly by the black activist and author Roberta Sykes.

> *The black community does have a problem ... just thinking about coping with a flood of white-looking and totally deculturated people poised to demand Aboriginal rights for themselves.*

David Foster, whose life is touched by these complex currents, is as unflinching about the strengths of Aboriginal civilisation as he is about the weaknesses. He regards the spiritual links that many Aboriginal peoples have with their country as the single greatest absence in Australia's dominant white civilisation. 'They have a spiritual connection with the landscape and their totem animals, so death is no big deal to them. That gives them their strength.

'We whites are settled pastoralists and we need a different dreaming. To me, the Irish landscape is a white dreaming landscape because there are myths around every pass, every valley, every rock. There was still an immense amount of wilderness in Ireland in St Patrick's day. The whole island was a wood of cecile oak with hardly a town or village ... White Australians haven't really bothered to know their own landscape sufficiently. I feel we walk in landscapes that have no resonance for us. We know nothing about them scientifically and they have no mythic meaning to us ...

'How long will we be the dominant force on this continent? Our record here is undistinguished and may be short-lived. I see Australia as a potential tragedy because it's a civilisation that has gone into premature decline.'

With his family spread to the Top End, to the Gulf, to Perth and to Sydney, Foster has travelled through the back country of Australia and found the most dangerous erosion of all, the widening divide between city and country. 'I found country people are outraged at how they are portrayed and treated in the city. It all began with the gun laws after the Port Arthur massacre, when country people perceived they were all portrayed as rednecks with rifles. It has just gotten worse since then. City people forget that country people are very hard up. And it's easy to mouth platitudes when you are not hard up against it in places like Bourke and Moree. The people in the bush now know they've got no back-up in the city.'

*It is unfair to expect rural whites to bear the full burden
of reconciliation. In the edicts of affirmative action and
restitutions from the High Court, rural white Australia,
prostrated by drought, abandoned by bankers, commodity
prices falling, sees only sanctimony from white lawyers
who've never had to face the problems they address.
Coming fast on the heels of a gun law that tells us we
cannot be trusted with our firearms, this, for many, is the
last straw.*

'The gun law quickly became a struggle between country
versus cities. It is so deeply offensive to country people. And
frankly, if you're going to disarm all the warriors, humiliate
them, you're going to disenfranchise that warrior spirit that is
required in times of trouble …

'All our current problems stem from overpopulation, and
no-one knows how to cope with it. Too much. Too many. Of
everything. We have exceeded the limits of a viable society
… Early in this century Australia was one of the most
promising of all civilisations—very democratic, very egalitarian, but also with a fierce racism that became
unacceptable. We had a very strong intellectual tradition.
Australia and New Zealand were among the first centres of
Western civilisation in the modern era. Geoffrey Blainey
called Sydney and Melbourne the first high-leisure Western
cities. I think a lot of that early advantage has been lost.

'Australia needs a stronger sense of its own identity. A
stronger faith in its own judgement. A willingness to mix
it with the neighbours. A spiritual dimension is crucial.

Spiritual hunger is a feature of the modern world and it's usually resolved in escapist activities. Drugs, more than anything else. Drugs are taking sacraments for gods you don't know the names of.

'Australians are becoming soft. Soft-minded. Soft people are usually knocked over by hard people. And they never thought it could come.'

15
A GRAND AND POWERFUL COUNTRY

IN 1911, ONE OF AUSTRALIA'S most highly regarded geographers, Griffith Taylor of Sydney University, predicted that by the year 2000 Australia might support a population of nineteen million people. The prediction ruined his career.

It was viewed as preposterous, even insulting, in a country that most people believed would become a second America. The harsh environment proved Griffin Taylor right, but his remarkable prescience—in the year 2000 Australia's population will be nineteen million—remained largely forgotten until the arrival of Tim Flannery, another environmental pessimist. Unlike Taylor, Flannery's pessimism was greeted by tremendous commercial and critical success when he published *The Future Eaters*, eighty-three years later in 1994.

Flannery quotes the great Charles Darwin who, after a visit to Australia in 1836, predicted with characteristic acuity that Australia's fragile environment would ultimately constrain the nation.

I formerly imagined that Australia would rise to be as grand and powerful a country as North America, but now it appears to me that such future grandeur is rather problematical.

One hundred and fifty years later, Flannery said the same thing for exactly the same reasons: Australia must give up its century-long delusion of becoming a large population country.

> *'We don't know what the real sustainable carrying capacity of this country is. When I wrote that it may only be twelve million people, it was an intellectually honest attempt to estimate the country's real capacity. Even with all of the benefits of irrigation and technology, our agriculture is at the mercy of the cycle that drives Australia's strange climate, the El Nino Southern Oscillation (ENSO), which brings cycles of drought, fire and flood. The critical difference between an Australian winter and a European winter is predictability. European farmers know almost exactly how long winter will last.'*

Flannery's estimate of twelve million people as Australia's sustainable carrying capacity seems absurdly low. Neither the CSIRO or the Australian Conservation Foundation come even close to agreeing with Flannery. They both put a figure of around twenty-three million, by which time Australia may no longer have a surplus of grain production, as the benchmark for imposing population limits.

Flannery, like Griffith Taylor, is a serious scholar not a green fanatic (well, maybe a bit fanatical). Even if he is wrong about the carrying capacity of Australia, he serves as a highly useful counterpoint to the ideology of unlimited growth. Griffith Taylor never backed away from his prediction, despite the ridicule heaped upon him, nor does Flannery. 'There is so much new science since then which supports the arguments in the book, and more is coming out all the time.'

Flannery has Taylor's capacity for stirring up trouble in the most gentlemanly way. At school, he was suspended twice, both times over a moral principle with the abortion debate then raging in Melbourne. 'I had a very unhappy education at St Bede's College, Melbourne. It was such an intellectually closed environment.' He qualified for every university, despite the convulsions at St Bede's, and he noticed an item in the *Catholic Advocate* which referred to Chisholm College at La Trobe University in Melbourne as a 'hellhole of sinners'. That was just the place for young Tim Flannery. 'I thought it sounded great.'

More than twenty years later, as principal research scientist at the Australian Museum in Sydney, he has warned in *The Future Eaters* that Australia is already overpopulated and eating its own future through sheer ignorance. Yet despite this urgent environmental pessimism, Flannery finds plenty to be hopeful about.

> *I find it fascinating to see the growing awareness about Australia's environment and its history. People are opening their eyes. They are going back to original documents that have been ignored. Watkin Tench is an example of someone who provides us with a superb original source.*

A GRAND AND POWERFUL COUNTRY

Captain Watkin Tench was an English officer who arrived in Australia with the First Fleet in 1788 and wrote two superb but largely forgotten eyewitness accounts of the first settlement, particularly the first interactions between the Europeans and the Aborigines. 'Watkin Tench challenges the negative myths that have grown up about Australia, especially about the relationship between the early white settlers and the Aborigines.'

Tench was the key witness of that crucial moment in Australian history when the two civilisations met as equals, with neither dependent on the other. 'It's a first-hand account of the origins of modern Australia. And it's a well-written account.' Tench writes at the outset of his first book, which generated tremendous interest in England when it was published in 1789: 'I have been careful to repress that spirit of exaggeration which is almost ever the effect of novelty on ignorance.' Flannery writes in the introduction of *1788*, the highly successful reissue of Tench's works:

Tench's evolving view of the Aborigines is of enduring interest. It is typical of the way humans react to new and different cultures. At first fearful, perhaps even contemptuous of these 'fickle, jealous, wavering' people, Tench gradually came to know them. When he left Sydney in 1791, he also left friends behind ...

[Tench] places in sharp focus just how distasteful the Aborigines found the English class system, a structure in which even fully initiated Aboriginal men were systematically relegated to the bottom of the social ladder. They

would simply not tolerate being treated so. Instead, they
laughed at and mocked the Europeans for their clumsi-
ness and stupidity in the bush. When the exhausted
Europeans (who in any case were carrying the supplies
of the Aborigines) showed ill-humour at this, the Aborig-
ines promptly called them gonin-patta—shit-eaters.

Flannery revels in what he calls 'unfashionable' history. He
has little regard for postmodernism. He does not think much
of the multicultural industry either. 'I hate tribalism in any
form.' He does not believe in the new academic vogue that
Australia is a postgenocidal society that must forever apologise for its existence. 'I think genocide is the wrong word.
Disease and social dislocation were more decisive than delib-
erate extermination.' While not trivialising the privations
visited upon the Aboriginal peoples, a subject about which he
feels deeply, he believes much contemporary Australian history is fixated on the cruelty directed toward Aborigines
while minimising the attempts to form bonds with them and
improve their conditions, however misguided, by the European settlers. The observations of Watkin Tench capture the
ultimate decency of the first settlers in regard to Aborigines
before the two civilisations were in a state of virtual war. Two
centuries later, some of the observations Watkin Tench made
in that first year of contact remain startlingly relevant:

With the natives we are hand in glove. They throng the
camp every day, and sometimes by their clamour and
importunity for bread and meat (of which they now eat

greedily) are become very troublesome. God knows, we have little enough for ourselves!

During the intervals of duty our greatest source of entertainment now lay in cultivating the acquaintance of our new friends, the natives ... [but] inexplicable contradictions arose to bewilder our researches which no ingenuity could unravel.

They walked stoutly, appeared but little fatigued, and maintained their spirits admirably, laughing to excess when any of us either tripped or stumbled. At a very short distance from Rose Hill, we found that they were in a country unknown to them, so that the farther they went the more dependent on us they became, being absolute strangers inland.

During this trial of their patience and courtesy ... they had manifested no ungenerous sign of taking advantage of the helplessness and dependence of our situation; no rude curiosity to pry into the packages with which they were entrusted ... let him whose travels have lain among polished nations produce me a brighter example of disinterested urbanity than was shown by these denizens of a barbarous clime.

I do not hesitate to declare that the natives of New South Wales possess a considerable portion of that acumen, that sharpness of intellect, which bespeaks genius.

But indeed the women are in all respects treated with

*savage barbarity. Condemned not only to carry the
children but all other burdens, they meet in return for
submission only with blows, kicks, and every other mark
of brutality. When an Indian is provoked by a woman, he
either spears her or knocks her down on the spot ...*

*It must nevertheless be confessed that the women often
artfully study to irritate and inflame the passions of the
men, although sensible that the consequences will alight
on themselves.*

Flannery agitated talk-back radio hosts and stimulated the letters pages of newspapers when he suggested that Sydney's
proper name was really 'Weerong' from an Aboriginal name
for Sydney Cove. The ridicule (the 'Weerong 2000
Olympics') was instant. His remarks were interpreted,
wrongly, as new age revisionism gone mad. What Flannery
was actually saying was not that we should rename Sydney,
but that we need a greater awareness of the city's underlying
history and environment. He had merely suggested the placing of some plaques around the city. 'We have to
fundamentally rethink the old ideas about the environment
that came from Europe. These old ideas are just not going to
serve us well in the long term.'

With a degree in English, a master's degree in geology, a
doctorate in zoology, and a high level of computer literacy,
Flannery has an exceptionally broad scholarly perch from
which he continues to stir the cultural pot. He remains a
senior scientist at the Australian Museum. He continues to
write books. He is on the advisory panel to the Minister for

Immigration—Flannery thinks Australia's high immigration intakes are crazy—and in 1998 he became visiting Professor of Australian Studies at Harvard University. When the *New York Times* reviewed *The Future Eaters*, Professor Paul Rabinow wrote: 'Mr Flannery tells an epic story with a sure-handed, personally implicated perspective … He tells a wondrous story of extinction, dwarfing, fire … ' *The Future Eaters* may be a wondrous story, but it is, above all, a warning, and Tim Flannery has declined to modify his warning in a time of material abundance.

> *The deception experienced by each wave of human immigrants into the 'new' lands is one of the great constants of the human experience in the region. To the earliest Aborigines, it must have seemed as if the herds of diprotodons stretched on forever. To the Maori, the moa must have appeared a limitless resource. European agriculturalists saw what they imagined were endless expanses of agricultural land. Early Chinese immigrants to Australia saw* san gum shaan *(new gold mountain), and now each new immigrant sees an opportunity to prosper in the land of plenty. In short, they have all seen cornucopia where there is very little …*
>
> *Yet these unoccupied spaces and apparent opportunities in fact represent something very different, for they are necessary accommodations in a hard land. For the Aborigines, it meant foregoing agriculture and hence leaving a very different mark on the land. For the Australians of European origin, it has meant leaving the*

centre and north largely empty and the creation of vast
national parks on what appears to be useable land. It
has meant the imposition of what are—by European stan-
dards—extraordinarily low stocking rates on rangelands.

These necessary accommodations have created a
sense of paranoia in living Australians. Perhaps because
of their own recent use of the concept of terra nullus,
many fear that people from Asia will perceive in Aus-
tralia, if not an empty land, then an under-utilised one.

Since the publication of *The Future Eaters*, the accumulation
of evidence by many other scientists confirms the need for
alarm and urgency. Among the most conspicuous of these
scientists is Doug Cocks, Senior Principal Research Scientist
with the CSIRO's Division of Wildlife and Ecology, who has
delivered sardonic assessments of Australia's ongoing degradation in two books, *Use With Care* (1992) and *People Policy*
(1996). Using extensive satellite mapping and an abundance
of geographic data, Cocks describes a continent with a thin
skin of soil, the most basic of all natural resources, which is
getting thinner all the time. He tells a story of erosion, salin-
isation and acidification. Less than ten percent of the
continent has rich productive soil. Even areas of deep soils
and good rainfall have poor tree growth because of nutrient
deficiencies. Pressures which drive artesian water to the surface are declining in large areas. In the Great Artesian Basin,
water has to be pumped up another half metre each year.
Imported weeds—thorny mesquite, rubber vine, bitou bush,
lantana, blackberries, bracken—have collectively wiped out

enormous amounts of native biota. The march of the cane toad is wiping out still more. Among Cocks's many diagnoses, warnings and recommendations, there is one subject that gets him agitated:

> *Australia must adopt a 'no immigration' policy. It is the one topic in this book on which I am prepared to take an unequivocal stand ... the economic argument for substantial immigration is in tatters.*

His agitation on this subject had not subsided by 1996 and the publication of *People Policy*:

> *It would not be difficult to assemble a long list of failures and embarrassments in the formulation and administration of Australian immigration policy going back to 1925 ... More recently, there have been significant failures ... the failure of the 'skills' program to deliver appropriately skilled people, the 'rorting' of the business migration scheme, increasing numbers of overstayers ...*

He lists the large number of constituencies which have self-interest in high immigration policies, which, collectively, explain the powerful forces behind large-scale immigration in Australia.

> *1. Migrant organisations.*
> *2. Migrant-dependent bureaucrats.*
> *3. Migrant-dependent entrepreneurs.*
> *4. Minority-group expansionists.*
> *5. Growth-oriented state governments.*

6. *Growth-oriented federal politicians.*
7. *Economic libertarians.*
8. *Open-door humanitarians.*
9. *The building industry.*
10. *Minority-dependent academics.*

Aligned against this battery of interests, writes Cocks, are several groups that want a reduction in immigration:

1. *Environmentalists.*
2. *The unemployed.*
3. *Aborigines.*
4. *Cultural protectionists.*
5. *Racists.*
6. *Off-shore humanitarians. (More foreign aid, not more refugees.)*

Obviously the high immigration groups have more economic firepower than the low immigration groups. The environmentalists provide the bulk of the counterbalance to the continued supremacy of high immigration.

Doug Cocks, Tim Flannery and most of the environmentalists who have appeared in this book believe Australia should stabilise its population immediately. Cocks advocates annual net migration of between zero and 50 000 people, which he says would produce a stable population of between twenty and twenty-three million by 2045. Growth of per capita national wealth and productivity would continue with minimal population increases. If Australia underestimates its carrying-capacity, it leaves future generations with freedom of choice to expand. Cocks describes most agricultural practices as the 'slow mining' of the soil.

More recent studies have shown that the 'slow mining' of Australia's soil resources is ongoing. Australian farmers are still clearing nearly 500 000 hectares of land every year. Professor Wayne Meyer of Charles Sturt University and the CSIRO warns: 'The day is fast approaching when we cannot afford to irrigate pastures to produce meat and wool because water will have become too expensive.' About seventy-five percent of Australia's water is consumed by agriculture and the rising cost of water is a hidden cost in food. He cites as an example the need for 730 litres of water to produce one kilogram of dry wheat.

When I asked Tim Flannery whether all these problems (most of which are still below the horizon of public concern) would preclude Australia from becoming an eco-superpower, he replied: 'No, providing we stop the policy of growth for the sake of growth. The high unemployment numbers show we already have a large surplus of workers.'

Flannery does not regard himself as a doomsayer, or a defeatist.

Australians have been shaped in a profound way, and in a positive way, by their environment. We are so fortunate that the Australian environment, through its poverty, has forced upon us an ethos of social obligation, of mateship. Australian mateship is a realisation that we either stand together in this environment or fall alone.

16
GREEN THUNDER

HIGH UNEMPLOYMENT IS KILLING young people. Research by people like Stephen Murrell at Sydney University shows a deep and abiding link between the rate of unemployment among young Australians and the rate of suicide.

The national unemployment rate passed through the 8 percent plateau in the 1980s and has stayed there for more than a decade now. It is roughly 30 percent higher than the unemployment rate in the United Kingdom—not long ago described as the Sick Man of Western Europe—more than 40 percent higher than the New Zealand rate, and about 60 percent higher than in the United States. Obviously, Australia needs a sense of national urgency and purpose about creating jobs and improving economic sovereignty.

Australia has one of the largest current account deficits in the developed world. The problem is not trade. Australia is performing well in trade and services. The problem is the drain of dividends and debt to foreign owners.

- Ninety percent of Australia's high current account deficit consists of interest payments and dividends to foreign owners.

- Australian assets owned by foreign entities total more than $300 billion, equivalent to sixty percent of Australia's total GNP.

- In the late 1990s, Australian overseas investments were bringing in around nineteen billion dollars a year, while foreign investments in Australia were taking out around thirty-nine billion dollars a year in dividends and interest payments. That twenty billion dollars deficit in investment income was bigger than the current account deficit. In other words, it *is* the current account deficit.

- The Foreign Investment Review Board, which has only minute investigative resources, receives about 4000 applications for foreign ownership of properties and businesses each year and about ninety-eight percent of applications are approved.

- Australia is one of the world's major food producers, but eighty percent of its food manufacturing industry is foreign controlled.

Among the issues facing Australia are structural unemployment; high youth suicide; drug abuse environmental degradation, and declining economic sovereignty. As Australians cast around for ways of tackling these problems there is a scheme which, at least potentially, could strike a blow at all of them. In January 1997 the Australian government allocated 41.6 million dollars to the Australian Trust for Conservation Volunteers to employ 440 young people aged between seventeen and twenty to help in the preservation and regeneration of the Australian environment. The program was to expand to employ 1700 people in the second year.

The idea was so unambiguously attractive that its only flaw was its size. It wasn't big enough. The Green Corps could be exponentially more ambitious. Obviously it would be exponentially more costly, but the cost of expanding the scheme would be an investment, not an expenditure. There are also ways the Green Corps can help pay for itself in the national accounts, especially as a form of foreign aid.

The Green Corps is not just another unemployment scheme. It is an overdue attempt to link two huge problems— the erosion of the physical environment, and the erosion of employment opportunities for young Australians. The old job-creating tools don't work as well any more. Technocrats and politicians would adjust the macroeconomic dials, cut interest rates, target waste, cut debt. But this has lost some of its job-creating impact. Advanced economies have seen a historic decoupling of economic growth and job-growth. Companies are expanding while shedding workers. Reinventing, reengineering, downsizing, outsourcing—all these buzzwords mean more efficiency, but they also mean that governments have to work harder to create work.

The Green Corps seeks to tap into the deep reservoir of commitment felt by the majority of young Australians to the cause of environmentalism. The urgent national issue of soil erosion and conservation, outlined by the CSIRO's Doug Cocks in the previous chapter, is one that the Green Corps could target. It could also help Australia project green power into its hemisphere. It could give Australians experience of the lives and cultures of our neighbours in the South-West Pacific and South-East Asia, the two areas where Australia must concentrate all of its foreign aid. Commitment to the environment would be a critical element in the selection process for applicants to the corps. Green Corps graduates would be expected to leave the program with training in skills ranging from bush regeneration techniques to habitat protection and environmental management. There is also the immeasurable benefit of the work done—thousands of small projects—and the work experience.

In its first year of operation, the Green Corps members worked on conserving vegetation along transport corridors, especially around conspicuous assets such as Sydney Harbour; on restoring habitats; creating sanctuaries, especially for endangered species; rehabilitating coastlands, wetlands, mangrove stands and coastal lakes. Green Corps members began work preparing Sydney for the 2000 Olympics. They were clearing and planting along the harbour foreshore, and along major transport corridors. A lot of Green Corps work is grinding, dirty, monotonous manual labour. It is not highly paid. In the first year, corps members were paid a training allowance of between $149 and $246 a week, depending on levels of schooling and time since leaving school.

But the work has a higher purpose and it is no more monotonous than many jobs. And if a tour of duty on the Green Corps is successful, its participants will graduate with a deeper knowledge of Australia and its soul, a sense of teamwork and camaraderie beyond the school environment. Those who are good enough and interested enough would then be ready for the next stage: duty on foreign aid. At the time of writing, Australia was spending 1.4 billion dollars a year on foreign aid, or just 0.29 percent of gross domestic product. The developed world average is 0.41 percent.

This is not exactly the behaviour of an eco-superpower. If Australia wanted to project its values, create jobs, help its poorer neighbours, build a multitude of personal links with South-East Asia and the South Pacific, and attack pollution and erosion problems that ignore national boundaries, we could not possibly make a better investment than expanding the Green Corps to regional aid. The single most potentially useful and practical government job-creating and value-creating project for young Australians seems to be the Green Corps. A commitment to a Green Corps employing and training thousands of young Australians on projects throughout Australia and its region would cost more than the 1.4 billion dollars in foreign aid budget but it would have a major impact on youth unemployment.

The Green Corps does need a budget blow-out.

(1) The Government has already set aside a one-billion-dollar environment fund from the sale of Telstra, part of which could be directed to the Green Corps.

(2) Part of the Green Corps's wage and training costs would be recycled as income taxes.

(3) Significant funding could come from within the existing foreign aid budget, substituting a portion of foreign aid with work and skills provided by Green Corps members, most of them trained professionals who would work on specific projects.

(4) Some of the ATSIC budget and work-for-the-dole funding for young Aborigines could be transferred to the Green Corps, which offers many possibilities for the indigenous population. Pilot programs involving young Aborigines working on conservation projects have already begun. Given the deep historic link between the indigenous peoples and the land, this would appear to be an obvious priority, though no doubt difficult to execute.

(5) Part of the Green Corps's work would be recycled as economic value as it slowed the process of soil and water degradation.

(6) The Public Service mentality of Australia's foreign aid, with its high overheads, needs to be replaced with an ethos of dynamic modesty. Economics writer Paul Cleary had first-hand experience of the need for change when he lived and worked in the foreign aid industry.

On top of the First World salary, there were all the 'expatri-ate-conditions-apply' trappings that tend to come with jobs in developing countries where wages are low. These include the cook, maid, driver and even a doorman ... for the French colonial villa costing several thousands of dollars a month to rent and maintain for one [aid] representative ... And many people who work for these organisations hold a fairly predictable set of politically correct values. Theirs is a definite mindset. The staff regarded anyone involved in business as bad, bordering on evil, and most of them rarely socialised with the business types.

This mindset, this illiteracy about where the money ultimately comes from, would need to be addressed in the training of Green Corps foreign aid workers. Overheads need to be measured and reported as a percentage of all aid budgets. Australians could be delivering specific aid for specific programs under a variety of nonmonolithic schemes, both government and nongovernment. They could replicate the projects of the domestic Green Corps; providing family planning and health services (a nurse can do almost as much good as a doctor where hygiene is poor); upgrading and training in horticulture and agriculture; contributing to fisheries protection; training local administrators, all of which, supplemented by scholarships for foreign trainees, would provide jobs for Australians, protect, step by step, the regional environment, and project the values of environmentalism that Australia must champion.

Birth control and the education of women are two causes Australia should do more to champion. 'Australia cannot consider population issues and foreign aid issues which fail to consider the global status of women,' says Jim Downey, executive director of the Australian Conservation Foundation. 'Ninety percent of the world's projected population growth over the next thirty-five years will take place in the developing world where the status of women and their access to education and birth control is of grave concern.'

Australia's aid budget has traditionally been spent on bloc grants to governments and on big construction projects that help Australian companies move into Asia's infrastructure boom. That is logical. It would be better if we sent more people instead, Green Corps members who could manage small-scale projects on conservation, agriculture, education, birth-control. Australia should also concentrate solely on its area of influence in the South Pacific and South-East Asia, an area which covers a quarter of the globe.

Before Australia can champion ecological diplomacy in its region, we need to lift our own game at home. However, the environmental needs of Australia's regional neighbours are even more urgent than our own. The smoke haze over South-East Asia in 1997, and the thousands starving in Papua New Guinea, made that abundantly clear.

Why do so many Asian countries have such poor environmental records? ask international law experts, Daniel Esty and Andre Dua. Because of 'the pervasiveness of market failures—the ability of producers and consumers to spill harm onto others, and not have to pay for it.' They write:

> The trends in China, Indonesia and Thailand remain
> unmitigatedly negative. China, for instance, is now home
> to three of the seven most polluted cities in the world.
> Indonesia suffered a loss of forest cover of almost 110
> million hectares between 1981 and 1990. In Thailand,
> the percentage of the population with access to fresh
> drinking water has actually fallen as the country's rivers
> have become fouled with a ten-fold increase in industrial
> waste.

The news is also bad in Papua New Guinea, Malaysia, Burma and the island-states of the Pacific. The ability of the world to deal with the mess is itself a mess. As Esty and Dua explain:

> *The global environmental regime, comprising the United Nations Environment Program, the Commission on Sustainable Development, numerous treaties and their secretariats, and the environmental work of many other international organisations, is deeply flawed. Authority is fragmented. Coordination across organisations is poor. Political and financial backing for serious initiatives is limited.*

Instead of attempting to be a second-rank power at the United Nations and multilateral forums—a pocket Britain or America—Australia should concentrate its diplomatic and foreign aid resources on becoming a first-rank nation in environmental diplomacy, research and foreign aid. In other words, an eco-superpower.

Daniel Esty has a brilliant idea:

> *The proper response to this chaos in international environmental management would be the creation of a Global Environmental Organisation (GEO) to bring coherence and structure to the set of environmental activities undertaken at the worldwide scale.*

Why not? The World Trade Organisation (WTO) has grown out of the General Agreement of Tariffs and Trade (GATT), which itself grew out of the multilateralism of the United Nations, and reflects the force of economic globalisation and integration. But the environmental problems facing the world are just as irrepressible, and they, too, need the authority and clarity that come from a forceful and mature world umpire like the WTO. Daniel Esty and Andre Dua have no illusions about the difficulty of setting up anything like a GEO:

> *Creation of a GEO does not presently seem politically feasible ... [In Asia] Korea has gotten no satisfaction from China in response to its entreaties for reduced [acid rain]; regional fisheries continue to fall precipitously; disputes among China, Taiwan and Vietnam have prevented the successful conclusion of the Regional Seas Agreement for the South China Sea ...*
>
> *The difficulty of achieving successful collective action in response to worldwide environmental harms does not diminish their significance ...*

Australia should push for a GEO. The United Nations is based in the United States. The World Trade Organisation is based in Europe. A third arm of international diplomacy should be based in the Asia-Pacific, the region where so much economic growth, and so much environmental damage, is taking place. The headquarters could be Sydney, with its direct flights to the world, its superb infrastructure, and Australia's environmental leadership in the region. There are two reasons for hope. Daniel Esty and Andre Dua explain one of them:

> *One of the major results of economic integration is that policies previously considered to be within the sovereign*

authority of domestic officials, especially environmental standards, have come under increasing scrutiny ...

GEO needs a champion, and it would need a headquarters, supported by the local government. In the wired global marketplace, Australia is entirely suitable. Daniel Esty and Andre Dua, both realists, both pessimists, believe GEO has enormous potential:

In contrast to trade, spectacular results are, without a doubt, achievable in the environmental sphere.

17
NOMADS

THE BATTLEGROUNDS OF Mabo and Wik were shrewdly chosen. Of all the hundreds of sites on which to fight for native title, these two places were perfect. Eddie Mabo's land was on a remote island, a distinct physical entity, where indigenous people had been living and fishing for generations. The idea that this island was *terra nullius*, land belonging to no-one, was indefensible.

Wik, too, was a careful choice. The leaseholdings in dispute had largely fallen into disuse for many years. There were no boundary fences, no buildings. The only cattle on one leasehold were feral cattle. Few leaseholdings in Australia could be more tenuous, a fact emphatically pointed out by the High Court's most indefatigable expansionist, Justice Michael Kirby:

> *The picture painted of the two leasehold properties ...*
> *is somewhat bleak. Each of them, in remote parts of*
> *Northern Queensland, offered to the lessee rudimentary*
> *and apparently unpromising conditions ... So unpromis-*
> *ing was the first Mitchelton lease that it endured for only*
> *three years and was forfeited for non-payment of rent.*
> *The second lease lasted an even shorter period before it*

was surrendered ... Members of the Thayorre continued living on the land in their traditional way. They would have no reason even to be aware of the grant of any pastoral lease over the land ... it would require very strong legal doctrine to deprive them of their native title.

The position of the Holroyd River Holding is not so extreme a case ... In such a large remote terrain, for most of the year, the Wik could go about their lives with virtually no contact with the lessee or the tiny number of stockmen, wood gatherers and occasional inspectors who entered their domain ...

To the contesting respondents, these facts are irrelevant ... The issue to be resolved was one of legal theory.

True. Australia at the end of the twentieth century is divided more by principles and theories than by anything else. The debate over these principles and theories has become so furious, so tilted with unchecked racial rhetoric, that it is taking the nation to the brink of genuine division and therefore to the brink of genuine cultural decline.

The Wik judgement, in so far as it applies to the specific circumstances before the court, was a victory for common sense and natural justice. The success of the Wik and Thayorre people hurt no-one. The dispute gave rights to real people—Chocolate Thomas, Sheba Dignari, Button Jones, Dodger Carlton, Paddy Carlton, Ben Ward and many others—in favour of absentee leaseholders with nothing at stake. The judgement protected access to land used by local indigenous people for many generations, at virtually no cost to anyone else.

Of course, the Wik judgement also opened the gates to a flood of litigation elsewhere. The most extreme result is in Western Australia, where Russell Lockyear's Mindara Station is facing fourteen separate native title claims in the wake of Wik. Another West Australian property, Barrie Sullivan's Melita Station, had eleven claims pending at the time of publication.

It is easy to forget amid the rhetoric and complexity surrounding Wik that the Australian people have the wealth and the means and the collective desire to restore the land, wherever possible, of indigenous people who have been deprived of their traditional land and the remnants of their traditional way of life. Indeed, a large proportion of traditional indigenous communities already have legal title to their own land. The area now held by traditional communities is larger than the combined size of the United Kingdom, France, Italy and Greece. It may mostly be arid land, but it is priceless to those who live on it. The federal Government's Indigenous Land Fund is being built up to 1.3 billion dollars to allow for the spending of up to 45 million dollars a year, in perpetuity, to purchase and manage land for indigenous communities. The process of completing this repatriation will take time and patience and bruise many participants but the resources and the goodwill are there despite the overheated rhetoric.

No clearer symbol of the broad goodwill most Australians have toward reconciliation is the changing attitude toward the ultimate national symbol, the flag. On Australia Day 1997, a nationwide McNair opinion poll asked Australians if they would support using elements of the Aboriginal flag as part of the design for a new Australian flag. The result was a surprise. (It was certainly a surprise to me, and I had commissioned the poll for the *Sydney Morning Herald* and written the questions). Fully sixty-six percent said they would consider such a move, 'if a suitable design for a new Australian flag were found' (this phrase had not been used in polling before and made a big difference). The level of recognition of the Aboriginal flag was universal: ninety-nine percent.

This open-mindedness about the flag and what it should symbolise became even more apparent on Australia Day 1998, when Ausflag, the private group which had long been trying to generate momentum for a new national flag, unveiled the hundred finalists in a national competition held among professional designers for a new flag. More than 2 500 entries were received and the overall quality was much higher than in two previous national competitions open to the public. This time the *Sydney Morning Herald* decided to reproduce all one-hundred new finalists, together with the Aboriginal and Australian flags and invited readers to vote for their preference through a phone poll. The paper also published the Internet address of Ausflag so people could examine the new designs.

Frankly, none of the new flag designs were strong enough to win majority support at a national referendum on the flag. The national blue ensign remains safe. However, we were not prepared for the response to our phone poll. Some 22 200 calls were registered in forty-eight hours, by far the biggest response to any opinion poll the newspaper had ever conducted. More than a hundred letters also arrived. In the week after publication of the Ausflag Internet address, more than 100 000 people visited the site. The phone poll was repeated by other newspapers and the results were similar.

What stood out was the public's open-mindedness about the national flag. Forty percent of the new Ausflag designs contained elements of indigenous culture. A clear majority of the 22 200 in our poll voted for flags with an element of indigenous culture. 'We've never had a response even remotely like this before,' the executive director of Ausflag, Harold Scruby, told me. 'I think the biggest change is the mood of reconciliation in the nation.' This was certainly true of the schools which contacted us.

Almost simultaneously, the Constitutional Convention in Canberra was taking place in an atmosphere of reasoned argument, logical debate, bipartisanship and an overall tone of good humour. Intelligent Australians of widely differing views conducted a dialogue about the soul of the nation and its democratic traditions. The Convention, which had seemed a recipe for inertia when it was announced by Prime Minister Howard, turned out to be a good idea. It clarified the difficulties of change but made clear the nation's mood for change. It set the stage for the one thing on which the majority of Australians appeared to agree—removing the legal fiction of the British monarch as Australian head of state.

Changes in the symbolism of the nation had become part of the political oxygen.

The other major cultural sea-change as the nation headed toward the year 2000 was a palpable awareness of indigenous culture. This was the cultural backdrop of the Wik debate. The goodwill was there. But there were enduring problems that mocked the sweet rhetoric of reconciliation. For a start, there was the Native Title Act itself, a bill whose many problems were set out by the former Chief Justice of the High Court, Sir Harry Gibbs, in a speech on Australia Day 1998:

'No-one of goodwill doubts that it is necessary to act justly to the Aboriginal people, as to all Australians, but one difficulty [with] reconciliation is that, in many instances, demands are not based on merit but simply on race.'

The former Chief Justice recognised the dangerous legal apartheid in the claim that the race power within section 51 of the Australian Constitution can be exercised only to enact laws which are beneficial to the Aboriginal peoples.

I cannot understand, how any political party which hopes to form a government could support such an inter-pretation ... [It] would have the result that a law which had mistakenly conferred an inappropriate benefit on the Aboriginal people ... could never be repealed.

He then listed other problems with the Native Title Act:

The 'right to negotiate', upon which the supporters of the Aboriginal cause place so much value is, of course, not a traditional right ...

> *Aboriginal claimants need not prove the existence of any*
> *interest before requiring negotiation, and need not have*
> *had any physical connection with the land in question ...*
>   *It is argued that the pastoralist has no problem, since*
> *the High Court has said his or her rights prevail if there*
> *is a conflict with native title. The problem is no-one*
> *knows what the rights of the pastoral lessee are until the*
> *Court has declared them.*
>   *It is also said that the Aboriginal people want nothing*
> *more than the right to go on their traditional lands for*
> *the purposes of hunting, gathering and visiting sacred*
> *sights. In fact, some want money, and a lot of it.*
>   *It is a defect in the law that the question who is an*
> *Aboriginal is undefined.*

In summary, Sir Harry asked:

> *It may be too much to hope that the public in general,*
> *and the media in particular, will accept that Aboriginals,*
> *who undoubtedly have special needs, should have those*
> *needs met simply because they are Australians. The two*
> *sections of society cannot be reconciled ... when one of*
> *those sections demands a special place and special privi-*
> *leges unrelated to need.*

Every problem that Sir Harry Gibbs foresaw has come to
pass. A mountain of overlapping, competing and dubious
native title claims, as well as simple and legitimate claims,
confront the holders of rural leaseholds across Australia. 'The
recent High Court's judgements make very clear,' wrote Bill

Hayden in 1997, 'that every case has to be considered separately and from a fresh start. This overall process will be extraordinarily complex and time-consuming and could go on exhaustively and without conclusion through the lifetime of generations of Australians ... Australia would have to be a very rich country to bear calmly the obvious large direct costs, as well as the substantial indirect costs, of projects which falter, even fail, because of [native title] objections.'

Mabo and Wik stand out like beacons of simplicity compared with many of these claims. 'There are now more than seven-hundred native title claims on pastoral leases in Australia and many of them are ambit claims, or overlapping claims,' Wendy Craik, Executive Director of the National Farmers Federation, told me in 1998. Almost identical words were used in a confidential ATSIC briefing paper written in February 1998 which not surprisingly, was not released to the press. 'All native title litigants are claiming an exclusive traditional connection with the land,' said Dr Craik.

A lot of pastoralists are despondent. Our members have been aghast when confronted with the paperwork. Some claims demand the right to 'possession, occupation, use and enjoyment of the claimed land and waters to the exclusion of all others' or to 'exclude strangers from the land' or to 'live on and erect residences and other infrastructures on the land'. Many of the farm families who have enjoyed private, voluntary agreements over access with Aboriginal people have received claims which demand much more than the right to hunt, fish and carry on traditional ceremonies.

It was always going to be a painful process. Australia is now sifting through the history of dispossession and dislocation. The process is made more complex by the ambiguous circumstances in which so many indigenous people left the land. Many indigenous groups have revived land claims despite a long absence from the land, and many of these absences occurred when clans left to follow an easier life around the pastoralists. The arrival of the European pastoralists created not merely, in the famous words of A.W. Howitt, a 'line of blood' in Australian history, but also a cultural revolution. Among innumerable examples that challenge the rhetoric of cultural annihilation and dispossession, the pathfinding anthropologist, T.G.H. Strehlow, a man fluent in the Aranda language and passionate in the indigenous cause, saw lands denuded of indigenous peoples for reasons that had nothing to do with dispossession:

> ... the Pitjantjatjara communities of the Petermann
> Ranges, whose lands I found almost completely deserted
> on my two visits of 1936 and 1939, despite the fact that
> their homeland had not been invaded by white settlers
> nor ravaged by police parties. They had merely 'drifted
> out' into areas of adjacent tribes, where white people
> had set up stations or settlements ... None of these
> drifters ever returned to their old homelands.

For all the political discussion of recent years about indigenous rights, the standards of health care and life expectancy among the indigenous peoples went nowhere during Labor's thirteen years in federal power even though Labor's heart was in the right place. Rates of imprisonment among Aborigines actually increased. In New South Wales, the Aboriginal proportion of the prison population rose from 5.8 percent in 1982 (the year before Labor came to power in Canberra), to 12.4 percent in 1996 (the year Labor lost power in Canberra). This increase partly reflected the growing lawlessness in New South Wales towns and the heroin trade in Sydney's Aboriginal communities.

The distinguished American scholar, James Q. Wilson, has noted that the advent in western society of genuine distaste for racism has not been matched by a significant improvement in community trust between blacks and whites:

> *If racist thinking has declined, why are relations between the races so bad? Why do so many whites who cannot be called racists in any fair meaning of the word so often treat blacks warily?*
>
> *Fear. Whites are afraid of young black males. It is not racism that keeps whites from exploring black neighborhoods, it is fear. It is not racism that makes whites uneasy about blacks moving into their neighborhoods, it is fear. It is not racism that leads white parents to pull their children out of schools with many black students, it is fear. Fear of crime, or drugs, of gangs, of violence ... Fear can produce behaviour that is indistinguishable from racism.*

Substitute the word 'Aboriginal' for 'black' and you have exactly the same problem in Australia. The state of life in country towns such as Moree, Bourke, Walgett, Brewarrina and Wilcannia is a state of permanent bubbling tension marked by stone-throwing, pub brawls, break-ins, bag-snatching, rapes, assaults, racist insults and intermittent riots.

On Australia Day 1998 the Premier of New South Wales, Bob Carr, announced he would visit the western town of Walgett in the wake of a riot in which shops were smashed and looted, the TAB robbed, and police showered with bottles and rocks by a crowd of Aborigines, many of them drunk. That same day, in Sydney's Redfern, a crowd of more than two-hundred Aborigines pelted police with rocks and bottles in Eveleigh Street after six police had sought to make an arrest. The previous week, in the New South Wales town of Moree, a general meeting was held after people were stabbed in two separate armed hold-ups. A month before that, an Aboriginal pub mob rioted in another western town, Bourke. And so it goes, a problem getting worse not better, as Aboriginal rights grow stronger.

The simmering problems at the grassroots are fanned from the top. Indigenous leaders maintain a drumbeat of comments about 'racists' and 'rednecks'. Aboriginal leader Noel Pearson described the Howard Government as 'racist scum' because it did not agree with him on Wik.

The Aboriginal legal activist Paul Coe was disbarred from legal practice on 3 July 1997 after the New South Wales Legal Services Tribunal found him to be, 'not a fit and proper person to remain on the roll of legal practitioners'. The finding was the latest and most fateful episode in twenty years of accusations and controversy. A few minutes after the judgement was handed down, Coe spoke to reporters on the steps of the court: 'It confirms my view that it is still a white man's world.' Asked what skin colour had to do with this case he simply repeated, 'It's a white man's world.'

Charles Perkins told Olympian Cathy Freeman she had 'symbolically turned her back on Aborigines' when she did not carry an Aboriginal flag during a lap of honour at the Atlanta Olympics even though such actions are expressly banned at the Olympics.

Mick Dodson used the Human Rights and Equal Opportunity Commission as a blunt political instrument and a platform for his high-octane blame-throwing. His influence is evident on the Commission's 1997 Report, *Bringing Them Home—Report of the National Inquiry into the Separation of Aboriginal and Torres Strait Islander Children from Their Families.*

Bringing Them Home is an important document. Australia must confront the mistakes of its past, not bury them. The heartache caused to thousands of Aboriginal families by the removal of children into foster homes is something Australians should acknowledge, not deny. That this was widely understood in the community was reflected in *Bringing Them Home* becoming a best-seller.

However, under the influence of Mick Dodson, the Report was also used to make the claim, the very grave accusation, that the treatment of Aboriginal children constituted 'genocide'.

Dodson received plenty of support from the news media, which did not blink at the obvious dubiousness of the accusation of 'genocide'. In the hands of the media, the Report mutated into the 'stolen' children. And even though the Australian *Year Book* showed that only ten percent of Aborigines had been taken away from their families, the media was uniformly enthusiastic in promoting the impression that entire generations of children were forcibly taken away.

Hundreds of thousands of words were written about *Bringing Them Home* and almost none of them were critical even though there was much to critically scrutinise. The role of the churches, for example, including the past behaviour of the President of the Human Rights and Equal Opportunity Commission himself, Sir Ronald Wilson, were fertile grounds for inquiry. But not a single critical inquiry was made. It was left to Dr Ron Brunton, an anthropologist, business consultant and former academic, to go where no journalist dared go.

In February 1998, the Institute of Public Affairs in Melbourne published Brunton's 16 000-word response to *Bringing Them Home*. Entitled *Betraying The Victims*, it was absolutely fearless.

Because *Bringing Them Home* received such an abundance of uncritical scrutiny in the media and because the same reporters and editors who devoted so much space to 'Stolen Children' showed a spectacular lack of interest in Ron Brunton's report, I will quote the main points of his critique:

> • Bringing Them Home *is a tendentious document [that] misrepresents a number of its sources and ignores crucial information, and readily makes major assertions*

which are either factually wrong or unsupported by appropriate evidence ...

• *Only nineteen of the individual witness accounts or their accompanying commentary provide any hint of the reason that was offered for their separation from their families ... [Yet] it is fair to state that the report attempts to give the impression that the bases for removal were nearly always unjustified.*

• *Many non-Aboriginal children who became wards of the state also had appalling experiences. From the late nineteenth century until the mid-1960s thousands of British children were sent to Australia and Canada ... and many of these children had families who had not consented to their migration.*

• *The most egregious aspect of the Inquiry is its 'finding' that the forcible removal policy constituted 'genocide' and 'a crime against humanity'.*

• *... the objective of assimilation is quite central to the 'genocide' argument in the report. Indeed, Mick Dodson, one of the two Commissioners with primary responsibility for the Inquiry, was specifically quoted as stating that 'assimilation is genocide' at a time when the Inquiry was still in progress ...*

• *Assimilation policies directed at indigenous or tribal people were strongly promoted by international bodies at least until the 1960s.*

• *Acknowledgement that major—and radical—Aboriginal leaders were publicly arguing for absorption ... would put a rather different perspective on many of the*

*claims and arguments in the report ... it would seem the
authors simply chose to omit such potentially damaging
information.*

Ron Brunton also makes two points about the then Chairman
of the Human Rights Commission, former high court judge
Sir Ronald Wilson. First, even though the churches were
prime agents in the removal of children, they receive only
light criticism in the report. Second, when Sir Ronald was a
Moderator of Assembly in the Presbyterian Church in Western Australia, he sat on the board of Sister Kate's home for
Aboriginal children and thereby played a role in the removal
of children from their families and communities.

*During the course of the Inquiry, [Sir Ronald] apolo-
gised ... He has also been quoted as stating 'I had no
knowledge of the wrongness of the practice', a remarkable admission given that he now claims that the
practice constituted 'genocide', which is generally seen
as the ultimate crime against humanity.*

Finally, Brunton makes the point that the unchallenged accusation of genocide has quickly metastasised into the
academic mainstream.

*Already it has become part of the conventional wisdom
of many academics who are blithely speaking of 'the cultural and biological genocidal policies of the stolen
generation years' ... These assessments will quickly find
their way into the texts which are used to give young
Australians their understanding of the past and they are*

*also likely to be thrown back in Australia's face when
complaints are made about human rights abuses in other
countries.*

It has already happened. Within a year of the publication of
Bringing Them Home, Amnesty International issued a report
critical of the government's response to the inquiry. Readers
may remember our punctilious European friend from the
opening chapter, Heinz Schurmann-Zeggel, the official from
Amnesty International who condemned the Warlpiri people
for imposing violent tribal law.

Now Schurmann-Zeggel is opining that the Australian
Government has failed to adequately respond to several
issues, and would also like to see the Government make a
formal apology. Mr Schurmann-Zeggel's unsolicited advice
is no less irritating in this final chapter than it was in the first.

As for apologies, we note that when the Canadian government made a formal apology to Canada's indigenous peoples
in 1997 it was thrown back in the Government's face. Sir
Harry Gibbs, the former Chief Justice, expresses an opinion
about apologies that is sharply at odds with his former
brother judge, Sir Ronald Wilson.

'It seems to be the fashion to demand apologies for
iniquities long past,' Sir Harry said in 1998. 'It is almost
beyond belief that the question whether the Prime Minister
should apologise for policies which neither his government
nor its predecessors instituted or had constitutional power
to prevent, should be a serious political issue ... surely the
discussion of this matter shows a lack of proportion.'

Lack of proportion? Sir Harry should know that the politicians who helped drive the Labor Government's race-based agenda—Nick Bolkus, Laurie Brereton, Gareth Evans, Simon Crean, Daryl Melham (with his references to 'white sheets' and 'burning crosses')—are, together with some indigenous leaders like Mick Dodson and Noel Pearson and their allies in the news media, at the centre of the so-called 'race election' in 1998 based on the Wik decision.

Despite the danger, despite the damage, Bolkus, Brereton, Crean, Melham, Dodson and Pearson are going to play, yet again, the race card.

And just in case the nation hadn't got the message, Gareth Evans, Deputy Opposition Leader, pronounced at the front door of Parliament House in Canberra on 2 April 1998: 'This bloke [Prime Minister Howard] seems to be never so happy as when he's bashing blackfellas.'

Nothing has changed.

The determination with which these men were prepared to put this nation on the rack of a race election, depict any reform as discriminatory, and raise the stakes to a destructive pitch, were exposed by Father Frank Brennan, Jesuit priest, son of Justice Brennan of the High Court (himself the author of the key opinion in the Mabo judgement), passionate and influential advocate of the indigenous peoples, and critic of the Howard Government. But Father Frank Brennan drew the line at Labor's Wik race strategy. In a letter written on 5 March 1998 to a Melbourne QC, he wrote:

As a Catholic priest involved in this issue, I have always

tried to be attentive to the conflicting claims of miners,
pastoralists and Aborigines, and to enunciate a decent
moral bottom line within the prevailing political context.
I have always regarded working relations with the Gov-
ernment of the day, whatever its political hue, as
essential in the political process ... For the ALP, which
coined the phrase 'unrepresentative swill', to craft 350
amendments to a bill and later inform its national con-
ference that, in government, it would call all parties to
the table (not having done so before presenting 350
amendments) is to strain the credibility of anyone com-
mitted to real legislative outcomes ...'

Father Brennan then reiterated his belief that the determination of Labor to make any Wik legislation subservient to
the Racial Discrimination Act was a prescription for chaos.

Labor's willingness to throw the race card does not sit well
with Bill Hayden, the former Governor-General and leader of
the Labor Party (and former holder of the seat of Oxley now
held by Pauline Hanson). Hayden now spends his time asking
the big questions that his own party prefers to avoid:

Why was Pauline Hanson so strong? Why did her issues
take off? Because people are sick and tired of being
screeched at by certain groups. Robert Tickner [a former
federal Minister for Aboriginal Affairs who lost his seat
in the 1996 election] was a classic case. He would say
'Racist, racist,' screaming it all over the ABC. So people
were not saying anything publicly but they were saying
a lot privately. And the tragedy of all this is that

Aboriginal policy can be set back enormously because of the way it has been run for so long.'

In Aboriginal welfare, there is a very serious alcohol problem, but if you raise it, there are well-meaning, fashionable, small-l liberals and lefties who will say, 'This is all exaggerated.' It is not. I have been in so many Aboriginal communities on what they call 'pay day', when the social security money comes in, and it's pretty awful. You don't want to hang around there for long. People say, 'There has been all this expenditure on health. Why hasn't is improved?' A lot if it [is self-inflicted] ... We need to be able to discuss these things without being accused of being racist. But a lot of the Aboriginal leaders, like Mick Dodson, I suspect, feel that once they allow that discussion to take place they will lose control of the direction of policy.

Many of the problems in Aboriginal Australia are the direct result of past mistakes by the dominant white culture. But many of the ongoing problems, notably the stark disparities in life expectancy and general health, reflect a chasm in value systems, a primal disparity between a hunter-gatherer civilisation and a mercantile-pastoral-industrial culture. The story told in the opening chapter of this book about Stephen Barnes Jungarrayi, the man who went back to his community to endure brutal traditional 'payback' tribal punishment, expressed the unease with which these differing universes co-exist.

The complexity of this uneasy coexistence and the need

for indigenous solutions to indigenous problems is largely ignored by those who portray all these problems as the result of white subjugation. In the words of Professor Kenneth Maddock, quoted earlier, we are witnessing 'the politics of embarrassment. The aim is to soften up your opponents by making them feel bad about themselves or their ancestors.' The 2000 Olympics in Sydney will be treated as the perfect platform for internationalising the politics of embarrassment.

All the strains caused by the strident politics of race and identity, the wear and tear of high and inefficient immigration, the toll of environmental stress, the hard-eyed efficiencies of economic rationalism and free trade, have exacted a toll on this prosperous nation. A 1996–1997 survey by the CSIRO found that the average Australian was five times wealthier at the end of the twentieth century than at the beginning of the century, but noted that material wealth was no longer enough to measure the progress and mental well-being of a nation:

> Material progress now presents developed nations with
> diminishing benefits and escalating costs. It appears to
> be becoming increasingly irrelevant, even hostile, to
> wellbeing and quality of life through the impacts on both
> the natural environment ... and social structures.

The nation that arduously won the 2000 Olympics must now endure those who will use this world event to pursue their domestic political agendas, including accusations of racism and genocide, ignoring the reality of Australia's fundamental tolerance. If those who are agitating are true to their word, when the world's news media descend on Sydney in 2000 to dispense instant analysis of contemporary Australia, the media will be fed an image of a racist nation. Australians will have to work hard not to allow this to happen. A successful Olympics would be the best way. We have already seen that Australia can be an eco-super-power; and Australia will likely play the role of sporting superpower in 2000. It is amazing what a nation can achieve when the people commit their hearts and minds to a national effort.

Sport is not a trivial subject. It is an arena which almost all the world takes seriously. It is the most important single form of cultural expression in the global marketplace. It matters more to more people than any other form of culture. Billions of dollars are spent in the cause of national pride on the sporting fields. It is the global surrogate for war and personal combat. And it is certainly not a trivial subject to many of Australia's Aborigines.

Anyone who doubts the potency of sport and sporting symbolism in the life of a nation need only remember the sight of Cathy Freeman, carrying the Australian flags in her moment of international glory at the 1996 Olympics and the Aboriginal and Australian flags after her victory in the 1997 World Championships, and the catharsis and joy these sights gave the nation. Freeman's reaction to those who called on her to boycott the 2000 Olympics and 'to stand and mourn with us' is instructive. She said she had not devoted her life to achieving international success so she could become a tool for moral blackmail.

The 1996 Olympics in Atlanta proved, once again, that Australians' passion for sport has made the nation a world sporting power, holding a position of prominence that most nations would like to achieve and few have attained. More than a hundred nations sent teams to the 1996 Olympics, and seventy-nine of them won medals. Thirteen nations reached the plateau of twenty medals. Only five reached the plateau of forty medals. One of them was Australia.

When the relative size of nations is taken into account, Australia becomes the singular performer of the 1996 Olympics. Not only did Australian men and women win forty-one medals but they won across a remarkable range of sports—fourteen—a breadth exceeded only by the United States. Above the plateau that defines a major Olympic nation—thirty medals would seem a reasonable benchmark—Australia's performance, in per capita terms, was dominant. Measured in medals (weighted for gold, silver and bronze performances) per million population, this is how the top nations performed:

1 Australia 3.78
2 Germany 1.46
3 France 1.27
4 Italy 1.22
5 Russia 0.92
6 United States 0.82
7 China 0.09

It was the perfect springboard for the 2000 Olympics where Australia would have the largest team, the home ground advantage and home waters. These advantages are tempered by the dangers of unrealistic expectations, excessive jingoism and political propaganda stunts.

The most spectacular difference between the staging of these Games and the 1956 Olympics in Melbourne will be the role of Australia's indigenous culture. Anyone perusing the newspaper clippings of 1956 would be struck by the invisibility of Aborigines, even in any token role in the Olympics. The opening ceremony was dominated by the presence of His Royal Highness the Duke of Edinburgh, who opened the games, and by the Russian team, which caused a stir during the ceremonial march into the Melbourne Cricket Ground when it failed to salute the royal box. 'REDS REFUSE SALUTE' said one headline.

Less than fifty years later, a white Australian Olympics is unthinkable. Indigenous cultural symbolism has become central to Australian cultural symbolism.

The world will come to a land of nomads, a rich mixture of characters, bush people who lived off the land, wanderers who traveled across the world, sojourners, immigrants, adventurers, a nation open to the world, a curious amalgam, a success. It is a nation where, when the Olympics first came in 1956, the athletes were encouraged to break from their national teams and mingle during the closing ceremony, a show of mass egalitarianism and informality that has endured ever since.

AFTERWORD
A DANCE WITH THE
THOUGHT POLICE

A POLITICAL BUREAUCRACY CAN work in subtle ways. In 1996, the Human Rights and Equal Opportunity Commission received a complaint about me from the editor of the *Chinese Post*, a small Chinese-language newspaper in Sydney. The editor of the newspaper, an immigrant from China, did not inform me he had complained to the Commission. I found out by accident when a Commission staffer let it slip during conversation.

The editor's complaint said that a front-page story I had written would cause:

(1) Severe and possibly irreversible damages to the group-image of the whole Chinese Communities.

(2) Cause the Australian general public to ferment and form an attitude and feeling of hostility, discrimination, or even hatred against the Chinese community.

(3) Instigating tensions and conflicts within the Chinese Community against Australian Society.

He wanted a front-page retraction by the newspaper and legal action by the Commission.

AMONG THE BARBARIANS

The story had been published in the *Sydney Morning Herald* on 1 July 1996 under the headline: FEDERAL LAWS BLAMED FOR SYDNEY'S WELFARE GHETTOS. Prior to publication, it had been read back to the source at Monash University. The Monash academics blanched at the use of the word 'ghetto', preferring the euphemism 'enclave', but journalism is antagonistic toward academic euphemisms. This is the story:

> *Racial ghettos are forming in Sydney as a result of federal government policies.*
>
> *Unpublished data from the Department of Social Security reveals the formation of ethnic enclaves marked by very high unemployment, welfare dependency and welfare abuse—the classic warning signals of ghetto-formation.*
>
> *One of the highest and largest concentrations of welfare dependency in the country is among Vietnamese-born immigrants in Fairfield, says Ernest Healy, who surveyed the data and published his findings in the latest issue of People and Place, the journal of the Centre for Population and Urban Research at Monash University.*
>
> *Other high concentrations of single-group welfare recipients in the city were found in Blacktown, Bankstown, Canterbury and Campbelltown.*
>
> *The ethnic concentrations in these enclaves are mainly Vietnamese, Lebanese, Turkish and Yugoslav-born populations, with the Vietnamese forming by far the largest single cluster.*

The Social Security data shows that just under 40 percent of all Vietnamese living in New South Wales are concentrated within a few postcodes in and around Fairfield, especially 2166 in Cabramatta.

The concentration of chronic welfare recipients in this small area is even higher—nearly half (47 percent) of all unemployed Vietnamese in the State are clustered in and around postcode 2166. Nearly two-thirds of these are long-term unemployed.

Not only are these figures very high, they are also bogus. The real unemployment rate among Vietnamese is much lower. This has been an open secret in Sydney for years, and it is acknowledged by Ernest Healy in his study:

> *'An exploitative informal labour market based on the clothing industry, and related to social security fraud, has assumed major proportions.'*

A Herald *source within the Department of Social Security says there is a culture of widespread welfare abuse within sections of the Vietnamese and Chinese communities.*

'About 90 per cent of the people I see are not entitled to the benefits they are claiming,' said the source, who added that the Vietnamese were not the worst abusers of the system: 'The most cynical groups are from the PRC, the People's Republic of China, [the so-called Bob Hawke special immigrants].'

... Healy's study found that among settler arrivals in

1994 who intended to work, the percentages still receiv-
ing unemployment benefits as of August 1995 were very
high among some immigrant groups:

Russians (62 percent unemployed), Lebanese (56),
Vietnamese (54) and Chinese, not including Taiwan (47).
In contrast, the figure for Hong Kong was 4.1 percent,
and for South Africa, 2.9 percent.

In lodging a complaint of racial discrimination, what the editor may or may not have told the Human Rights and Equal Opportunity Commission is that he had a vested economic interest in the matters broached by the story. The *Chinese Post* is a newspaper whose primary market is the so-called Bob Hawke special immigrants from the People's Republic of China. Front-page stories published in the *Post* at the time the complaint was being lodged included, '*The Howard government has been in office six months and new immigrants face fierce attacks,*' and, '*Ruddock guarantees that students whose 816 applications were refused will no longer be sought by the immigration department.*'

The response of the Commission was interesting, especially as its senior officials had already expressed irritation at 'The multicultural myth', published several months earlier. Nothing was ever heard from the Commission, but not long after the complaint from the *Chinese Post,* the 'ghetto' story was included in a media handbook compiled by the Commission.

Without ever checking with the *Herald* about the accuracy of the story, or informing the *Herald* that it had received a complaint, the Commission determined that the piece was inaccurate and, by clear implication, racist. It was included prominently in a handbook on the Racial Hatred Act to be distributed to news media and journalism faculties throughout Australia as an example of how *not* to write a news story. The chapter began:

> *Partly due to their necessarily reductionist nature, news stories created from reports on complex research findings, surveys and polls are often inaccurate and misleading. In many cases misinterpretations may be the inadvertent result of carelessness or deadline pressures, but there are clearly instances where journalists have deliberately misinterpreted and manipulated reports to reflect their own opinion and agenda.*

Exhibit number one was the *Herald*'s front-page 'ghetto' story. It was placed next to another story, from the *Illawarra Mercury*, which began: 'Claims that "ethnic ghettos" similar to those in American cities were springing up in Sydney and Melbourne were inaccurate and irresponsible, the *Vietnamese Herald* newspaper editor said yesterday.' Even though the factual accuracy of the *Herald* story had never been challenged, it was used as an example of a story that was 'reductionist', 'inaccurate', 'misleading', 'careless', 'manipulated' and 'irresponsible'.

This is how the Thought Police work.

The Human Rights and Equal Opportunity Commission, together with its allies in the State Ethnic Affairs Commissions, State Ethnic Community Councils and State anti-discrimination tribunals, are now armed with the broad and amorphous weapons of the Racial Hatred Act and various anti-discrimination statutes. These laws give power to control or sanction what people say by legal action, legal threat or professional rebuke. As part of this broad trend to constrain freedom of speech, the Human Rights and Equal Opportunity Commission seeks to be a media judge and jury, a role for which it is ill-equipped. The Commission even dispenses annual media awards.

The historian and columnist Gerard Henderson attended the Commission's annual awards ceremony on 10 December 1997, and described a luncheon event which lasted long into the afternoon punctuated by speeches which he found to be, 'self-congratulatory and self-righteous self-indulgence'.

> *This year's highlight occurred when a somewhat long winded Avril Henry presented the awards in the corporate division. To the astonishment of some, she proceeded to bag what she called 'corporate Australia' for its alleged indifference to 'sexual harassment, gender discrimination and racial discrimination'.*
>
> *Much of corporate Australia was at work, rather than at lunch, so it missed Henry's overstated missive. Nevertheless, her outspokenness was not lost on those representatives from corporate Australia which had financially supported the 1997 HEROC awards.*

Self-congratulatory. Self-righteous. Self-indulgent. Back

in the chapter of this book called 'The Billion Dollar Bluff', there is a scene where lawyers from the Commission give a briefing on the Racial Hatred Act at the Ethnic Community Council of New South Wales. The meeting led to a chorus of censorious outrage from activists who made it clear they wanted the law changed so that Pauline Hanson—and therefore many others—could be jailed for their beliefs.

A telling moment at that meeting came after I identified myself and asked the three visiting lawyers how the Commission handled malicious complaints and vexatious litigants.

There was a brief pause, a silent stutter.

The concept of a malicious, mischievous or gratuitous accusation, or a vexatious litigant, is not of top priority at the Human Rights and Equal Opportunity Commission. In a culture concerned with victimisation, all accused are guilty until proven innocent. And this is despite the obvious potential for misuse, and the obvious power of the mere accusation of racism or discrimination.

After considering the question for a moment, one of the lawyers pointed out that the vast majority of cases are mediated or dropped, and only a small percentage are litigated. The other lawyers nodded in agreement.

So what? Every year, hundreds of Australians receive letters from government bureaucracies or corporations informing them they have been accused of discrimination or, worse, racism and need to explain themselves. This is a powerful ideological weapon. Given the wide definition of discrimination used by some of the people quoted in this book, the possibility for misuse of this power is overwhelmingly obvious.

Fortunately, before the Human Rights and Equal Opportunity Commission could smear me as a racist, it was obliged under copyright law to ask the *Sydney Morning Herald* for permission to run the 'ghetto' article. At this point the *Herald*'s lawyers saw a copy of the proposed handbook. They were appalled. However, rather than withdraw the piece, I negotiated—mediated, as the Commission would say—and wrote an explanation to accompany the story of why I had used the word 'ghetto'. I also got the Commission to soften, but not remove, the insulting language at the beginning of the case study. But most people don't work for large media companies with their own defamation lawyers. They don't have much leverage.

More than a year after the offending 'ghetto' article appeared, the award-winning journalist Craig McGregor, author of *Class in Australia*, wrote a feature published on 13 October 1997 entitled 'The new ghettos of Sydney' about the growing divides in Australian society:

Ghettos? In Sydney? Aren't they a phenomenon of American cities? Answer: Sydney, which is now well on the way to becoming a global city, is also developing one of the most brutal characteristics of the planet's First World metropolises. It is developing ghettos.

Not just racial ghettos, either. Ghettos of poverty, unemployment, violence, social distress and

*desolation which are only too familiar in Los Angeles
and in Brasilia, but which the Australian Dream always
thought it could avoid. And, worst of all, there is now a
permanent underclass which is being concreted into
these ghettos from generation to generation.*

*If you redefine the term 'ghetto' a little, Sydney
also has developed—ahead of all other Australian
cities—ghettos of wealth and privilege which are
visibly transforming themselves into American-style
redoubts ...*

*Some of the contrasts are stark: reliance on the maxi-
mum rate of Family Payment ranges from 60 per cent in
Auburn to zero in leafy, waterfront Pittwater, on the Palm
Beach peninsula ...*

*This is brave new Australia, in the era of globalisation
and post-modern capitalism. While some surf the new
technowealth, others end up in social compounds where
a culture of poverty, joblessness and low expectation
means people are trapped there for generations. If this
isn't a ghetto, what is?*

Soon after, the Centre for Population and Urban Research at
Monash University released hundreds of pages of detailed
census analysis which showed, in unambiguous detail,
concentrations of ethnic clusters around Sydney, many
of them low-income and high-welfare. Unlike previous classic patterns in the immigrant stream, where initial
concentration is followed by dispersal, these concentrations
were hardening over time.

As for my own 'ghetto' story, yes, there was a problem. It contained no mention of the heroin trade, or gangs, or extortion, or rampant crime—all classic ingredients in ghetto formation—all of which exist in abundance in some urban clusters around the country. I had censored myself. It is the only thing I regret.

The immigration scholar, John Atchison, is one of the many people who sees the most insidious problem coming not from the xenophobes and racists in society, who have a voice but little real power, but from those censorious forces who seek to control the debate and have considerable power. Atchison wrote in 1997:

> *One of the most disturbing features of the so-called and inaccurately described Blainey debate was the associated latent fascism in the labeling of opponents as racists.*

The problem of ideological orthodoxies imposed through the agencies of the bureaucracies and the legal system was foreshadowed with remarkable clarity more than a 150 years ago, in Alexis de Tocqueville's *Democracy in America*, one of history's most enduring works of social insight. He believed that once a democratic society had been built, the greatest threat to individual freedom was the insidious dominance of the state:

> *Government extends its embrace to include the whole of society. It covers the whole of social life with a*

network of petty, complicated rules that are both minute
and uniform, through which even men [and women]
of the greatest originality and the most vigorous
temperament cannot force their heads above the
crowd. It does not break men's will, but softens,
bends, and guides it; it seldom enjoins, but often
inhibits action; it does not destroy anything, but
prevents much being born; it is not at all tyrannical,
but it hinders, restrains, enervates, stifles, and
stultifies ...

Of all the political problems facing Australia, the growing power to suppress and constrain freedom of expression is the most sinister. Given the tremendous achievements of Australia, it should be a time of national confidence, but it is not. Thirty years of poisoning of the nation's history has taken its toll. Many histories now parrot a hatred of Australia. The politically-motivated accusations of racism, made hollow by overuse, have been pumped up to include 'genocide' and 'holocaust'.

The mud has stuck. The nation's sense of certainty at the end of the century has been eroded by the politics of stealth and division. Australians are caught in a moment of collective hesitation, still exuberant, hedonistic, open-minded, successful, yet their everyday freedoms are being eroded behind the rhetoric of equity.

The real methods of political control have become subtle, evasive, sweetly ruthless, a billion-dollar lie, an inability to see that Australians have built a prototype for a new way in the twenty-first century, an eco-superpower and a culture that transcends tribalism.

SOURCES

THIS IS A BOOK OF reportage. It is a depiction of Australia at a moment in time. The primary sources were telephone and face-to-face interviews. These were supplemented by *Hansard*, court records, annual reports, scholarly papers, government reports, and newspaper articles.

Most direct quotations are from interviews with the author. Most sources are noted at the time they are quoted.

I am indebted to colleagues at John Fairfax, publishers of the *Sydney Morning Herald*, notably defamation lawyer, Mark Polden, economic writer Max Walsh, and librarians Helen Bayliss and Franca Bopf. Thanks to the Editor-in-Chief, John Alexander, for the time and space to write stories which later expanded into the chapters 'An Empire Of The Soul', 'White Dreaming', 'The Man Who Wasn't There', 'Strip Mining', 'The Vote Eaters' and 'A Grand and Powerful Country'.

Particular thanks go to Susan Wyndham.

Four scholars—Richard Basham, Tim Flannery, David Foster and Bob Birrell—contributed significantly to this book. Another scholar, Stephen J. Pyne is quoted through his book, *The Burning Bush*.

Sang Ye, journalist and oral historian, has made an important contribution to the understanding of Chinese immigrants to Australia and to this book.

David Reid, formerly of the Department of Social Security, stuck his neck out by agreeing to be interviewed. Given his new career as a school teacher and the ad hominem treatment meted out to critics of immigration rorts, I changed his second name.

William Whitworth, Editor of *The Atlantic Monthly*, and, in my opinion, the finest editor of his era, has provided many years of unobtrusive excellence, some of which has guided this book.

The following court judgements were used extensively:

Equal Opportunity Tribunal of New South Wales, *The Hellenic Council of NSW v The Macedonian Youth Association* (10/1995), Sydney, 1997.

High Court of Australia, *Mabo and others v State of Queensland* (FC 92/014), Canberra, 1992.

High Court of Australia, *The Wik Peoples and Thayorre People v the State of Queensland and others* (FC 96/044), Canberra, 1996.

Industrial Relations Court of Australia, *Battese and Election for Communication Workers Union (Postal and Telecom branch)* (169/96), Sydney, 1996.

Industrial Relations Court of Australia, *Cook v Australian Postal Corporation* (NI4428/1995), Sydney, 1997.

The following books all provided material for *Among The Barbarians*:

Atkinson, Alan, *The Europeans in Australia*, Volume One, Oxford University Press (Melbourne), 1997.

Barmé, Geremie, *In The Red: Chinese Contemporary Culture*, Columbia University Press (New York), 1998.

SOURCES

Bernstein, Richard and Munro, Ross, *The Coming Conflict With China*, Knopf (New York), 1997.

Birrell, Robert, *A Nation Of Our Own*, Longman (Sydney), 1995.

Browne, Janet, *Charles Darwin—Voyaging*, Random House (London), 1995; Pimlico, 1996.

Carew, Edna, *Paul Keating: Prime Minister*, Allen & Unwin (Sydney), 1992.

Caruana, Wally, *Aboriginal Art*, Thames and Hudson (London), 1993.

Cocks, Doug, *People Policy: Australia's Population Choices*, NSW Press (Sydney), 1996.

Cocks, Doug, *Use With Care*, University of NSW Press (Sydney), 1992.

Daws, Gavan, *Prisoners Of The Japanese*, William Morrow (New York), 1994.

Dodd, Helen, *Pauline: The Hanson Phenomenon*, Boolarong Press (Brisbane), 1997.

Fitzgerald, Stephen, *Is Australia An Asian Nation?*, Allen & Unwin (Sydney), 1997.

Fitzgerald, Tom, *Between Life and Economics*, [The 1990 ABC Boyer Lectures], ABC Books (Sydney), 1990.

Flannery, Tim, *The Future Eaters*, Reed Books (Melbourne), 1994; George Braziller (New York), 1995.

Foster and others, David, *Crossing The Blue Mountains*, Duffy & Snellgrove (Sydney), 1997.

Foster, David, *Mates of Mars*, Penguin, 1991; Vintage (Sydney), 1996.

Foster, David, *The Ballad of Erinungarah*, Vintage (Sydney), 1997.

321

Foster, David, *The Glade Within the Grove*, Random House (Sydney), 1996.

Frost, Alan, *Botany Bay Mirages: Illusions of Australia's Convict Beginnings*, Melbourne University Press (Melbourne), 1994.

Gammage, Bill, *The Broken Years,* ANU Press (Canberra), 1974; Penguin Books (Australia), 1975.

Gill, Alan, *Orphans of the Empire*, Millennium Books (Melbourne), 1997.

Grant (editor), Bligh, *Pauline Hanson—One Nation and Australian Politics*, University of New England Press (Armidale, NSW), 1997.

Grover, John, *The Struggle For Power*, E.J. Dwyer (Sydney), 1980.

Hanson, Pauline, *The Truth*, Pauline Hanson's One Nation (Adelaide), 1997.

Hayden, Bill, *Hayden*, Angus & Robertson/HaperCollins (Sydney), 1996.

Horne, Donald, *The Lucky Country,* Penguin Books (Melbourne), 1964.

Howitt, A.W., *The Native Tribes Of South-East Australia*, [first published 1904], Aboriginal Studies Press (Canberra), 1996.

Hughes, Robert, *The Culture of Complaint*, Oxford University Press (New York), 1993.

Hughes, Robert, *The Fatal Shore*, Knopf (New York), 1986.

Irving, Helen, *To Constitute A Nation*, Cambridge University Press (Melbourne), 1997.

Jacobs, Bruce and Yu, Ouyang (editors and translators), *Bitter Peaches and Plums: Two Chinese Novellas (My Fortune in Australia*, by Liu Guande, and *Australia—Beautiful Lies*, by Huangfu Jun), Monash Asia Institute (Melbourne), 1995.

SOURCES

Lingle, Christopher, *The Rise and Decline of the Asian Century*, Asia 2000 (Hong Kong), 1997.

Lines, William, *Taming The Great South Land: A History of the Conquest of Nature in Australia*, Allen & Unwin (Sydney), 1991.

Little, Reg and Reed, Warren, *The Tyranny Of Fortune*, Business & Professional Publishing (Sydney), 1997.

Murray, Les, *Subhuman Redneck Poems*, Random House, 1997.

Pyne, Stephen J., *The Burning Bush: A Fire History Of Australia*, Henry Holt (New York) 1991; Allen & Unwin (Sydney), 1992.

Reynolds, Henry, *Aboriginal Sovereignty*, Allen & Unwin (Sydney), 1996.

Reynolds, Henry, *Fate Of A Free People*, Penguin (Melbourne), 1995.

Samuelson, Robert, *The Good Life and Its Discontents* (The American Dream in the Age of Entitlement, 1945-1995), Times Books (New York), 1996.

Ye, Sang, *The Year The Dragon Came*, University of Queensland Press (Brisbane), 1996.

Schama, Simon, *Landscape And Memory*, Knopf (New York), 1995.

Seagrave, Sterling, *Lords Of The Rim*, Bantam (London), 1995; Corgi (London), 1996.

Shelton, Judy, *Money Meltdown: Restoring Order To The Global Currency System*, The Free Press (New York), 1994.

Sleeper, Jim, *Liberal Racism*, Viking (New York), 1997.

Spillman, Lyn, *Nation and Commemoration (Creating National Identities in the United States and Australia)*, Cambridge University Press (Cambridge), 1997.

Tench, Watkin, *1788*, [first published 1789, 1793], edited and introduced by Tim Flannery], Text Publishing (Melbourne), 1996.

de Tocqueville, Alexis, *Democracy In America*, [first published in this edition, 1848], Doubleday/Anchor (New York), 1983.

Vasta, Ellie and Castles, Stephen (editors), *The Teeth Are Smiling (The Persistence of Racism in Multicultural Australia)*, Allen & Unwin, 1996.

Viviani, Nancy, *The Indochinese in Australia, 1975-1995*, Oxford University Press (Melbourne), 1996.

Walsh, Peter, *Confessions Of a Failed Finance Minister*, Random House (Sydney), 1995.

White, Mary E., *Listen ... Our Land Is Crying*, Kangaroo Press (Sydney), 1997.

Wright, Alexis, *Grog War*, Magabala Books (Broome, WA), 1997.

The following reports, scholarly papers and journal articles were also used:

Amnesty International, *Australia—Silence on Human Rights: Government responds to 'Stolen Children' inquiry*, Amnesty International Secretariat (London), 1998.

Atchison, John, 'The Sad State of the Immigration Debate,' in *Pauline Hanson—One Nation and Australian Politics*, University of New England Press (Armidale, NSW), 1997.

Bureau Of Statistics, Australian, *Australian Agriculture and the Environment*, Report 4606.0 (Canberra), 1996.

Bureau Of Statistics, Australian, *Australian Social Trends, 1997*, Report 4102.0 (Canberra), 1997.

Bureau Of Statistics, Australian, *Labour Force—and The Youth*

Labour Market, Catalogue no. 6203.0 (Canberra), November 1997.

National Audit Office, Australian, *Follow-up Audit, Department of Immigration and Multicultural Affairs, 1997-98*, Canberra (1997).

Basham, Richard, *Australia and Asia: Race, Ethnicity and the Golden Triangle*, Graduation address, Bond University, June, 1997.

Birrell, Bob, Spouse Migration to Australia, *People and Place* (Monash/Swinburne), vol 3, no 1, 1995.

Birrell, Bob, Policy Implications of Recent Migration Patterns, *People and Place* (Monash/Swinburne), vol 3, no 4, 1995.

Birrell, Bob, Our Nation: The Vision and Practice of Multiculturalism Under Labor, *People and Place* (Monash/Swinburne), vol 4, no 1, 1996.

Brunton, Ron, *Betraying The Victims: The 'Stolen Generations' Report*, Institute for Public Affairs, February, 1998.

Downey, Jim, *Population Policy and Ecological Sustainability*, AESP national conference paper (Sydney), 1997.

Dua, Andre, and Esty, Daniel, *APEC and Sustainable Development*, Yale Center for Environmental Law and Policy (New Haven, CT), 1996.

Eckersley, Richard, *Perspectives on Progress: Is life getting better?*, CSIRO Resources Futures Program (Canberra), 1997.

Ethnic Affairs Commission of NSW, *Annual Report 1993-94*, (Sydney), 1994.

Ethnic Affairs Commission of NSW, *Annual Report 1994-95*, (Sydney), 1995.

Federal Bureau of Investigations, *Overview—Asian Criminal*

Enterprises in the United States, Department of Justice (Washington DC), 1993.

Fitzgerald Report, The, *Immigration, A Commitment to Australia*, Dr Stephen Fitzgerald (Chairman), Australian Government Publishing Service (Canberra), 1988.

Gibbs, Harry, Sir, *Australia Day Message 1998*, The Samuel Griffith Society, January, 1998.

Gruen, Fred, 'The Quality of Life and Economic Performance', in *Dialogues On Australia's Future*, Centre for Strategic Economic Studies (Melbourne), 1996.

Healy, Ernest, *Ethnic ALP Branches—The Balkanisation of Labor Revisited*, People and Place (Monash/Swinburne), vol 3, no 3, 1995.

Healy, Ernest, 'Welfare Benefits and Residential Concentrations Amongst Recently-Arrived Migrant Communities', *People and Place* (Monash/Swinburne), vol 4, no 2, 1996.

House of Representatives Standing Committee for Long Term Strategies, *Australia's Population Carrying Capacity: one nation—two ecologies*, Australian Government Publishing Service (Canberra), 1994.

Human Rights and Equal Opportunity Commission, *Bringing Them Home, Report of the National Inquiry into the Separation of Aboriginal and Torres Strait Islander Children from Their Families*, (Canberra), 1997.

Human Rights and Equal Opportunity Commission, *The Racial Hatred Act: A Guide for People Working in the Australian Media*, (Sydney), 1996.

Human Rights and Equal Opportunity Commission, *Annual Report 1995-96*, (Canberra), 1996.

SOURCES

Human Rights and Equal Opportunity Commission, *Annual Report 1994-95*, (Canberra), 1995.

Hunter, J.C. and Altman, B., Welfare Assistance and the Indigenous Labour Force: An Analysis, *People and Place* (Monash/Swinburne), vol 4, no 2, 1996.

Joint Standing Committee on Electoral Matters, *Report on the inquiry into the role of the Australian Electoral Commission in conducting industrial elections*, Parliament of Australia (Canberra), October, 1997.

Jones, Barry, *Political Challenges of Population Planning*, AESP National Conference Paper (Sydney), 1997.

Jones, Barry, *Australia's Population 'Carrying Capacity': One Nation—Two Ecologies*, Australian Government Publishing Service (Canberra), 1994.

Kaufman, Henry, *Structural Changes in the Financial Markets: Economic and Policy Significance*, Henry Kaufman & Co. (New York), 1994.

Joske, Stephen, *The Economics of Immigration: Who Pays?* and *The Economics of Immigration: A Postscript*, Parliament of Australia Legislative Research Service, (Canberra), 1990.

Malouf, David, Foreword to the Third Edition of the *Macquarie Dictionary*, Macquarie University Press (Sydney), 1997.

Moore, Des, *How Labor Targeted Votes And Opinion*, Institute of Private Enterprise (Melbourne), 1996.

Morrisey, Patrick, 'Undermining Rural Sustainability', Policy, Winter 1997.

Nagle QC, John, *Report Of The Special Commission Of Inquiry Into The Police Investigation Of The Death of Donald Bruce Mackay*, (NSW Government Printer), 1986.

Department of Corrective Services, NSW, *NSW Inmate Census 1996*, Statistical Publication, October, 1996.

Government Green Paper, NSW, *Building on our Cultural Diversity*, Draft Report, NSW Government, May 1996.

Price, Charles, *Immigration and Ethnicity*, Department of Immigration (Canberra) 1996.

Price, Charles, Net Immigration and Population Growth, *People and Place*, (Monash/Swinburne), vol 1, no 2, 1993.

Russell Bill, and Nicholas de Roos, *Towards an Understanding of Australia's Co-movement with Foreign Business Cycles*, Reserve Bank of Australia (Sydney), 1997.

Ye, Sang, *Unfair Competition*, Heat 6 (Sydney), 1997

Stilwell, Frank, *Economic Policy and Population Policy: is Stability Uneconomic?*, AESP national conference paper (Sydney), 1997.

Sullivan, Lucy, and Maley, Barry, and Warby, Michael, *State of the Nation*, Centre for Independent Studies (Sydney), 1997.

Sullivan, Lucy, *Rising Crime in Australia*, Centre for Independent Studies (Sydney), 1997.

World Bank, The, *Expanding the Measure of Wealth*, (Washington D.C.), 1997.

World Bank, The, *Monitoring Environmental Progress: A Report on Work in Progress*, (Washington D.C.), 1995.

Year Book Australia, *1997*, Australian Government Publishing Service (Canberra), 1997.

Zubrzycki, Jerzy, *The Evolution of the Policy of Multiculturalism in Australia, 1968-1995*, Global Cultural Diversity Conference, April, 1995.

SOURCES

A number of rigorously researched magazine articles are also quoted in the text:

William Calvin, 'The Great Climate Flip-Flop', *The Atlantic Monthly*, January, 1998.

Cassidy, John, 'The Melting-Pot Myth', the *New Yorker*, July 14, 1997.

Hertsgaard, Mark, 'Our Real China Problem', *The Atlantic Monthly*, November, 1997.

Kaplan, Robert D., 'Was Democracy Just A Moment?', *The Atlantic Monthly*, December, 1997.

Schwarz, Benjamin, 'The Diversity Myth: America's Leading Export,' *The Atlantic Monthly*, May, 1995.

Soros, George, 'Toward a Global Open Society', *The Atlantic Monthly*, January, 1998.

Thurow, Lester, 'Asia: The Collapse and the Cure', *The New York Review of Books*, February 5, 1998.

INDEX

INDEX

INDEX

INDEX